EXPERIENCES IN INQUIRY: HSGP and SRSS

EXPERIENCES IN INQUIRY: HSGP and SRSS

Prepared by   The High School Geography Project and
Sociological Resources for the Social Studies

Sponsored by   The Association of American Geographers and
The American Sociological Association

Supported by   The National Science Foundation

ALLYN AND BACON, INC.   BOSTON

Experiences in Inquiry: HSGP and SRSS was prepared by the High School Geography Project (sponsored
by the Association of American Geographers) and Sociological Resources for the Social Studies (sponsored
by the American Sociological Association) and supported by the National Science Foundation.

Printed in the United States of America
Library of Congress Catalog Card Number 73-87822

Acknowledgments

The following staff members of the High School Geography Project (HSGP) and Sociological Resources for the Social Studies (SRSS) collaborated as authors of this book:

Joan W. Barth (SRSS)
Sociological Resources for the Social Studies
Ann Arbor, Michigan

Ronald J. B. Carswell (HSGP)
The University of Calgary

Robert M. Cason (HSGP)
Fulton County School System
Atlanta, Georgia

James S. Eckenrod (SRSS)
Biological Sciences Curriculum Study
University of Colorado

Dana G. Kurfman (HSGP)
Prince Georges County Public Schools
Maryland

Ina V. S. Mullis (HSGP)
University of Colorado

Salvatore J. Natoli (HSGP)
Association of American Geographers
Washington, D.C.

Robert W. Richburg (HSGP)
Colorado State University

Thomas J. Switzer (SRSS)
The University of Michigan

Everett K. Wilson (SRSS)
University of North Carolina

Supporting Staff:
   Susan J. Beasley (HSGP)
   Jane F. Castner (HSGP)
   Claudia L. Flory (SRSS)

Contents

PART III   INSTRUCTOR'S GUIDE 103

PART IV   EVALUATION 229

Preface

While sitting back and resting on the seventh day, the social science curriculum projects looked at their creations and thought, "Well, now that we have developed new materials for use in the schools, how can we make sure that they will be used wisely and well?" They thus began the second week of their existence by facing the pressing problem of implementation.

During their final year of operation, both Sociological Resources for the Social Studies, a curriculum project sponsored by the American Sociological Association and supported by the National Science Foundation, and the High School Geography Project, sponsored by the Association of American Geographers and, also funded by the National Science Foundation, turned their attention to the recurrent problem of teacher education. Although numerous summer institutes, workshops, and in-service training sessions had been helpful in preparing teachers to use the new materials, it became obvious that only a small fraction of interested teachers could be reached by these methods. Perhaps there was another way to broaden the base of potential users. Members of both project staffs felt that pre-service and in-service teachers might benefit from a systematic exposure to the instructional materials developed by the two projects. It was also believed that experience with the inquiry methods presented by these projects would help teachers deal more effectively with instructional materials developed by other social science and social studies projects, materials that have been loosely defined as "the new social studies." Thus this volume was conceived. It is the culmination of a cooperative effort to provide samples of the materials produced by HSGP and SRSS — samples that we hope will be useful in training pre-service and in-service teachers in inquiry methods.

Mandated by the National Science Foundation to create instructional materials for high school students that would reflect the interests of the disciplines, both HSGP and SRSS spent their early years producing experimental units that were then tested in high schools across the country. Following these national testing programs, the units were revised on the basis of the test results and were then published for commercial distribution. The sociology materials have been published by Allyn and Bacon, Inc., of Boston, and the geography units have been published by The Macmillan Company of New York.

Sociological Resources for the Social Studies has produced three kinds of instructional materials designed to acquaint students with the sociological perspective: the "Episodes in Social Inquiry Series," *Inquiries in Sociology*, and the "Readings in Sociology Series." The "Episodes in Social Inquiry Series" is composed of twenty-three short inquiry units, each on a topic of interest to high school students and representative of the field of sociology. They are designed to be inserted into existing social studies courses and vary in teaching time from one week to three weeks. *Inquiries in Sociology* is a one-semester sociology course suitable for the eleventh or twelfth grade. By using various episodes along with *Inquiries in Sociology*, a full year's course can be created. The "Readings in Sociology Series" comprises seven paperback books, each of which is composed of professional readings, rewritten for the high school student, that explore a broad sociological topic. The readings provide source materials for social studies courses. A comprehensive "Instructors' Guide" accompanies each episode and the course. Optional transparencies are available for certain of the episodes and for the course.

Under the auspices of the High School Geography Project, a year-long geography course entitled *Geography in an Urban Age* was produced. Designed and developed as an integrated whole for ninth and tenth-grade levels, the course consists of six sequential units, each of which has been published separately. The full set of published materials for each unit contains separate softcover books for teacher and students, together with a series of supporting teaching materials. In addition to *Geography in an Urban Age* (the basic set of classroom materials), HSGP has produced a reference volume for teachers, *The Local Community: A Handbook for Teachers*, and a comparatively shorter publication, *Sources of Information and Materials: Maps and Aerial Photographs*. A final report on the project's work, *From Geographic Discipline to Inquiring Student*, was published by the Association of American Geographers. In addition, teacher-education kits have been developed to assist the teacher in analyzing teaching strategy, clarifying his role, and applying the strategy to a new situation.

On the basis of the knowledge gained from developing new curriculum materials, the authors of this volume concluded that the best way to acquaint teachers with inquiry methods of teaching would be to use the same principle of inquiry in this book that was employed in the high school materials — that is, more learning occurs through active involvement. Thus this book strives to involve the pre-service and in-service teacher in the inquiry process. By experiencing the activities in the role of student, it is hoped that teachers will become better guides of inquiry. To convey this notion of student role, the word "participant" was chosen for use in this book.

Although many excellent instructional materials have been created by the curriculum projects — and we believe that they contribute to better teaching and learning today — the millennium in educational resources has not arrived. What is of utmost importance, however, is that these new products be viewed as catalysts that will spur teachers to a deeper understanding of broad educational objectives and to creative ways of achieving such goals.

It would be impossible to acknowledge here the hundreds of people who have participated in the work of both the HSGP and the SRSS projects. Suffice it to say that this volume would not have been possible without their talented contributions.

High School Geography Project
Sociological Resources for the Social Studies

PART I

Introduction

SAMPLE ACTIVITIES

1. Site Diagrams

Assume that the five areas shown in Figure 1-1 are within the continental United States. Circle the letter representing the site at which you think a settlement is most likely to develop in the year indicated. Be prepared to give reasons for your choices.

FIGURE 1-1. *Site Diagrams*

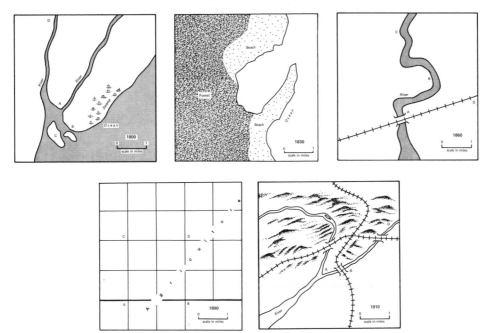

SOURCE: "Geography of Cities," in *Geography in an Urban Age*, Unit 1 (New York: The Macmillan Company, 1969), Student Manual, p. 2.

2. Poverty Pictures

Look at Figures 1-2 and 1-3 and answer the question under each. In what way are the pictures similar? In what way are they different?

FIGURE 1-2.   *Where Will This Family Go for Their Summer Vacation?*

SOURCE: From "The Shame of the Nation" by P. M. Stern and G. De Vincent, © 1965. By permission of Astor Honor, Inc.

FIGURE 1-3.   *Where Is the Father?*

SOURCE: Office of Economic Opportunity.

Discussion

What did you learn from the sample activities presented above? How did you learn it? What kinds of teaching and learning experiences could you develop by using the data presented in these examples? Could you develop an original teaching activity using similar data?

How did you feel about taking part in the two activities? Since you were plunged into the experience without advance preparation, were you ambivalent and uncertain about what to do and what was expected of you?

Assume that you are a high school student who has had little or no formal education in either geography or sociology and that your teacher has asked you to examine the data presented in the two activities. As you look at Figure 1-1, you may wonder about the meaning of "site" or "map scale" or the symbols in the diagrams. For a moment, you might even think that there are correct answers — real places that the teacher expects you to identify. The teacher, however, tells you that there are no "correct" answers, that you are only expected to consider the *most likely* places where settlements would occur. Furthermore, the teacher tells you that, if you so desire, you can discuss your possible choices with one or more of your fellow students! On the other hand, the teacher will be expecting a variety of responses because of the variety of situations built into the activity. For example, of the five site diagrams illustrated on page 3, only three — 1860, 1890, and 1910 — give any indication of human settlement. In only two — 1830 and 1890 — are there any indications that the climate will support vegetation or agriculture. Each site illustrates only a very limited area — twenty-five square miles. Some of the sites seem to have an amazing similarity to specific locations in the United States. Some sites provide more clues than others to possible settlements. Therefore, your response to the site diagrams will range from the very general to the very specific. In addition, the *general* responses may range from those based upon either a lack of knowledge or sophistication about the sites or a healthy skepticism because of the many variables that are necessary to shape an intelligent specific response. Some of the *specific* responses may be based upon as limited knowledge as the general responses. It is therefore necessary that the teacher focus upon a searching inquiry into the reasons why you as a student respond as you do.

Thus as a student you begin to discover that a problem may have more than one solution, and that other people's thoughts can help you enlarge your ideas about solutions. By reasoning with others and coming to conclusions about specific sites, you have advanced to another level of learning — you have begun to ask significant questions about the way man organizes his activities with respect to his geographic location.

When you examine the photographs in Figures 1-2 and 1-3, you may wonder where the pictures were taken, and then realize that they tell you something about poverty in different places. As you ponder the question under Figure 1-2, you may feel that it is a ludicrous one to ask because the answer seems so obvious. The people depicted, however, are part of our society and they, like everyone else, are bombarded with advertisements offering family package trips to faraway places or elaborate vehicles and equipment for camping. You become aware of the discrepancy between what these people have and what is available in our society, and you ask yourself how one accounts for the unequal distribution of the good things in life. You reflect upon the life of a family whose living quarters provide less adequate shelter than someone's camper and whose most important priority is simply providing enough food for tomorrow's needs. Moreover, you may realize that this family's chances of emerging from a poverty-level existence are very slight.

As you study the black family in Figure 1-3, you ask yourself if you are looking at a poor family whose father is at work or a poor family that has no father. If it is a fatherless family, then the problems associated with being poor are likely to be compounded, and more questions tumble around in your head: How common is this family's situation? Who will pay for the basic necessities of life? What part should the government play in softening the impact of poverty? Are day-care facilities available for the children? Is a tenement neighborhood an unhealthy environment? What type of medical care is available to this family? What part does the church play in enriching such people's lives? By now you are involved in a heady introduction to questions about the organization of society and the roles of individuals and institutions in that society.

Now reverse roles for a moment. You are the teacher and you have asked your students to complete these activities. How well-prepared are you to guide them through these activities?

HOW TO USE THIS BOOK

The two learning activities presented above were adapted from materials produced by the High School Geography Project (HSGP) and by Sociological Resources for the Social Studies (SRSS). The selected activities are in no way unique to these two projects. They are, in fact, representative of inquiry-oriented materials developed in the 1960's by a number of physical and social-science curriculum projects. Since teachers are encountering the new curricular materials at an ever-increasing rate, it was felt that they might benefit from a systematic exposure to materials from two of the social-science projects. Thus this book was designed to be used in the training of pre-service social-studies teachers or as part of in-service training programs for teachers preparing to use new social-studies curricular materials.

Twelve teaching activities selected from instructional materials developed by SRSS and HSGP form the basic structure of this volume. The twelve activities were chosen with the idea that they would be used primarily for teaching-demonstration purposes. However, one can benefit by simply reading about each activity. Based on the activities theme, the book is organized into four parts: Introduction, Participant Materials, Instructor's Guide, and Evaluation.

Part One began with two sample activities, chosen for the purpose of immediately involving participants (pre-service or in-service teachers) in an inquiry-learning experience. Participation in these activities is now being followed by descriptive information on the organization of this book. The larger educational context is then examined. Arguments in favor of using teaching strategies that provide for active student-involvement are presented, and some of the advantages accruing from the development of materials by national curriculum projects are discussed. The section ends with a consideration of the effects of the national projects on local curriculum-development efforts.

Part Two contains the twelve activities that participants will experience. The participant materials have been separated from the instructor's materials so that the twelve activities can be used for demonstration purposes if so desired. All the information required for participants is included in this section. (In a few instances, as noted in the Instructor's Guide, additional data are provided in handouts.)

Part Three, Instructor's Guide, presents detailed information on how each activity is to be carried out. In addition, information on how to analyze the activity from two perspectives (substantive content and teaching strategy) is given, and suggestions for applying the new learnings are made. Participant objectives — those objectives that participants should learn from experiencing and analyzing an activity — are identified. (Content objectives are listed in regular type, whereas pedagogical objectives are listed in italic type.)

The final section of the book, Part Four, deals with evaluation by exploring the procedures appropriate for use with these and other social-studies curricular materials. Many teachers realize that conventional evaluation methods will not suffice for the new curricular materials. In addition, students must become accustomed to new forms of evaluation and to the significance of the results. Thus evaluation procedures for measuring student achievement and course effectiveness are discussed.

The authors of this book hope that its users will give free rein to their imagination and creativity. The twelve activities in Part Two do not appear in a preferred sequence. Decisions on which activities to use and the sequence of use are left to the instructor.

Although there are many ways to use this book, it is designed so that pre-service or in-service teachers can actually participate in each activity — i.e., so the activities can be conducted as teaching demonstrations. Although the activities have been adapted from those designed for high school students, it is not necessary for participants to play the role of high school students. If an activity is used as a teaching demonstration, participants should read the appropriate material in Part Two but should *not* read the corresponding material in Part Three: to do so would limit the effectiveness of the demonstration. The instructor, however, should read the appropriate participant materials (Part Two) and instructor's materials (Part Three) prior to conducting the demonstration. After completing the demonstration, the instructor should engage the participants in an analysis of the activity. Following this analysis, participants can read the appropriate information in Part Three which, until now, has been reserved for the instructor. Although the person conducting the demonstration is likely to be the instructor in a college methods class or the director of an in-service program, it is possible for a pre-service or in-service teacher to act as instructor. Thus experience could be gained from teaching an inquiry activity while at the same time presenting other participants with a different teaching behavior for analysis.

Although we believe that participants will benefit most by participating in the activities, we also feel that the book will be of value if simply read by pre-service or in-service teachers. If read as part of a group project, discussion of each activity could follow its reading. Or some activities might be read and others used for demonstration purposes. As stated earlier, the only limits on how the materials in this book might be used are the limits of the instructor's imagination and creativity.

It is well to keep in mind that this volume does not contain a systematic or logical presentation of geography or sociology learning units. The authors' basic objective was to provide social-studies methods teachers and directors of in-service teacher training programs with materials that will facilitate the introduction of a variety of inquiry-oriented teaching activities into their programs. However, the concern for strategy should not evolve into a preoccupation with teaching methodologies at the expense of cognitive and affective learning goals. The end product of each activity is not only a better understanding of a teaching strategy but also a better understanding of the behavioral science concepts and affective outcomes that may emerge from the experience.

Before beginning the activities, however, it might be well to consider the broader context of inquiry teaching by looking at some of the characteristics and purposes of the products developed by national curriculum projects.

CHARACTERISTICS OF NATIONAL CURRICULUM PROJECTS

Student Participation

An important characteristic of materials developed by SRSS and HSGP, as well as a distinguishing feature of this book, is active student-involvement in the learning process. Both reason and experience support the view that learning and interest are promoted when students are actively engaged in gathering and analyzing data needed to answer the questions they consider important. More than fifty years ago, A. I. Gates found that "learning scores jumped 100 percent when four-fifths of the subjects' time was devoted to recitation rather than to passive reading." [1] Haggard and Rose, after reviewing a large number of learning studies, concluded that ". . . when an individual assumes an active role in a learning situation (a) he tends to acquire the response to be learned more rapidly, and (b) these response patterns tend to be more stably formed than when he remains passive." [2] And when Gordon Allport asked 250 college students to recall their experiences in the eighth grade, three-fourths of the memories were for situations in which the subject himself was actively participating. Facts of this sort, Allport says, "prove to us

[1] A. I. Gates, "Recitation as a Factor in Memorizing," *Archives of Psychology*, Vol. 6, No. 40 (1917). Cited in Gordon W. Allport, "The Psychology of Participation," *The Psychological Review*, Vol. 53, No. 3 (May 1945).
[2] E. A. Haggard and R. J. Rose, "Some Effects of Mental Set and Active Participation in the Conditioning of the Autokinetic Phenomenon," *Journal of Experimental Psychology*, Vol. 34 (1944), pp. 45–49.

that people have to be active in order to learn, in order to store up efficient memories, to build voluntary control, to be cured when they are ill, restored when they are faint." [3]

Student participation usually promotes student interest. Data from the national testing of the SRSS sociology course, *Inquiries in Sociology*, shed light on expressed student interest in materials calling for active student involvement. These data show that 75.4 percent of the students who took the sociology course felt that it was more interesting or as interesting as other courses they were taking.[4] One trial teacher in an all-black school reported in her teaching log:

> . . . Pacing was one of the problems . . . vocabulary was difficult for students . . . they responded best to activities. . . . One thing I noted was interesting . . . sometimes "A" students couldn't perform unusual experiments too well. . . . But this is where the poorer student . . . seemed to blossom.[5]

Similar comments were made during the school trials of HSGP activities. For example, an Educational Testing Service Report, prepared in 1966 for HSGP, included the following comment on the Portsville activity: "Many teachers and most observers noticed that most students who were not actively participating in building the large map were less stimulated than those who were." As a result, the large single-board map in the activity was replaced by four smaller ones. This facilitated the involvement of all the students in the class rather than a select few.[6]

Such evidence may not persuade the skeptic, but it does give us some confidence that to pose significant questions, to pursue and analyze data that yield tentative answers, and to engage actively in the learning process may indeed be more effective than learning from exposition methods of teaching.

The Inquiry Environment

How does one ensure a proper setting for inquiry? What behaviors might we expect from the serious teacher who wants to provide such a setting? What kind of administrative support is necessary? Will there be a community reaction if students inquire into some of the so-called "closed areas"? What might we expect from students who are given the chance to be active inquirers instead of rote learners?

Inherent in the new social-science materials is the assumption that the role of the teacher must change. Unfortunately, many teachers teach the way they were taught or

[3] Allport, "Psychology of Participation," p. 20.

[4] Graeme S. Fraser and Thomas J. Switzer, "Inquiries in Sociology: Responses by Teachers and Students," *Social Education*, Vol. 34, No. 8 (December 1970), pp. 923–924.

[5] Thomas Switzer and Everett K. Wilson, "Nobody Knows the Trouble We've Seen: Launching a High School Sociology Course," *Phi Delta Kappan*, Vol. L, No. 6 (February 1969), p. 350.

[6] Dana G. Kurfman and Robert W. Richburg, "The Role of Evaluation," in *From Geographic Discipline to Inquiring Student*, Final Report on the High School Geography Project (Washington, D.C.: Association of American Geographers, 1970), Chapter 4, p. 42.

even in ways they think their administrator or community members might want them to teach. Few teachers care to admit that their lectures dominate a class period. It is not uncommon, however, for a teacher to claim more than seventy percent of the class time for himself. Such teacher-domination is inconsistent with the inquiry emphasis found in materials developed by the social-science curriculum projects. In contrast to the teacher-dominated and sometimes authoritarian classroom climate that exists in some schools, a democratic and relaxed classroom atmosphere is called for by the new materials. This does not mean that a teacher should take a laissez faire approach to classroom control and planning, but it does mean that the atmosphere must be nonthreatening, enabling the student to feel free to experiment, test out ideas, and explore beliefs.

All the responsibility for change should not be placed on the teacher, however, for he operates in a complicated and highly interrelated network of social relationships. Because roles and role expectations are interrelated, we can assume that any significant change on a teacher's part will be accompanied by a change in the role of student and in the role of administrator, and perhaps even in the community's conception of what constitutes quality education. It would be absurd, for example, to expect a teacher to be flexible, democratic, imaginative, and inquiry-oriented when the reward structure of the school and community honors rigidity, strict classroom discipline, and a "don't rock the boat" teaching philosophy. If opportunities for student inquiry are to exist, school administrators, school-board members, and the community in general must join the teacher and student in providing a receptive learning environment.

We must be prepared, however, to cope with the consequences of using inquiry methods. When we speak of inquiry, we are talking in part about an attitude. We want students to develop the habit of asking questions and of being skeptical. But if students are to raise questions, suggest possible answers, gather data, make tentative conclusions, and test the outcomes — if we accept these as goals of social-science instruction — then we cannot expect them to confine their curiosity to the classroom. The school itself, school policies, or perhaps aspects of community life become fair game for investigation by inquisitive students.

It is important to note that in the new social-science curriculum materials, transfer of learning is central to the process of education. Students are expected to transfer the skills acquired through active investigation to solutions of actual problems. Some problems will be of immediate concern to students and may be of such a nature that students can actively participate in their solution. Other problems suitable for inquiry are related to the larger social order. When faced with trying to deal with these societal problems, students may feel that they are so massive and complex that they are beyond solution or at least beyond any action program that students can implement. This is not altogether bad, however. In their frustration, students learn that the complicated nature of many of our great social problems preclude any simple answers. Although student action cannot actually solve the problem under investigation, as might be the case with a more immediate problem, it should not deter consideration of possible solutions and, when practical, the testing of proposed solutions in the local community.

Advantages and Disadvantages of National Projects

One characteristic of much new instructional material, loosely defined as "the new social studies," is its development by national curriculum projects. These projects are thought of as national in scope, since they are not usually associated with a particular school system, and since they are supported by private foundations or by government organizations, such as the National Science Foundation or the U.S. Office of Education. In many cases, they are sponsored by one of the scholarly disciplines. These projects view their role as being producers of material for national consumption.

The way in which instructional materials are developed by local school systems is different from the way in which they are developed by national projects. Although particular school systems vary in their approaches to curriculum development, the conventional pattern has been for an administrator to charge a committee of teachers with the development of a curriculum guide for a certain subject. The committee examines other curriculum guides and appropriate textbooks and sometimes receives advice from local universities and colleges. A course outline or syllabus is then prepared, containing general suggestions for appropriate teaching activities. The syllabus is distributed to teachers in the local school system.

In contrast, the national project has a full-time staff, composed of many specialists, that develops a variety of interrelated materials and, in addition, is able to test and evaluate its products before final national distribution occurs.

The process by which instructional materials are developed by national projects seems to have several advantages over the traditional, local method. First, *national projects are more efficient mechanisms than are local committees for developing instructional materials and translating abstract ideas into practical teaching units.* One major problem faced by the high school teacher asked to work on local curriculum development is lack of time. Although released time has become more common in recent years, most local curricular work takes place after classroom responsibilities are fulfilled. Thus classroom teachers often have insufficient time and energy to devote to the complicated task of creating instructional materials, whereas staff members of national projects can devote their complete attention to thinking about emerging trends in education and then to developing appropriate new instructional devices. Thus the gap between what is thought by the scholar and what is taught in the classroom is reduced.

A second advantage of national projects stems from the first one: *In reducing the gap between scholarship and classroom practice, the amount of time that it normally takes an innovative idea to find its way into the schools is shortened.* For example, the rapid acceptance of materials produced by both the Biological Science Curriculum Study project and the School Mathematics Study Group project, and the initial favorable responses to the SRSS and HSGP materials, prove that project materials can move quickly into the schools. Furthermore, national projects tend to legitimize innovations. If a national curriculum project sponsored by a learned society suggests that inquiry is the way children learn, or that the structure of the discipline is what should be taught, and *then develops instructional materials to implement these suggestions,* the impact on school systems is greater than if a local curriculum committee recommends similar changes. The weight of authority comes into play.

A third advantage of the national curriculum projects over local curriculum efforts is that in addition to speeding up the change process, *national projects make it easier for teachers to deal with the so-called "closed areas."* In the past, social-studies teachers were reluctant to explore such "closed area" topics as race, sex, politics, etc. Materials developed by the social-science curriculum projects treat such topics in a straightforward, intellectually honest fashion and thus do not generate much negative community reaction. This is not to say that negative reactions will not occur, but it has been the case that topics such as overpopulation, race relations, stereotyping, and cultural relativity have been successfully introduced into the classroom by way of HSGP and SRSS materials.

Fourth, *national projects can recruit talents that are not available to local curriculum groups.* Since most national social-science curriculum projects are sponsored by professional associations, and since the prestige of the association devolves upon the project, outstanding scholars in a field can be recruited as staff. In addition, curriculum specialists and talented teachers are employed in the common effort. The outcome of this collaboration between specialists in subject matter and specialists in education has been instructional materials of high quality — materials that present recent research in the discipline, cast in workable teaching strategies of interest and value to students.

Yet another benefit from bringing teachers and scholars together is *the development of better relationships between the university scholar and the classroom teacher.* Most national projects have found that when scholars and teachers work toward a common goal, the scholar develops a more positive view of teachers and a greater appreciation for the many problems faced in the classroom.

A fifth advantage of national curriculum projects is that *a well-funded and adequately staffed national project can carry out a testing program for its materials, whereas local school systems can seldom afford to do so.* Much of the evaluation work of the national projects has been of the formative type.[7] That is, evaluation takes place during the course of developing materials and has as its primary emphasis the gathering of information for making revisions. This type of evaluation can improve an educational product during the course of its development, whereas assessment of a finished product does not contain this potential for change. Yet it is just this "after-the-fact" evaluation that most school systems use if they evaluate their curricular materials at all. Most local efforts concentrate on evaluating students rather than materials. The tacit assumption is that if the student is unsuccessful, it is his fault and not the unsuitability of the courses. In contrast, the major national projects have employed full-time staff evaluators, have devised varied testing procedures, and have spent thousands of dollars evaluating each product

[7] See Michael Scriven, "The Methodology of Evaluation," in *Perspectives of Curriculum Evaluation*, AERA Monograph Series on Curriculum Evaluation, American Educational Research Association (Chicago: Rand McNally and Company, 1967).

prior to its publication.   Thus, information gathered during the evaluative process is used to revise the materials so that the best educational product possible can result.

A sixth advantage of national projects is *in the important area of teacher training and retraining.*   Despite the change and ferment in education today and despite the new materials produced by the social-science projects, many departments of education continue to train teachers as before.   Although the national projects have not made the training of teachers one of their prime responsibilities, they have been active in in-service training by conducting short workshops, participating in institute programs, and preparing teacher-training materials such as this book.   Virtually all the projects provide elaborate teachers' guides to accompany their student materials.

Implications for Local Curriculums

Given the advantages of national curriculum projects and assuming that such projects will continue to develop instructional materials, what are the implications for local control of the curriculum and for local curriculum development efforts?

That instructional materials are being developed by *national* projects has made some local and state educators fearful of losing control over curriculum decisions.   There are several reasons, however, why national projects pose no threat to local control.   Of primary importance are the facts that (1) the many curriculum projects are independent of each other, and (2) they have had no government direction or interference regardless of sources of support.   Indeed, it has been argued that the taxpayer's money is being wasted because there has been so little communication among the projects despite the similarity of objectives.   Such a belief might suggest that there is need for more central planning, not less.   The reality is, however, that projects compete with each other for space in the school curriculum — an important factor in preserving local control.   As long as schools can choose from a wide variety of high-quality materials, there is little danger that a national curriculum will be imposed.

It is important to distinguish between local efforts to develop instructional materials and the responsibility of schools to structure local curricula.   To argue that national curriculum projects are well-suited for developing instructional materials is not to contend that decisions about the structure of a curriculum should be removed from local control.   Each school system must and should retain responsibility for identifying values, selecting objectives, deciding on curricular organization and content, and selecting appropriate instructional materials.   Because of the "authority" aspect (discussed earlier) of national project materials, schools should be alert to one potential danger — curriculum directors and teachers adopting such materials without careful scrutiny.   With the many diverse products now available from national projects, it is necessary for each school system to develop a systematic way of selecting the most appropriate materials for its purposes.

To view the teacher as selector rather than creator of instructional materials may run counter to the professional image that some teachers hold of themselves. Teachers imply this view of creator when they say, "I must do my own thing." "Doing one's own thing," however, does not mean that one must start from scratch. The national projects cannot possibly produce materials and teaching strategies that are useful for every possible situation. Thus creativity comes into play as the teacher adapts the materials to his own classroom needs. This process is analogous to the orchestra conductor who, though he did not write the music, nevertheless plays a vital role in the creation of the final product.

The national projects show great promise for improving instructional materials in elementary and secondary schools, and, significantly, they can accomplish their goals without disturbing local control of the curriculum or threatening individual teacher creativity. However, curriculum reform is not achieved simply by developing superior instructional materials; change depends on the wise selection and implementation of those materials. Thus ways must be devised to help teachers work effectively with the new products. This book is one attempt toward that end.

PART II

Participant Materials

The Eye of Childhood

In the early 1960's, a psychiatrist tried to find out how children in recently integrated schools in the South felt as they went through this new and very different experience. One method that he used to uncover the feelings of younger students was to have them create pictures for him.

The four drawings shown in Figures 2-1, 2-2, 2-3, and 2-4 (see insert opposite page 36) were made for this psychiatrist by a six-year-old girl at a New Orleans school. Ruby, like the other students being studied, was attending a school that was admitting Afro-Americans for the first time. For the first several weeks, crowds of whites outside the school swore and screamed at the black children and the few white children who entered the building. (A boycott by local whites kept white attendance at a minimum.)

Your task is to analyze the four drawings to see if you can tell (1) how Ruby feels about herself and (2) how she feels about blacks and whites. The following questions should help you with your analysis:

1. Compare Ruby's feelings about blacks and whites as they are revealed in the four drawings. Be sure to explain your answer.
2. Describe three ways in which Figure 2-1 differs from Figure 2-2.
3. Why do you think Ruby drew Figure 2-1 differently from Figure 2-2? List as many reasons as you can.

Based on material in Part 3 of *Inquiries in Sociology* (Boston: Allyn and Bacon, 1972). Copyright © 1972 by the American Sociological Association. Reprinted with permission. The basic idea for this teaching activity was formulated by Gary T. Marx of Harvard University and Richard W. Sprague of Newton High School, Newtonville, Massachusetts.

4. Describe three ways in which Figure 2-3 differs from Figure 2-4.
5. What is the most likely explanation of the differences between Figures 2-3 and 2-4?
6. Three of the four pictures have suns in them. What could you hypothesize about Ruby's feelings on the basis of the three suns?
7. Figure 2-3 has no sun. What type of sun do you think Ruby would draw for this figure?
8. On the basis of the four drawings, would you say that Ruby is a white girl or a black girl? Explain your answer.

ACTIVITY 2

Metfab

INTRODUCTION

You are part of the management team of a new metal fabricating company called "Metfab." Although each member of your team has a specific job that entails individual interests, you must make a group decision about where to locate your new factory. A brief description of each member of your management team follows:

PRESIDENT: Gregory Williams, age 53, is responsible for all facets of the factory's operation. He is particularly interested in locating in a market area that will have the best long-range prospects for the company.

SALES MANAGER: Ralph McNeil, age 45, is primarily concerned with a location that will provide the best sales for Metfab. Thus he is interested in present market conditions and in the shipping costs of finished products to this market.

PRODUCTION MANAGER: Samuel Dubrowski, age 41, is responsible for the production aspects of the company. His interests include maintaining a productive labor force and minimizing the cost of raw materials.

PERSONNEL MANAGER: Frank Greenstein, age 37, is concerned with the availability of an adequate but inexpensive labor force. He is also interested in an area that will be attractive to middle and upper management.

From Unit 2: "Manufacturing and Agriculture," in *Geography in an Urban Age* (New York: The Macmillan Company, 1969). Copyright © 1969 by the Association of American Geographers. Reprinted with permission. The original idea for this activity was contributed by Howard A. Stafford of the University of Cincinnati.

TREASURER: Henrietta Engle, age 48, is anxious to locate in an area where good financial contacts and credit at low interest rates will be available. She also feels that low corporate taxes are important.

In addition to the knowledge particular to your job, you are aware of the general nature of production for the new company. Your factory will be a medium-sized one, with a total work force of about two hundred. The company will purchase raw materials from copper and steel manufacturers and will sell your products, steel and copper containers, to producers of agricultural and industrial chemicals. You also know that a rather high proportion of the company's employees must be skilled workers and that such a labor force is both difficult to find and expensive to maintain.

In previous meetings your management team has decided to locate your factory in the United States. To date, you have narrowed the list of potential sites to the following eight cities:

Atlanta	Los Angeles
Cincinnati	New Orleans
Detroit	New York
Houston	Pittsburgh

You have all agreed that it is likely that in each city an adequate supply of workers and specialized suppliers will be available. You also know that each area is able to provide the services your operation requires, such as rail and truck transportation facilities, and fire and police protection. These eight cities, as well as copper and steel production locations, are shown on the map in Figure 2-5.

On the basis of the information provided up to this point, decide among yourselves which role each of you will assume. If there are less than five people in your group, you can omit any role but the president's. When roles have been assigned, each member of your team should take ten or fifteen minutes to read his role description carefully (see pages 22–27). Although the data presented in the role descriptions are in many cases limited and fictitious, this should not affect your ability to decide on the best location for the Metfab plant.

After reading the description of your role, choose the city or cities that you feel would be best for the factory location. In addition, be prepared to present your reasons for your choices.

As participants, you probably possess additional information and background about these cities that go beyond the limited statements provided in the role descriptions. Feel free to use or share this information as you make your initial choices and subsequently participate in the group decision. However, you should not attempt to redefine your role.

Your responsibility in the meeting of your management team will be to help choose the best city in which to locate the factory. Each member of the team has one vote; a unanimous decision is desirable. The president will serve as group chairman for the twenty-minute meeting. After your session, you will join the other teams to present and support your group decision.

FIGURE 2-5.

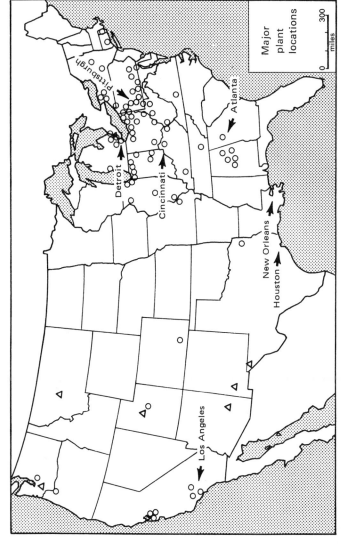

O Major Steel-making Locations

△ Copper Refining

➤ Potential Locations for Metlab

Major
plant
locations

miles
0   300

ROLE DESCRIPTIONS

President Gregory Williams

You have gained much valuable experience from working as a management officer in a competing firm and are thus well-informed about the many different factors that must be considered in making a wise choice of location. To ensure the best possible future working situation, you want all your management team members to agree on the final choice. Each member, including yourself, has one vote. You may be called upon to support your management decision publicly.

You believe that the best location for your firm would be one that is some distance from your competitors, if such a location is feasible otherwise. You think a distance factor would tend to ensure a local market that competitors would find difficult to invade — their costs would be greater to ship products into such an area, their service would be slower, and their knowledge of the territory would not be as good as yours. Conversely, you would be able to serve this local market efficiently and thus be able to pick up a larger proportion of its business.

Table 2-1 shows the anticipated average tons of the product that will be sold annually in each of the eight cities. When this figure is divided by the sum of the number of competitors in the area plus one (your factory), a figure is obtained that indicates the anticipated number of tons you are likely to sell in that market region — your share of the market. For example, according to Table 2-1, three competitors are already located in New York. If you choose to locate in New York, there would then be four metal fabricating plants in the area. Thus, the market for the area (1,600 tons) is divided by four to determine that your share of the market would be 400 tons.

Because of contacts in the industry, you believe that the greatest potential growth in your markets (agricultural and industrial chemical industries) will be in the Gulf States

TABLE 2-1. *Share of Market*

Metropolitan Area	Tons of Product Sold Annually	Number of Competitors Already There	Share of Market (Tons)
Pittsburgh	600	0	600
Houston	1,100	1	550
Atlanta	1,000	1	500
Cincinnati	1,500	2	500
New York	1,600	3	400
Los Angeles	800	1	400
Detroit	600	1	300
New Orleans	300	0	300

region. Since you are considering the long-range prospects for the company, you think that the Gulf States should be given greater weight than indicated by the present geographic pattern of markets. In addition, you favor locating in the Gulf States because many of your relatives, including several grandchildren, live there.

Sales Manager Ralph McNeil

You are in charge of the sales force of the new company. You have great faith in the quality of your products. You are also confident that your crack salesmen can outsell any of the competitors' salesmen, no matter what location decision is made. However, you believe that the way to build a strong company is to pick a spot that is best for supplying the majority of your customers — the closer you are to the largest number of customers, the better your chances for outselling the competition. The market for each of the eight cities is shown in Table 2-2.

In addition, you believe that an important way to increase profit is to save money in distributing your product. Information about shipping costs is found in Table 2-3. The figure for each city represents the cost of shipping your finished product from that city to customers across the country.

Another consideration you want to take into account in making the location decision is the availability of air transportation. It is important to be able to reach potential customers quickly. Also, good airline transportation will enable you and your salesmen to spend more time with your families. The number of passengers served by the airlines in each city is shown in Table 2-4.

Production Manager Samuel Dubrowski

You are in charge of gathering together the necessary materials, primarily finished steel and copper, for the production of the company's chemical containers. You are also responsible for the production processes in the factory.

TABLE 2-2. *Market Table*

Metropolitan Area	Tons of Product Sold Annually
New York	1,600
Cincinnati	1,500
Houston	1,100
Atlanta	1,000
Los Angeles	800
Pittsburgh	600
Detroit	600
New Orleans	300

TABLE 2-3. *Annual Costs for Shipping Finished Product to Market Areas*

Metropolitan Area	Product Shipping Cost
Houston	$1,500,000
Cincinnati	1,500,000
New York	1,550,000
Pittsburgh	1,600,000
New Orleans	1,650,000
Atlanta	1,800,000
Detroit	1,900,000
Los Angeles	2,900,000

TABLE 2-4. *Airline Passengers for Selected Metropolitan Areas*

Airports	Number of Passengers Inbound and Outbound
New York	1,089,822
Los Angeles	480,218
Pittsburgh	225,740
Detroit	166,947
Cincinnati	160,000
Atlanta	145,574
Houston	112,120
New Orleans	81,390

Your major concern is with the transportation costs of your two major materials: copper and steel. You have noted that all copper suppliers absorb transportation costs and sell at a uniform delivered price regardless of location. Therefore your main consideration in choosing a site is the availability of steel at a low cost. The total cost of getting the necessary steel from the nearest source of supply to each city is shown in Table 2-5.

Your other worry is the availability of a hard-working and productive labor force for the plant. Such a force can be expensive. You are aware that Mr. Greenstein, the personnel manager, is quite concerned with the wage rates that he must pay for labor. However, you believe his viewpoint is shortsighted. You know from actually running a shop that the most important factor is the productivity of the labor force. A more productive labor force will turn out more finished products in a given amount of time than will a less productive labor force. In Table 2-6, the eight cities are ranked from highest to

TABLE 2-5. *Costs of Shipping Raw Materials to Selected Metropolitan Areas*

Metropolitan Area	Steel Shipping Costs
Pittsburgh	$ 0
Detroit	62,000
Cincinnati	120,000
Los Angeles	148,000
Atlanta	182,000
New York	188,000
New Orleans	206,000
Houston	300,000

TABLE 2-6. *Labor Productivity Index*

Metropolitan Area	Productivity Index
New York	7.23
Houston	7.18
Pittsburgh	7.15
Atlanta	6.99
Cincinnati	6.66
New Orleans	6.40
Detroit	6.20
Los Angeles	6.10

lowest according to their labor productivity. You will want to select a city with a high productivity index, if possible.

Personally, you would like to locate as close as you can to the ski areas in New England since you and your chief assistants are in the habit of skiing these areas during the winter.

Personnel Manager Frank Greenstein

As personnel manager, you are responsible for obtaining an adequate supply of qualified workers at a reasonable cost. Each metropolitan area is ranked in Table 2-7 in terms of anticipated labor costs for your 200 employees.

You would prefer also to locate in a city that does not have too "tight" a labor supply. The right kind of skilled labor needs to be available for hire. In a city with a tight labor supply, you might have difficulty finding workers. You know that productivity is important too, but you are suspicious of so-called "productivity indexes" that seem to have no clear monetary meaning. Estimates of the availability of labor for each city are shown in Table 2-7.

Another major consideration for you to take into account is a city's attractiveness to middle and upper management personnel. You are aware that competition for plant managers is becoming fierce. You know that when people have a choice, they tend to prefer warm climates to cold climates. Another factor in attractiveness is the amount of air pollution a city has. Table 2-8 ranks the eight cities from least to most air pollution.

Treasurer Henrietta Engle

As treasurer of the company, you believe that any good decision requires a long, hard look at the profit picture. Furthermore, you believe that although a long-term profit is nice to dream about, a substantial profit in the short term is absolutely necessary. You will be most impressed with cities that promise the greatest immediate profit for Metfab.

In order to increase the new company's chances for short-term gains, you are interested in locating in a city with low corporate taxes. The annual average corporate taxes in each city are shown in Table 2-9.

TABLE 2-7. *Labor Costs and Supply Index*

Metropolitan Area	Total Wage Costs	Labor Supply Index[a]
Houston	$1,182,000	C
Atlanta	1,204,000	C
New York	1,229,000	A
Cincinnati	1,295,000	B
Pittsburgh	1,346,000	B
New Orleans	1,375,000	A
Los Angeles	1,398,000	C
Detroit	1,416,000	B

[a] A = Tight; B = Moderately tight; C = Moderate surplus.

TABLE 2-8. *Air Pollution Ranking*

1.	New Orleans	5.	Detroit
2.	Atlanta	6.	Pittsburgh
3.	Houston	7.	Los Angeles
4.	Cincinnati	8.	New York

TABLE 2-9. *Corporate Taxes for Various Cities*

Metropolitan Area	Corporate Taxes
Cincinnati	$100,000
Houston	110,000
Atlanta	120,000
Pittsburgh	130,000
Los Angeles	150,000
New Orleans	175,000
Detroit	195,000
New York	200,000

TABLE 2-10. *Bank Deposits for Various Cities*

Metropolitan Area	Total Bank Deposits
New York	$51,829,321
Los Angeles	9,130,527
Atlanta	4,915,659
Houston	3,829,317
Pittsburgh	3,756,934
Cincinnati	1,357,332
Detroit	1,325,435
New Orleans	1,091,174

You are also aware of the advantages of having good contacts in the banking world. The ability to obtain future financing, if needed, and the ability to invest profitably are enhanced by close contact with banking interests. Bank deposits in the various cities are indicated in Table 2-10.

One immediate financial fact you must consider is the prevailing interest rate in each city. Your company will need to borrow about $2,000,000 for factory construction and equipment. Interest rates are known to be higher in the West than in the East by as much as two percent.

ACTIVITY 3

Occupational Prestige Rating Questionnaire

How do you rate the *social standing* of persons who work at each of the following occupations? Pick the adjective that describes the rating you would give each occupation and put a check in the corresponding box.

SOCIAL STANDING

Occupation	1 Poor	2 Below Average	3 Average	4 Good	5 Excellent
Artist					
Banker					
Bookkeeper					
Building Contractor					
Carpenter					

SOCIAL STANDING

Occupation	1 Poor	2 Below Average	3 Average	4 Good	5 Excellent
Clergyman					
College Professor					
Electrician					
Garage Mechanic					
Gasoline Station Attendant					
Janitor					
Mayor of a Large City					
Physician					
Plumber					
Public School Teacher					
Reporter on a Daily Newspaper					
Shoeshine Stand Attendant					
Soda Fountain Clerk					
Taxicab Driver					
U. S. Supreme Court Justice					

From the Instructor's Guide for *Class and Race in the United States*, SRSS Episodes in Social Inquiry Series (Boston: Allyn and Bacon, 1972). Copyright © 1972 by the American Sociological Association. Reprinted with permission. Designed by Melvin Tumin of Princeton University, Edward Tumin of Weequahic High School and Israel Tumin of South Side High School, both in Newark, New Jersey.

ACTIVITY **4**

Hunger

THE PROBLEM OF HUNGER

Sometime during 1961, the earth's population reached three billion people, half of whom never had enough to eat. It now seems likely that in 1980 the number of people on earth will be four billion, and half of them will never have enough to eat either. In fact, these two billion people probably will be even hungrier than the billion and one-half were in 1961.

Two developments could change this bleak outlook. A disaster — famine, pestilence, or war — might occur, killing hundreds of millions of people. Or the food supplies of hungry countries might be increased. This second possibility poses a serious challenge to the world's agriculture.

In Asia, where more than half the world's population lives, two out of every three people are hungry or suffering from one of the sicknesses caused by "diet deficiencies." Such diseases shrivel the muscles, swell the stomach, and damage the bones. In addition, they may dull the mind and weaken the body. Large parts of Africa and Latin America suffer from a food shortage, too. Today's challenge to agriculture is to produce not only more food for two-thirds of the world's people but also more of the right kinds of food.

The problem of hunger is both old and new. Mass starvation and famines are part of the earliest history of man. China is said to have had at least 1,800 famines since 108

From Unit 2, "Manufacturing and Agriculture," in *Geography in an Urban Age* (New York: The Macmillan Company, 1969). Copyright © 1969 by the Association of American Geographers. Reprinted with permission. Walter M. Kollmorgen of the University of Kansas was the originator of the idea for this activity.

B.C. More than fourteen million people died in the 1876–1878 famine that reached from India to China. England suffered at least seven famines every century from 1200 to 1600. Food shortages were so severe throughout Europe in the middle 1800's that a whole decade is called "the hungry forties."

Crop failures caused these famines. Even today in much of Asia, Africa, and Latin America, the best crop years yield only enough to keep most people barely alive. Three million people die of hunger or the diseases caused by hunger every year. Crop failures can cause twice this many deaths in a single country, as happened in India in the drought years of 1965 and 1966.

However, Asia, Africa, and Latin America have no monopoly on hunger. A 1968 film report, *Hunger USA*, revealed that of the billion and one-half hungry people in the world at that time, ten million lived in the United States, mostly in the South and on Indian reservations. They were victims of a new phase of hunger that began when modern sanitation and medicine reduced the number of deaths caused by plague and disease.

FOOD ON THE FAMILY TABLE

A diet of only cereals, potatoes, and sugar can support life but not health. In South Asia, these foods make up sixty percent of the average diet; in North America, they make up less than ten percent.

The contrast between your diet and that of a South Asian's may be clearer if you imagine that you are an ordinary person in a South Asian village. A bowl of rice or cereal (wheat, corn, or other grains) would be the main dish at every meal — with only one

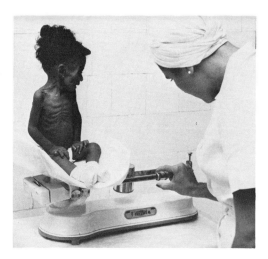

When this picture was taken, this little Brazilian girl named Leci was one year old and weighed nine pounds — half of what she should have weighed. In Brazil, three out of every ten babies born alive die by the end of their first year, with most deaths occurring from diseases associated with hunger. Brazilian authorities and the United Nations Children's Fund are trying to do something for Leci and for other children like her. (Photograph by Jean Speiser; courtesy of UNICEF.)

serving. You would eat two meals a day, not three. With the rice or cereal you would have about two tablespoons of a green vegetable or as much fruit as half a small apple, but not both; you would also have one tablespoon of nuts or beans, one of sugar or a sweet, and one of oil or fat. Once a week you would add to your diet enough meat or fish to make a hamburger the size of a golf ball. Your ration of dairy products would be equal to one glass of milk a day. You would have no seconds and no between-meal snacks or soft drinks.

This amount of food would keep you alive, at least until you had a serious illness. But your resistance to disease would be low, your capacity for study or work severely limited, and your height would be less by several inches than it is now.

Figure 2-6 shows how much and what kinds of food the North American eats in comparison with the South Asian. The North American's food weighs 1,744 pounds per year and the South Asian's 603 pounds.

FIGURE 2-6. *Comparison of Diets in North America and South Asia*

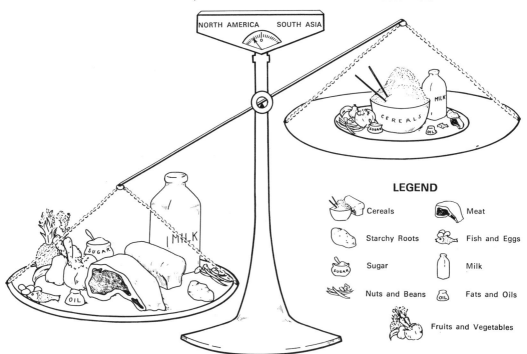

Measuring Nutrition

The unit commonly used to measure diets is the calorie. One recent study[1] divided countries into low-calorie groups and high-calorie groups. People in the low-calorie nations — two-thirds of the world's population — average 2,150 calories a day. People in high-calorie countries average 3,050 calories a day. The low-calorie countries grow about fourteen percent of the world's food and the high-calorie countries about fifty-nine percent.

However, calories measure only energy and a healthy diet is more than just the number of calories a person consumes. (Many Americans cut down to 2,000 calories a day when they want to lose weight and are all the healthier for it.) The kinds of foods that supply the calories are important to good health. Proteins and fats are two essential elements of a good diet. Low-calorie countries have a per capita consumption of only one-fifth the protein and one-third the fat of that consumed in high-calorie countries. Certain vitamins and minerals are also valuable to good health, and they too are present in greater amounts in the diets of high-calorie countries than in the diets of low-calorie countries.

BACKGROUND ON HUNGER

The United Nations' *Third World Food Survey*, from which the comparisons shown in Figure 2-6 were taken, grouped the nations of the world into two classes: well-fed and poorly fed. The second group have been poorly fed for generations and are at least as bad off now as in the past. Perhaps they are in even worse straits today. The well-fed countries had twenty percent more food of all kinds in the early 1960's than they had before World War II. The poorly fed countries had ten percent less.

The map in Figure 2-7 shows where the "diet deficient areas," the poorly fed countries, are located. Figure 2-8 shows the distribution of the world's population. Population in the poorly fed regions is increasing more rapidly than in the well-fed regions. A United Nations' survey gave the population figures shown in Table 2-11. They are percentages of the total world population.

Little evidence exists that the farmland (land now cultivated and land that could be cultivated) of the hungry regions is naturally less productive than the farmland of the well-fed areas. The total land area of the earth is nearly thirty-three billion acres. About one-tenth of it is used for agriculture — not quite three and one-half billion acres, according to a recent estimate of the Food and Agriculture Organization of the United Nations. Figure 2-9 shows the cropland areas of the world.

[1] *Third World Food Survey*, Food & Agriculture Organization of the United Nations, Rome, 1963.

FIGURE 2-7. *Well-Fed and Poorly Fed Countries*

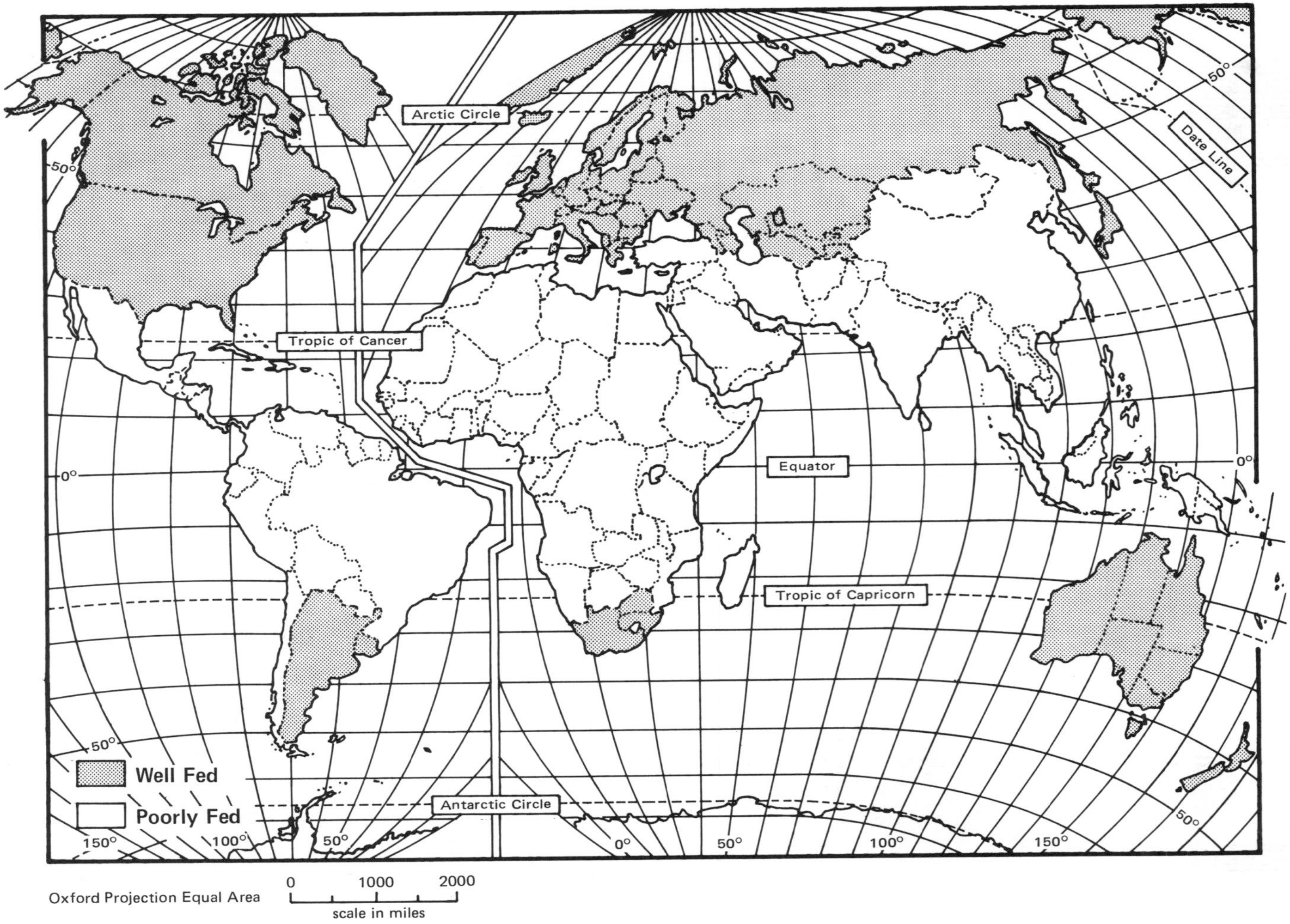

Arctic Circle
Date Line
Tropic of Cancer
Equator
Tropic of Capricorn
Antarctic Circle
Well Fed
Poorly Fed
50°
0°
150°
100°
Oxford Projection Equal Area
0
1000
2000
scale in miles

FIGURE 2-8. *Population*

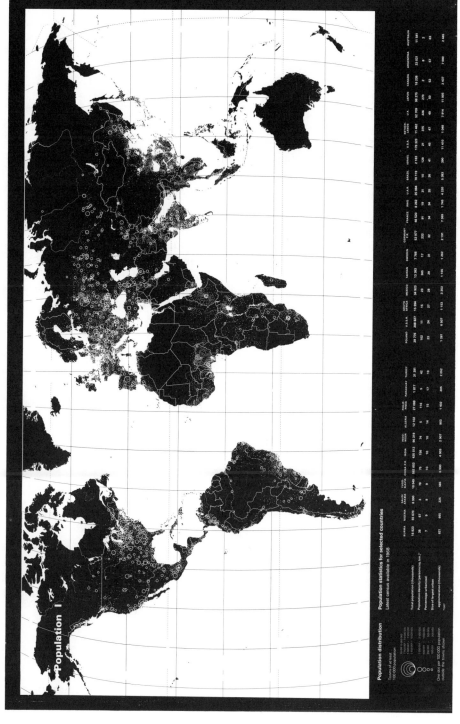

From the *Oxford Economic Atlas of the World*. © Oxford University Press.

TABLE 2-11.

	1938	1960
Poorly Fed Countries	66.5%	70.8%
Well-Fed Countries	33.5	29.2

Farmers in the hungry regions generally grow less food per acre than those in the well-fed regions. Many still scratch the soil with a pointed stick to plant seeds. They reap their crops with a big knife or sickle and carry loads on their backs or heads. Among the reasons for their agricultural primitiveness are the following:

1. Lack of Education. Almost every suggestion for raising food production in the hungry countries calls for more literacy and more technological training for the people. Education is needed before the farmers can handle better tools and seeds, improve storage and transportation, and use their land more efficiently.
    In the poorly fed countries, more than forty percent of the people are less than fifteen years of age, compared with about thirty percent in the United States. Teaching that many people to read and write and how to use better farming techniques requires many more schools and teachers than exist now.
2. Lack of Capital. Poor countries cannot afford commercial fertilizers, simple modern farm equipment, high-yield seeds, rural electric power, elaborate irrigation works, roads to get food to market quickly, and proper storage to prevent losses from spoilage and vermin. (Improper storage accounts for half the crop losses in some areas.)
3. Lack of Energy. Hungry people are tired people. A farmer on a diet that is half of what he needs for full health has barely enough energy to scratch the ground with a stick to plant his seeds. He does not have the strength to guide a plow, even if he had one, knew how to use it, and could afford a draft animal to pull it.
4. Dislike of Change. People are reluctant to do things in ways that are different from the ways they have always done them. The less they know about the rest of the world and the fewer visitors there are from abroad to talk to, the more reluctant people are to adopt something new when they hear about it.
    You do not have to go to Asia or Africa to observe a dislike of change. There is an old story of a midwestern American farmer who refused to buy a patented hog feeder because his grandfather never used one. Told that his pigs would grow as fat in six weeks with the new feeder as they did in six months by using his grandfather's methods, he shook his head and demanded, "What's time to a hog?"

Snowballing Effects

As population increases, the gap widens between the need for food and the supply of food. Workers on the land grow barely enough food for their own families; less and less is left for

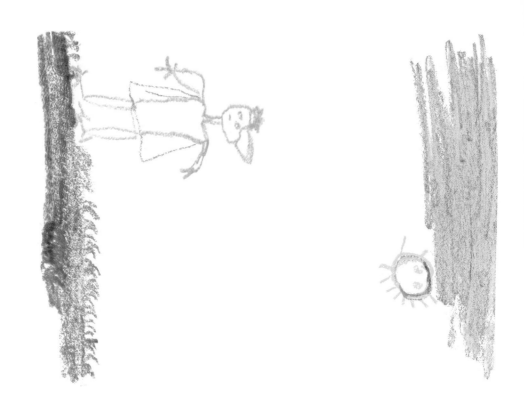

FIGURE 2-1. *Ruby by Ruby at Age 6.*

FIGURE 2-2. *A White Girl by Ruby at Age 6.*

FIGURE 2-4. A Negro Boy Jimmie's Age by Ruby at Age 6.

FIGURE 2-3. Jimmie by Ruby at Age 6.

FIGURE 2-9. *Approximate Cropland Area*

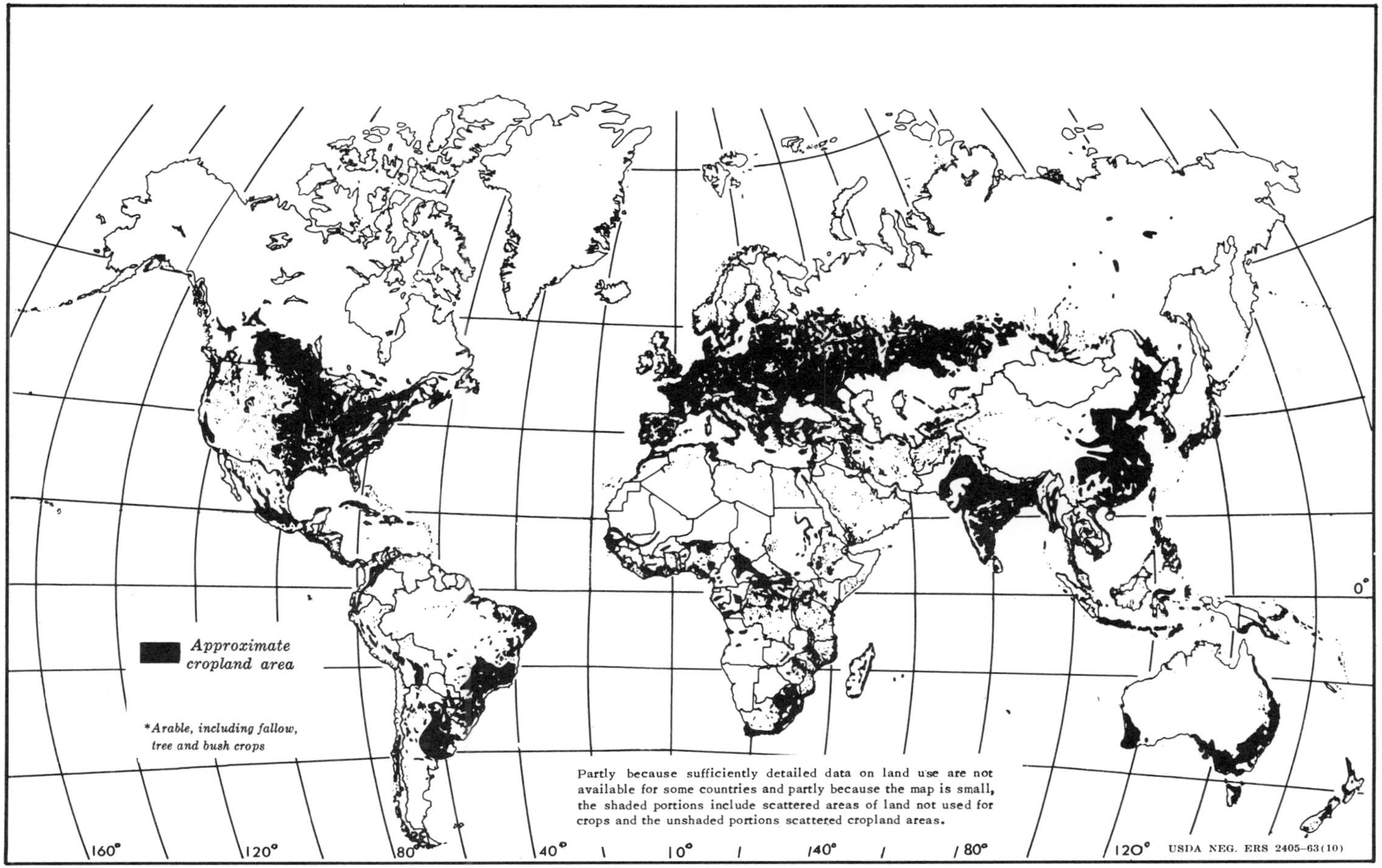

Approximate cropland area
*Arable, including fallow, tree and bush crops
Partly because sufficiently detailed data on land use are not available for some countries and partly because the map is small, the shaded portions include scattered areas of land not used for crops and the unshaded portions scattered cropland areas.
160°
120°
80°
40°
10°
140°
180°
120°
0°
USDA NEG. ERS 2405-63(10)

the cities.   Countries in the Far East that used to export rice to other lands now must import enough for their needs.

Even farms that use only human labor have work for a limited number of hands. Some of the farmers' children must go to the city; there they swell the ranks of the unskilled unemployed.   To keep them alive, a nation must use money it could otherwise spend on improving both industry and agriculture.

In the developing regions, scarcity of food often sends prices so high that even workers with good jobs cannot afford to eat very well.   We might compare the amount of time a factory worker in India and one in the United States have to work to feed themselves and their wives three meals a day of the quality Americans regard as a minimum diet for health.   At going prices and wages in the two countries, the Indian would have to work almost sixty-three hours a week and the American five and one-half hours to buy the food needed for a minimum American diet.   To buy the food that the Indian family actually eats, the Indian has to work twenty-nine and one-half hours and the American has to work two hours and forty-five minutes.   Such information provides comparisons on the relative standards of living in developed and less developed regions of the world.

ACTIVITY 5

Dilemma of the Tribes

In this activity, you will play a game that simulates a social conflict situation that occurred in some African nations shortly after they became independent. These countries had formerly been colonies of European nations, such as France and Great Britain.

Before the European nations arrived in Africa, the tribes had established the boundaries of their own territories. Some tribes cooperated by sharing territory for hunting, herding, or farming. Other tribes were hostile and strictly guarded the boundaries of their territories.

Later in time the European nations conquered African lands and set up colonial governments. They did not recognize the already established tribal boundaries. Therefore the colonial boundaries did not always correspond to the territory of a single tribe or to the territory of a closely related set of tribes. Moreover, when the colonies gained their independence, these colonial boundaries became the actual boundaries of the new independent nations. Here the dilemma arose. Sometimes tribes that were hostile to one another found themselves citizens of the same new state. Often when only two or three powerful tribes were involved, each of them was strongly tempted to try to dominate the new government.

"Dilemma of the Tribes" is a game simulating a situation in which two tribes of about equal strength are located in one nation. Both tribes want to protect their own interests and to control the policies of the new nation. We will call the tribes the *Golos* and the *Mantas*, and we will call the country *Equatoria*. Most participants will play the

From "Dilemma of the Tribes: Version 1," *Simulating Social Conflict*, SRSS Episodes in Social Inquiry Series (Boston: Allyn and Bacon, 1971). Copyright © 1971 by the American Sociological Association. Reprinted with permission.

role of chief of one tribe or the other. These players will be paired so that the two members in each pair represent the two tribes in Equatoria. There will be referees who will work with several of the pairs. You can imagine the referees as being United Nations observers or other uninvolved foreigners in a real-life situation.

The simulation is divided into twenty "rounds" of play, which might represent time intervals such as weeks in real life. In each round each member of a pair has to make a decision: whether to be cooperative (Choice A) or whether to be belligerent (Choice B) toward the chief of the other tribe. Each chief's choice is hidden from the other. The score on each round is determined by the *combination* of moves made by the two chiefs. After each round the referee records each player's score on the player's score sheet. The scoring system will be explained to you before you begin play.

ACTIVITY **6**

School Districts
for Millersburg

INTRODUCTION

In this activity, you will work in groups to make a decision about redistricting the city of Millersburg so that you can determine the locations of six new high schools. In so doing, you will experience this simulation in much the same way that high school students in a geography class would experience it. Begin by reading the following background material on the city of Millersburg.

THE CITY OF MILLERSBURG

Settlement of Millersburg began in 1819 when a fur trader established an outpost at the crossing of an Indian trail and the Shenango River. Shortly thereafter, pioneers built a dam and a mill on the site, and numerous settlers from western New York State moved into the new village. Millersburg was chosen to be the county seat in 1836, and it grew as a trading center for the surrounding valley farming area. In 1855 Millersburg was incorporated as a city. By 1860 it had a population of 5,162.

From Unit 4: "Political Geography," in *Geography in an Urban Age* (New York: The Macmillan Company, 1970). Copyright © 1970 by the Association of American Geographers. Reprinted with permission. Roger Kasperson, in cooperation with the Department of Geography at Clark University, Worcester, Massachusetts, was the originator of this activity.

In 1852 a plank road was built to connect Millersburg with the state capital. Then, shortly after the Civil War, railroads were constructed that linked the city with the rest of the state. These transportation facilities and plentiful woodlands nearby contributed to the growth of Millersburg between 1860 and 1885 as a lumbering center and as a center for the manufacture of agricultural tools. By 1885, however, the local pines were depleted and the industries declined. Manufacturing shifted to the production of small steam engines and, in 1903, a new factory was established to build "horseless carriages." Millersburg grew rapidly thereafter as an automotive center.

Population growth accompanied this industrial expansion. Between 1900 and 1920, the population of Millersburg increased from 19,000 to 65,000. By 1965 the city's population had reached 150,000.

Between 1900 and 1965 the composition of the city's population changed also. In 1850 the population was predominantly of western European extraction, made up of people who had migrated from New York State and from Canada. Between 1910 and 1920, however, large numbers of eastern Europeans settled in Millersburg. The eastern Europeans tended to band together in small, neighborhood communities, maintaining the traditions and the languages of their old countries. The children of the immigrants spoke their native language at home and with their neighborhood friends, and learned some English (their second language) at school. Most of the children found school difficult because of their limited ability with English.

In the 1920's American immigration laws were tightened and few immigrants found their way to Millersburg. The next influx of people were blacks who came from the southern United States. Although these people blended well with the mix of people already in Millersburg, there was a major racial disturbance in 1967, touched off by grievances against low wages, inferior schooling, and poor living conditions.

The city boasts a branch of the state university, a city community college, a technical training college, and a state school for the blind. The city recently built a new civic center and a new combined city hall and police building. The growth of cultural facilities has matched the growth of the population.

At present, Millersburg is still growing and trying to deal effectively with many problems. It has a total high school population of more than 12,000. The elementary school population is about 44,000. The high school population is bound to increase in the future as more people move to Millersburg and as the elementary students enter high school.

A unique situation exists with regard to the schools. An independent consultant group was selected by the school administration to study existing school facilities and to make recommendations for the future. Although it found some high schools in the area too old to be safe, the group did not recommend restoration or modernization of these buildings. Instead, the committee recommended that the city take a fresh look at its need for secondary schools and redistrict the city, building new high schools and phasing out those now in existence. The group estimated that six new high schools would be needed. School-board members, city officials, and interested citizens are now examining the implications of this proposal.

HIGH SCHOOL DISTRICTS FOR MILLERSBURG

In class, you will be part of a group that will undertake the task of redistricting the city — the proposal facing the civic leaders of Millersburg. The problem is to divide the city into six school districts and then determine the location of a high school in each district. It is not often that a city can begin fresh, unhampered by decisions made in the past, but this is the case now in Millersburg. Consequently, you will not have to take into account the high school district boundaries as they now exist.

Millersburg does not plan to have any junior high schools, only eight-year elementary schools and four-year high schools. There are no private high schools in the city.

On pages 44–47, you will find various kinds of information in the form of maps to help you make thoughtful decisions about the school districts. Figure 2-10 shows the locations of the industrial and business areas in Millersburg; Figure 2-11 gives information on the location of high- and low-income areas; Figure 2-12 details areas where minority groups live; and Figure 2-13 provides data on population densities in the city. As you undertake this exercise, remember that each of the six high schools will be an all-purpose school, each preparing students for business, a trade, or college.

PROFILES OF CERTAIN MILLERSBURG CITIZENS

William Kent

William Kent, age forty-three, is president of the Millersburg school board. His family has been in business in Millersburg for three generations, and he will assume the presidency of the city's leading department store when his father retires. Meanwhile, he is a member of the board of directors of City Bank and generally finds time to frequent the country club's golf course. The product of private schools himself, he has yielded to public pressure and has permitted his children to attend the public schools. This is quite a concession for socially minded William, but he is willing to work for quality education. His motivating drive for serving as a school-board member is to see that his ideals are included in policy decisions.

William lives at a prestigious address in a part of town where families are financially able to send their youngsters to college. Although the Kent children are still in elementary school, William is looking toward the day when they will attend high school. He envisions a school for his part of town that will be devoted primarily to preparing students for college. The districting problem that is facing the community has the potential for fulfilling that dream.

FIGURE 2-10.   *Millersburg: Industrial and Business Areas*

MILLERSBURG

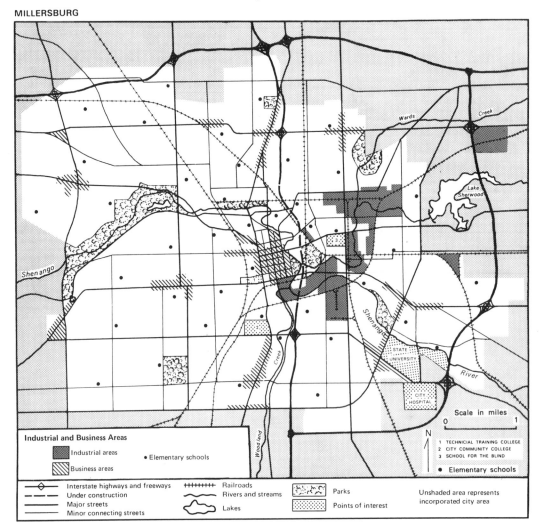

FIGURE 2-11. *Millersburg: Income Areas*

MILLERSBURG

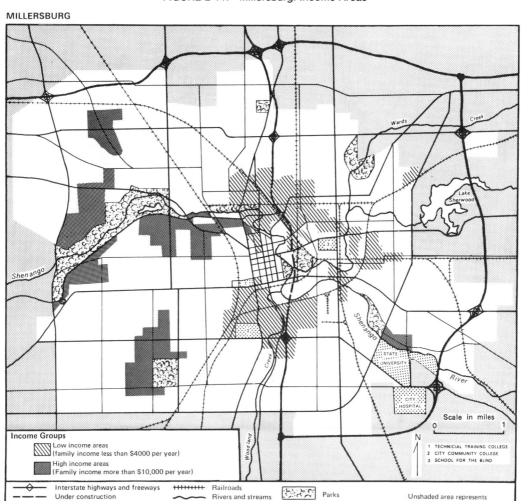

Income Groups

Low income areas
(family income less than $4000 per year)

High income areas
(Family income more than $10,000 per year)

Scale in miles
0 — 1

1 TECHNICIAL TRAINING COLLEGE
2 CITY COMMUNITY COLLEGE
3 SCHOOL FOR THE BLIND

	Interstate highways and freeways		Railroads		Parks	Unshaded area represents
	Under construction		Rivers and streams		Points of interest	incorporated city area
	Major streets		Lakes			
	Minor connecting streets					

FIGURE 2-12. *Millersburg: Minority Groups*

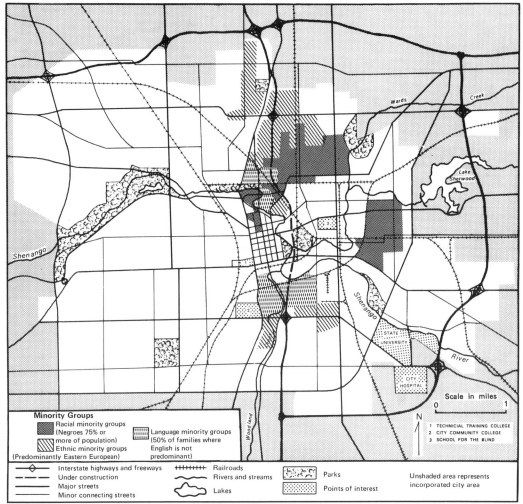

FIGURE 2-13. *Millersburg: Population Density*

MILLERSBURG

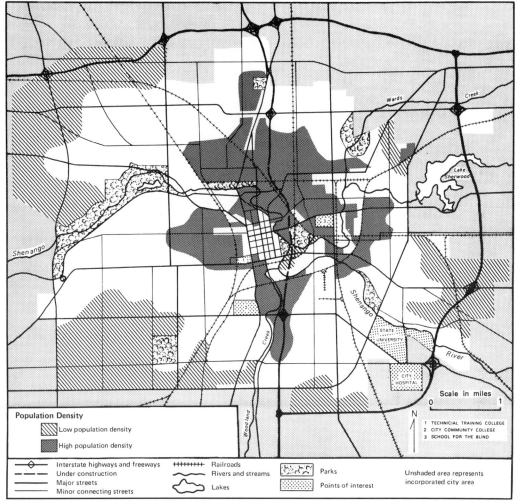

Melvin Paine

Melvin Paine is left of center in his political and social convictions. At age twenty-nine, he is a regular contributor to the Sunday editorial page of the conservative *Millersburg Tribune*. He is the spokesman for the oppressed and downtrodden. After graduating from college, where he was a champion debater, he went on to spend two years with the Peace Corps in West Africa. He returned to his home town to take up the banner of social injustice and to accept a low-paying job at the Community Center. Every civic group has felt Mel Paine's presence.

Mel has begun to believe that change will occur only through political action and he now has aspirations for a city or a state office. Mel fully realizes the consequences that can befall minority groups as a result of school districting decisions. He wants to do his best to protect their interests and, in the process, perhaps to further his political career.

Frank Sarma

Frank Sarma, age fifty-five, was about to leave the family farm to attend college when the Great Depression hit. He knew hard work and hard times and learned the value of a dollar. In the late 1930's, he and his young wife moved to Millersburg where Frank worked in a mill during the day and studied accounting at night. Frank earned his certification when the children were small and entered an established accounting firm as a junior member. He earned a reputation for careful work and conservative advice. His work with certain accounts brought him into contact with Millersburg's power elite and later Frank found himself running unopposed for the office of city treasurer, a position he has held ever since.

Frank, of all people, knows the condition of the city's finances. The proposed new high school system will be a drain on existing funds and will raise the question of a school bond. Since he wants to keep costs as low as possible, he feels that schools should not have swimming pools and other extras. Nor does he think the city should be burdened with providing school buses. He is interested in working on the problem of establishing school-district boundaries since there may be a solution that will save the taxpayers' money.

LeRoy Washington

LeRoy Washington, age thirty-four, is the leader of the black community. LeRoy dropped out of school at age sixteen and learned the code of the streets. On chilly afternoons he often sought refuge in the public library where he staked out a table facing the door. There he read everything from Karl Marx to biographies of famous blacks. For a time, LeRoy came under the sway of the Baptist leader, Reverend Evans, who advocated passive approaches for the integration and betterment of black people. The slowness of the movement for black improvement irritated impatient LeRoy, especially as he caught the rumblings of the black militant movement. LeRoy has let his hair grow long and bushy, wears African print shirts, and takes great pride in his ancestry and cultural heritage. He does not want to see his people submerge their identity in white middle-class values.

LeRoy's interest in the school districting question is to see that his people get their own high school with all the modern facilities a good school should have. He hopes that, if the area gets a facility of its own, the black community can work to solve its own problems and the school can help to meet the needs of the adolescents there.

ACTIVITY 7

Settling Accounts

When the Chinese Communist party came to power in 1949, it faced two major tasks in the rural areas: one political and one economic. Politically, it wanted to establish control over the people at the village level. At the same time, it wanted to win the confidence and support of the peasants for the new government of China. The government had to solve the economic problem of producing enough food to feed China's large and growing population. Land reform was the first large attempt at solving these problems.

The following reading is excerpted from near the end of Part 1 of a short story about land reform in Tungmao (pronounced doong-mah-o), a village in northern China. It is typical of land reform in much of China. The characters and setting are taken from Chou Li-po's novel *The Hurricane*,[1] but the story itself is based on other land reform accounts, both Chinese and Western. It attempts to provide a vivid example of how land reform was actually carried out.

[The story picks up where a Communist party land reform team leader by the name of Hsiao is organizing the peasants of Tungmao into a Peasants Association.]

From "Land Reform: Part 1," *Social Change: The Case of Rural China*, SRSS Episodes in Social Inquiry Series (Boston: Allyn and Bacon, 1971). Copyright © 1971 by the American Sociological Association. Reprinted with permission. Designed by Ezra Vogel, Harvard University; Philip West, Indiana University; David L. Grossman, Brookline High School, Brookline, Massachusetts; Suzanne Davenport, Hamilton-Wenham Regional High School, Hamilton, Massachusetts; and John C. Williams, Weston High School, Weston, Massachusetts.
[1] Published by the Foreign Language Press (Peking), 1955.

Pronunciation Chart

Chao Yu-Lin	(jah-o yo leen)	Li	(lee)
Han	(hah-n)	Pai	(bah-ee)
Hsiao	(see-ah-o)	Tungmao	(doong-mah-o)
Kuo	(gwoh)	Wang	(wah-ng)

Team Leader Hsiao was pleased with Little Wang's new friend Chao. In fact every team member had made valuable friends in the village. Chao suggested to Hsiao and Little Wang that they should go visit Kuo (pronounced Gwoh), another peasant, who was anxious to meet the land reform team members. And so they started out on another day, gathering stories, befriending the peasants.

They met Chao's friend at the well outside the gate of Goodman Tu's, for Kuo was hired by Tu to keep his horses, and Kuo drew water for them from the well. Kuo smiled as Little Wang introduced Hsiao and himself. Then the men walked to Kuo's room which was attached to the horse barn. They passed Big Li's house on the way, but Kuo did not seem to be afraid. The men sat in the tiny room, chatting.

Kuo was only twenty-four, but his face was heavily wrinkled. He was very poor. His mother died when he was eight. His father hired himself out to Han Number Six as a farmhand, and took the boy along. As Hsiao listened quietly, Kuo told his story:

"One evening Han was playing cards, and he called to Old Kuo, my father, to come and play a hand with him for small stakes. 'I can't play,' my father said politely. Han shook him by the arm and said, 'How dare you refuse me, you pig!' And though my father really did not know how to play cards, he could not refuse. As he sat at that table until morning, his mind dozed, for he was very tired. Han would not let him leave. Well, when it was through, Old Kuo had lost a whole year's wages. Han laughed at him as he left. It broke my father's heart, for now he had no way to put food in our mouths. The next day he got sick, groaning and sweating in his bed. Han heard that he was ill, and he told his bodyguard, 'It's New Year's Day! Tell him to stop that damned groaning.' In two weeks' time Old Kuo was nearly dead. The snows blew in on him through the cracks in our lean-to next to Han's house. Goodman Tu had come one night to drink with Han beside his warm fire, when Han's bodyguard rushed in and said: 'Old Kuo is dying fast!' 'Well, get him out-doors,' ordered Han. 'Get him out of the house, it's bad luck to let him die inside!' 'Yes,' said Goodman Tu, 'get him into the yard. His breath will stink up the whole place.' The bodyguard dashed away, and in another minute he was carrying Old Kuo out into the winter storm. I fought him as hard as I could, but he pushed me off despite my sobbing and yelling, for I was only a little boy. Very soon my father was frozen to death. I knelt there beside him, hugging him, crying. 'What can I do now, Father? You die, and you leave me nothing. What can I do?' Han saw me through the window and ordered his servants to chase me away. 'Throw him out! We won't have a howling brat around here.' That was in 1934. After that, until 1940, I did what small jobs I could, just to get a bit of food on my tongue."

After pausing to catch his breath, and to think again about his troubled life, Kuo told Hsiao how he had come to work for Goodman Tu. Tu had approached Kuo one day and he said:

"You work for me, Young Kuo. I've known you since you were a boy. You know how to work. I'll pay you well, and give you whatever you ask."

"I want six hundred dollars a year."

"All right, I'll give you six hundred."

And so Kuo began slaving for Goodman Tu, dawn to dusk, in wind or rain, pushing and pulling and straining. But when the end of the year came, Tu did not pay him. Instead, Goodman Tu killed a single pig and shared it among his farmhands. Young Kuo got five pounds of pork. He tried to refuse the gift, for he knew what was coming. "If you refuse, then you can go elsewhere for work," said Goodman Tu. So Kuo accepted, and he began another year working for Tu.

When winter came, Kuo needed a jacket. He went to Tu to ask for the last year's wages. Goodman Tu only shouted at him, "Didn't you eat my pork? What more do you want?"

When Kuo heard this, he was blinded with anger. He grabbed a meat chopper, but the bodyguard blocked his way.

"What do you think you're doing, you communist?" said Big Li.

He beat Kuo to the ground and made him repent, and Goodman Tu added another ten months' labor to Kuo, for punishment.

When he finished his story, Young Kuo said to Little Wang:

"Han and Tu are our enemies — my father's and mine."

"Then why didn't you speak up at the meeting?" asked Little Wang.

"Who dared to speak up? The landlords sent their spies, and they kept staring at us."

"Why don't you join with friends and fight together? Join with all the poor who have suffered at the hands of Han and Goodman Tu? Together you can move mountains. Alone, you are nothing."

"Yes, we must join together."

And Kuo jumped up and led them across town to another poor peasant, Pai (pronounced Bah-ee), who he thought would be eager to help with the land reform.

Pai was a lazy little man who would rather sleep than do anything else. His wife constantly screeched at him, but it did no good. He had had hard times, and he grew to expect the worst, so he did not strain himself to get anything better. He owned a small rocky piece of land which barely gave them enough to eat. But Pai's humor was always good and he would sit all day by the kang, smoking a cigarette, taking his wife's harsh words without a groan.

Pai greeted Kuo warmly and ushered the land reform workers into his house. Mrs. Pai, who had just been quarreling with her husband about work, listened as the men began talking together. Little by little Pai discovered the reason for their visit, and he obliged Hsiao and Little Wang by telling some of his own history, as each peasant was urged to do.

In 1935, Pai settled in Tungmao. He was a hard worker then, and he cleared fifty mou of wasteland. That year he had a good harvest. He began to make his way, so he got married. But the next year Han's horses were let loose upon his land just as the crops were ready for harvesting. Nearly everything was lost. Pai got into a fierce fight with Han's bodyguard and the bodyguard reported it all to his master. Han was furious at the nerve shown by this peasant. He galloped up to Pai's hut and, without a word, smashed everything in the house, pots, kettles, pans, everything. Pai made a complaint to the village government about it, but Han bought them all off, and before Pai knew what was happening he was thrown into prison for "doubting the honor" of an "innocent" citizen. His wife had to sell most of the land to get him out. Everything was lost. It was then that he became devoted to laziness. "I only want enough to keep alive," he would say, crawling back into bed. He never bothered about food and clothing, and his wife quarreled with him long into the night, day after day. But to no avail.

"Yes, you work hard," he would say to her. "But does it get you anywhere? Where are your chickens? They all died. And look what happened to your pig, my dear Shu-ying!"

Whenever he mentioned the pig, his wife would burst into tears. For, with the pig, there went perhaps the saddest story of all the peasants, and Pai, seeing the eager faces of Little Wang and Hsiao before him, told each detail of that story.

His wife had bought a suckling pig, intending to fatten it up and sell it to get a little money. Every day she would carry her baby boy in her arms as she gathered leaves and fodder for the animal. By August the pig had filled out. But one day it strayed into Han's garden and trampled down a few flowers. By the time Mrs. Pai caught up with the pig, Han Number Six had his gun aimed at the porker's head. Mrs. Pai pushed the gun aside and begged Han to pardon the animal.

"If you want to save your pig, you must pay for my flowers!" yelled Han, and he swung the gun around so hard that it threw her to the ground on top of the child. The boy's head was cut deeply at the temple, and he was unconscious. Mrs. Pai, horrified at the sight of blood pouring from her limp son, rushed home to care for the child. As she ran, BANG! Han shot the hog. A few days later the poor child died, having lost too much blood. A child's life had been taken to pay for a few flowers. It was a price that Pai and his wife had never overcome, and their grief still hung upon them.

When Pai was finished, Little Wang asked:

"Will you help us tackle Han?"

"He's too lazy to lift a toe," said his wife.

"That's right, keep howling at me, woman," retorted Pai.

Little Wang turned to Mrs. Pai.

"If we tackle the landlords," he asked her, "will you accuse Han Number Six in public?"

She was silent for a moment, then she said:

"I've never done it before. I'm afraid I couldn't speak well."

"Can't speak?" laughed Old Pai. "She's yacking from daylight to dark." Then he added, touching the shoulders of the workers, "Yes, she will speak. And that's settled."

Hsiao and Little Wang returned with Kuo to his shack by Goodman Tu's stables, where the three of them continued to talk hour after hour. They were elated, for the first winds of land revolution had already begun to blow, and they could feel it gathering strength in the village. Who could tell how soon Tungmao would be blown clean of the fat and evil landlords?

[The Communist party program of land reform had the following basic effects:

1. Changed power relationships between the landlords and peasants. The power of the landlords was destroyed, while that of most of the peasants, especially those who cooperated with the Communist party, was increased through the organization of the Peasants Association.
2. Changed the ownership of land and possessions. The land and surplus possessions of the landlord were confiscated and redistributed among the peasantry.
3. Effected a consolidation of Chinese Communist control in rural China through the organization and control of the Peasants Association.]

ACTIVITY 8

Culture Change:
A Trend toward
Uniformity

In this exercise, you will analyze a series of photographs to reach some tentative conclusions about the cultural characteristics of cities. You will then analyze the learning experience in terms of the concepts developed and the teaching strategy used.

For the first part of the activity, study Figures 2-14, 2-15, 2-16, 2-17, 2-18, 2-19, and 2-20 — pictures of seven cities from around the world. After you have studied the photographs, name the country and the continent in which each city is located, listing the locations next to the figure numbers. Keep in mind the clues that helped you make your decisions. When you have completed this part of the exercise, your instructor will provide you with the correct answers. Score one point for each country you identified correctly and one point for each continent you identified correctly, for a possible total score of fourteen points.

After you have identified and discussed the first set of photographs, study the pictures in Figures 2-21, 2-22, 2-23, 2-24, 2-25, and 2-26. Again, identify the country and the continent in which each city is located. You may find it more difficult to make decisions about these pictures since there are fewer clues given in them. However, do not worry too much about the correctness of your answers — simply give your first impression of where each city might be located. Score this activity in the same way you scored the preceding one.

From Unit 3: "Cultural Geography," in *Geography in an Urban Age* (New York: The Macmillan Company, 1970). Copyright © 1970 by the Association of American Geographers. Reprinted with permission. Richard F. Hough and Max C. Kirkeberg of California State University, San Francisco, were the originators of the idea for this activity.

FIGURE 2-14.

© 1961 National Geographic Society

FIGURE 2-15.

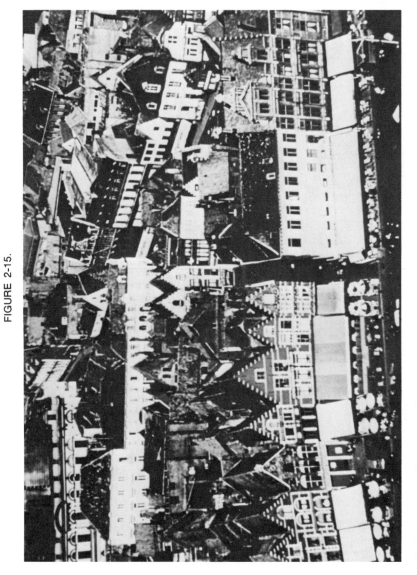

FIGURE 2-16.

© National Geographic Society

FIGURE 2-17.

FIGURE 2-18.

FIGURE 2-19.

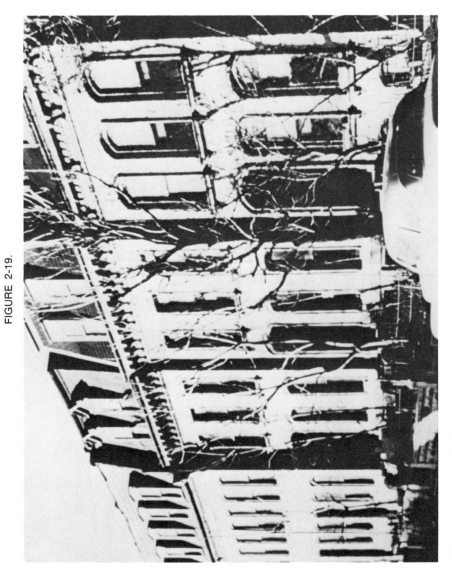

FIGURE 2-20.

© 1967 National Geographic Society

FIGURE 2-21.

© National Geographic Society

FIGURE 2-22.

© 1962 National Geographic Society

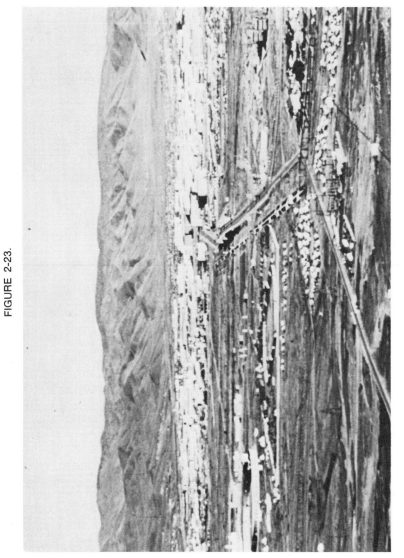

FIGURE 2-23.

FIGURE 2-24.

© National Geographic Society

FIGURE 2-25.

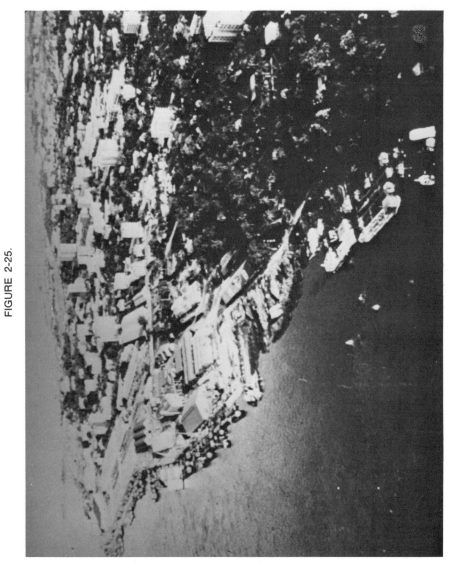

FIGURE 2-26.

ACTIVITY 9

The Decision-Maker

Below you will find some information about Robert Metky, an up-and-coming business executive with a large Kansas City–based firm. Bob is currently faced with a difficult decision: where to build a new twenty-million-dollar cement plant. Although the story of Bob's life and the data he has to consider concerning the location of the new plant are fictitious, the problem he faces is quite typical of those actually faced by business executives. As you read about Bob Metky and examine the information he must consider in arriving at his decision on the plant location, try and place yourself in his position. What would you do if you were THE DECISION-MAKER?

ROBERT METKY

Robert Metky is on his way up. At forty-four, he is vice-president for research and development for Compac Industries, a large and highly diversified firm based in Kansas

From Part 2 of *Inquiries in Sociology* (Boston: Allyn and Bacon, 1972). Copyright © 1972 by the American Sociological Association. Reprinted with permission. This teaching activity was created by Graeme S. Fraser and Thomas J. Switzer of Sociological Resources for the Social Studies.

City. Success did not come easily for Bob. High school graduation was followed by a stint on his parents' Iowa farm, after which he spent four years with Uncle Sam's Navy. The decision to enter business school at the University of Iowa was difficult, given the fact that Bob was virtually ten years the senior of the other freshmen. He often commented to his wife Pat that he was old enough to be teaching the courses. Three children did not make matters any easier. Money was hard to come by. But hard work and perseverance paid off. Bob got his degree in business administration, though he is quick to admit that he was not at the top of his class.

Graduation from Iowa was followed by two years as office manager for a small aircraft firm in Des Moines, where Bob first met John Nicholls, president of Compac Industries. John took an immediate liking to Bob and finally persuaded him to make the move to Kansas City. Bob started with Compac as a salesman, but both he and John knew that this job was only temporary. Bob was marked for bigger things. At each opportunity John saw to it that Bob was promoted, usually to the consternation of those being bypassed. Bob seemed to get along all right with those under him, but his rapid upward movement in the company left a small trail of bitterness.

Bob's current position makes him one of three vice-presidents immediately responsible to John. To say the least, competition is keen among the vice-presidents. John is approaching retirement age and there is speculation that he might step down sometime this year. Pat is pushing hard for Bob's promotion to president of the company. With Jeff away at the University of Wisconsin, there is no question that they could use the money.

Bob's image in the community is very good. He has purchased a fine, but not elaborate, home in Rolling Ridge, a suburb of Kansas City. Pat is active in school and community programs, and Bob in church and civic work, although he does not always have as much time as he would like to devote to it. His interest in civic improvements resulted in the suggestion by some that he run as a Republican candidate for city council. Bob gracefully declined the offer, claiming that his church and other community activities would suffer should he be elected. And, anyway, business seems to take more and more of his time.

Now he is especially busy, with the final decision on the location of a cement factory less than a month away. For six months he has been gathering information on where to build the plant in the Kansas City area. Two possible sites have finally been selected, both north of St. Joseph, Missouri, but tracking down the bits and pieces of information on the properties has been a lot of work. If it were only a matter of which site would most benefit the company, the decision would not be so hard. But other considerations have come to light. The residents of St. Joseph oppose the plant and are even bringing pressure to bear on state officials to prevent building such a factory so close to the city. In fact, so many factors and so many people are involved that Bob is not sure which way to turn.

HOSLER AND HONSBERGER   —MANAGEMENT
                                                  CONSULTANTS

918 CLARK BUILDING
KANSAS CITY, MISSOURI 64110
Telephone (818) 786-2096

October 7, 1969

TO: Robert Metky
FROM: Dan Hosler
SUBJECT: St. Joseph (Missouri) Cement Works: A Preliminary Report

Analysis of the feasibility of constructing a $20,000,000 cement works in the vicinity of St. Joseph, Missouri, was completed September 30, 1969. A final comprehensive report is being prepared. It will be completed October 20, 1969.

The preliminary findings are as follows:

- Two sites appear to be possible. The first site (hereafter called S-1) is located in Buchanan County approximately one and one-half miles northwest of the St. Joseph city limits and adjacent to the Missouri River. The second site (hereafter called S-2) is in Andrew County, close to Amazonia and some eleven miles from St. Joseph.

- At S-1, forty-six acres of flat, well-drained land are available for immediate purchase. Prospects for site development and future plant expansion are excellent. Access to the river is good, and existing road and rail access is adequate.

- At S-2, sixty acres of cheap, level, well-drained land are available for purchase. Prospects for site development and plant expansion are adequate. Access to the river is barely adequate. Road access to the site is poor. Improvement of access and transport facilities would be costly and time-consuming.

- The analysis indicates that S-1 is the better location. S-1 has available to it a larger limestone deposit and better (developed) transport facilities. Further, the Buchanan County Board of Supervisors is willing to negotiate (i) sharing the cost of site development and (ii) granting tax concessions.

- On the basis of past experience, we feel that you might run into adverse reaction from authorities and the public in St. Joseph regarding air pollution. Such reaction could prejudice consideration of S-1 as a possible site. At this time, the cost of installing the necessary anti-pollution equipment would make the total cost of developing S-1 prohibitive.

DONAHUE AND DONAHUE
ATTORNEYS-AT-LAW
503 FIRST NATIONAL BUILDING   KANSAS CITY, MISSOURI 64112
Telephone (818) 798-3456

November 3, 1969

TO: Robert Metky
FROM: William Donahue

This memo is in response to your inquiry regarding the air pollution laws of the State of Missouri. Air pollution laws are in effect for the St. Louis area and for the Kansas City area. These laws are not applicable outside the specified areas. St. Joseph and Buchanan County are not included in the legislation applying to the Kansas City area. At present, then, there are no state pollution laws that must be complied with if you decide to build the proposed cement plant in Buchanan County.

We would like to point out, however, that St. Joseph has indicated an interest in having the boundaries of the Kansas City Air Pollution District extended so as to include St. Joseph and its surrounding area. In the event that this happens, your plant will, of course, have to meet state pollution standards as specified by the State Code of Missouri.

The appropriate sections from the State Code are attached to this memo for your information.

CITY AND COUNTY SPLIT ON NEW CEMENT PLANT
(Article from the *St. Joseph Examiner*, November 12, 1969)

JEFFERSON CITY — A committee of St. Joseph residents, including Mayor Delmar Marks, today presented arguments to the State Air Conservation Commission in opposition to a proposed twenty-million-dollar cement plant to be located north of St. Joseph by Compac Industries of Kansas City.

Mayor Marks argued that because of prevailing winds, the cement plant will pollute the air of northern St. Joseph and prevent further expansion of the city in that direction. Charles Wright, chairman of the Air Conservation Commission, informed the concerned citizens that Missouri has no state-wide air pollution laws, thus preventing state interference with the building of the plant.

The Commission also heard from Don Rathe, county supervisor for Buchanan County. Mr. Rathe stressed the benefits to be gained from having the cement plant built in Buchanan County. He specifically cited increased tax revenue and job opportunities.

The Air Conservation Commission took the matter under advisement and agreed to meet with Robert Metky, vice-president of Compac Industries, to discuss the company's plans for controlling air pollution from the proposed factory.

ARE WE CONCERNED?
(Editorial from the *St. Joseph Examiner*, November 16, 1969)

Concern by government, the media, and the public about problems of law and order, drug abuse, racism, and inflation has often been expressed. But alarm about another problem that most surely threatens the well-being of us all is just beginning to be felt. In most of our large cities today, more wastes are being discharged into the atmosphere than are dissipated under certain weather conditions. The result is air pollution. Polluted air can contribute to sickness, disability, premature death; it can soil and damage buildings and materials of all kinds; it can injure and destroy farm crops and other vegetation; it can blight our cities and degrade the quality of our lives. In addition, the more distant future holds the ominous possibility of radical changes in climatic conditions.

The idea that St. Joseph could be plagued by the blight of air pollution seems ridiculous. Murk and smog — terms that may be less troublesome than air pollution — are facts of life in huge industrial cities like Chicago, Los Angeles, New York, and Cleveland. Here, in St. Joseph, there has been no need for concern or action about the ravages of air pollution. But is this now true?

The recent announcement that Compac Industries is considering a building site on the Missouri River just outside the city limits for the construction of a $20,000,000 cement factory is a case in point. Should this plant be built, it undoubtedly will provide some jobs for local workers; over the long term it may even stimulate further industrial development in the area. Without question, it will bolster the sagging finances of the county. But what about the threat such a plant would pose to the clean air of our city: the noxious fumes and the destructive grey dust? Since Missouri does not have state-wide laws governing air pollution, we can only hope that any industries locating here will take steps to control the discharging of dangerous wastes into the atmosphere. But is hope sufficient? The experience of other cities suggests otherwise. Before it is too late, laws to control air pollution in this region must be enacted. Moreover, the manpower and technology to enforce them must also be made available.

A large cement works is only a beginning. Other factories, other sources of pollutants, will follow. Clearly, we should not hobble industrial development. An expanding economy is essential. Nevertheless, we cannot be blind to nature's limited capacity to absorb wastes. Air pollution is a serious and growing problem. Steps to control the problem must be taken now; the near future may be too late.

ACTIVITY 10

Watchung

You are going to study relationships between man and the surface of the land by looking at part of the Watchung Mountain area in north central New Jersey. After you learn a few simple characteristics of the land forms, rocks, and soils of the area, you should be able to make some "educated guesses" or predictions about where agriculture, settlement, transportation routes, and industry would most likely be found. After you have made these predictions and checked them against a topographic map and an aerial photograph, you will then look at how man's changing technical abilities and desires have led him in recent years to respond differently to some of the habitat features of the Watchung landscape.

The map in Figure 2-27 shows the general location of the Watchung area. The concentric ridges, indicated by the solid black areas, are the Watchung Mountains. These ridges contrast sharply with the lower-lying country (dotted on the map) between and beyond the mountains.

The ridges of the Watchung Mountains are composed of igneous rock called basalt. Basalt is a very resistant and massive rock which weathers well and does not erode easily. The areas between and around these basalt ridges are composed of shale — a very different kind of rock. Shale is much softer and more easily weathered and eroded than basalt. Thus the basalt areas have remained as high, steep ridges for many millions of

From Unit 5: "Habitat and Resources," in *Geography in an Urban Age* (New York: The Macmillan Company, 1970). Copyright © 1970 by the Association of American Geographers. Reprinted with permission. Melvin G. Marcus of The University of Michigan and Buckley F. Robbins of East Tennessee State University developed the original idea for this activity.

FIGURE 2-27. *Physiographic Regions of New Jersey*

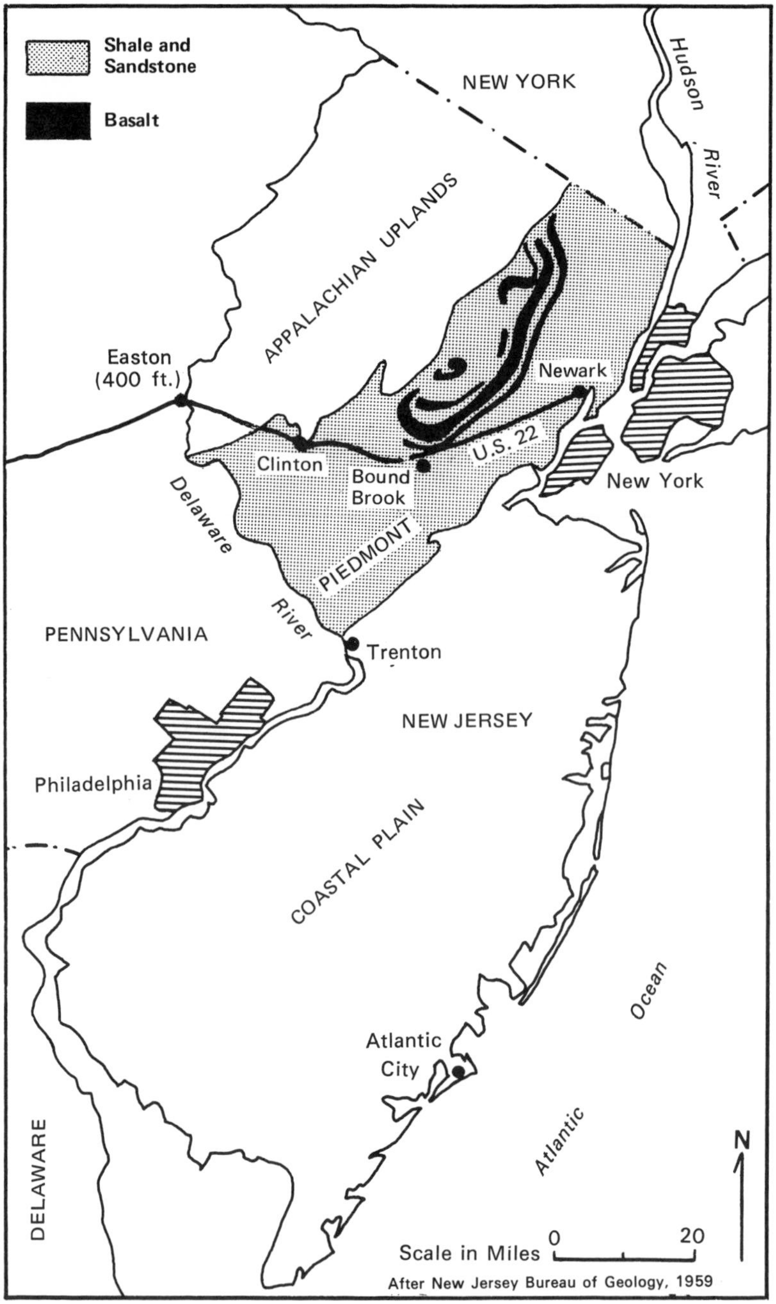

Scale in Miles 0   20

After New Jersey Bureau of Geology, 1959

years whereas the shale areas have worn down into low-lying, somewhat level expanses. The cut-away diagram of the Watchung Mountains in Figure 2-28 shows that the steep ridges of the mountains are composed of slanting layers of basalt sandwiched between worn-down shale layers.

The difference in hardness between shale and basalt accounts not only for the contrasting landforms but also for differences in the soils that have developed from the two kinds of rock. Because basalt is so hard and dense, it is not readily affected by the processes of weathering. In weathering, rocks decompose and disintegrate. Weathering ultimately changes rocks into fine, loose matter from which soils are formed. Basalt breaks up very slowly and produces only thin, stony soils. Also, what little loose material it does produce is easily eroded — that is, the material is carried away by water flowing down the slope or it simply slides off the steep slopes.

In contrast, the softer shale provides an excellent base for soil formation. Weathering of shale produces large amounts of fine particles. These are not subject to such rapid erosion as in basalt areas, since shale areas tend to be fairly level. Thus soils that have formed over shale areas are deeper and less stony than soils in basalt areas. They are potentially more productive for farming than soils in basalt areas.

How do these closely interrelated physical characteristics and processes affect the

FIGURE 2-28. *The Watchung Mountains*

THE WATCHUNG MOUNTAINS

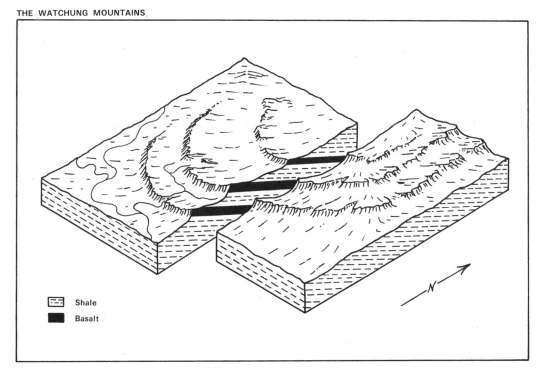

Shale

Basalt

N

choice of locations for certain human activities? To answer this question, you will make location predictions (and then verify them) for different types of activities. Think about the following questions in preparation for this activity:

1. Does steepness of slope affect the choice of location for farming?
2. Which type of area, basalt or shale, would have the best soils for farming?
3. In which type of area would it be easiest to use farm machinery?
4. In which type of area would it be easiest to build houses and farm buildings?
5. In which type of area would it be easiest to obtain water? Why?
6. Part of the Watchung area is covered with forests. Would you expect to find forests mainly on the basalt areas or the shale areas?
7. Do steep slopes affect the location of roads? In what way?
8. What factors are important in deciding the particular routes of main highways?
9. Which type of area, basalt or shale, would be best for the construction of industrial plants?
10. Which type of area would be best for urban development?

PREDICTING 1956 SETTLEMENT PATTERNS AND HIGHWAYS

Figure 2-29 ("Participant's Work Map") shows a contour map of the Watchung Mountain area. You will use this map to register your predictions for the following four land use activities: agricultural areas, rural settlement, U. S. Highway 22, and urban and industrial areas (1956).

Figure 2-30 ("Agricultural Areas") shows four potential choices (labeled A, B, C, and D) for agricultural areas. Select the one that you think would most likely be used for agricultural purposes and shade that area on your work map (Figure 2-29).

Next look at Figure 2-31 ("Rural Settlement"). You will see that there are again four choices. Choose the one you think would be the best rural settlement and shade the area on your work map.

Follow the same procedure for Figure 2-32 ("U. S. Highway 22") and for Figure 2-33 ("Urban and Industrial Areas, 1956"), choosing one of the four potential sites in each figure and registering it on the work map (Figure 2-29).

When you have completed your work map, turn to pages 206–7 and look at Figure 3-7 ("Watchung Mountain Area Topographic Map") and at Figure 3-8 ("1956 Aerial Photograph of Watchung Mountain Area") to confirm your predictions. Be prepared to discuss the reasons for your choices.

FIGURE 2-29. *Participant's Work Map*

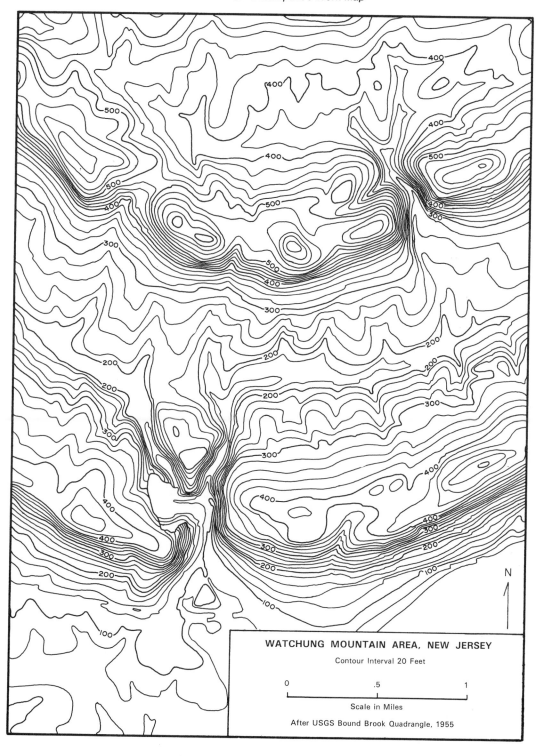

WATCHUNG MOUNTAIN AREA, NEW JERSEY

Contour Interval 20 Feet

0 .5 1

Scale in Miles

After USGS Bound Brook Quadrangle, 1955

FIGURE 2-30. *Agricultural Areas*

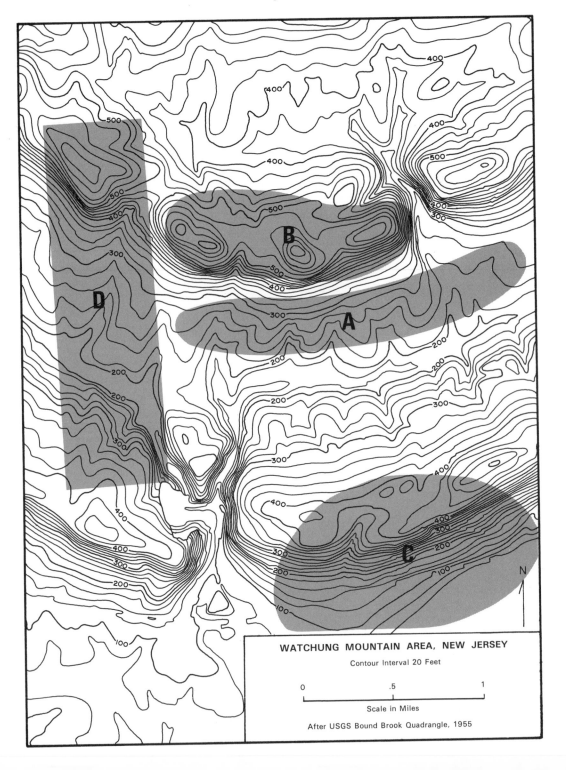

WATCHUNG MOUNTAIN AREA, NEW JERSEY

Contour Interval 20 Feet

0   .5   1

Scale in Miles

After USGS Bound Brook Quadrangle, 1955

FIGURE 2-31. *Rural Settlement*

RURAL SETTLEMENT

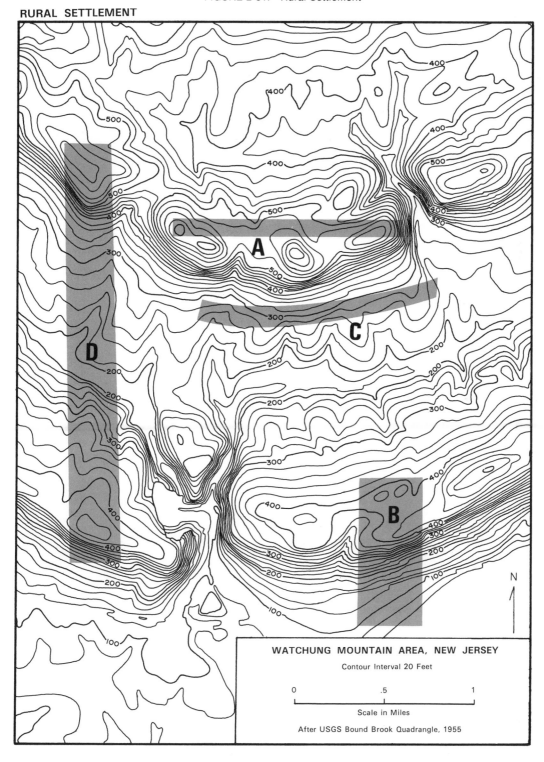

WATCHUNG MOUNTAIN AREA, NEW JERSEY

Contour Interval 20 Feet

0 .5 1

Scale in Miles

After USGS Bound Brook Quadrangle, 1955

FIGURE 2-32. *U.S. Highway 22*

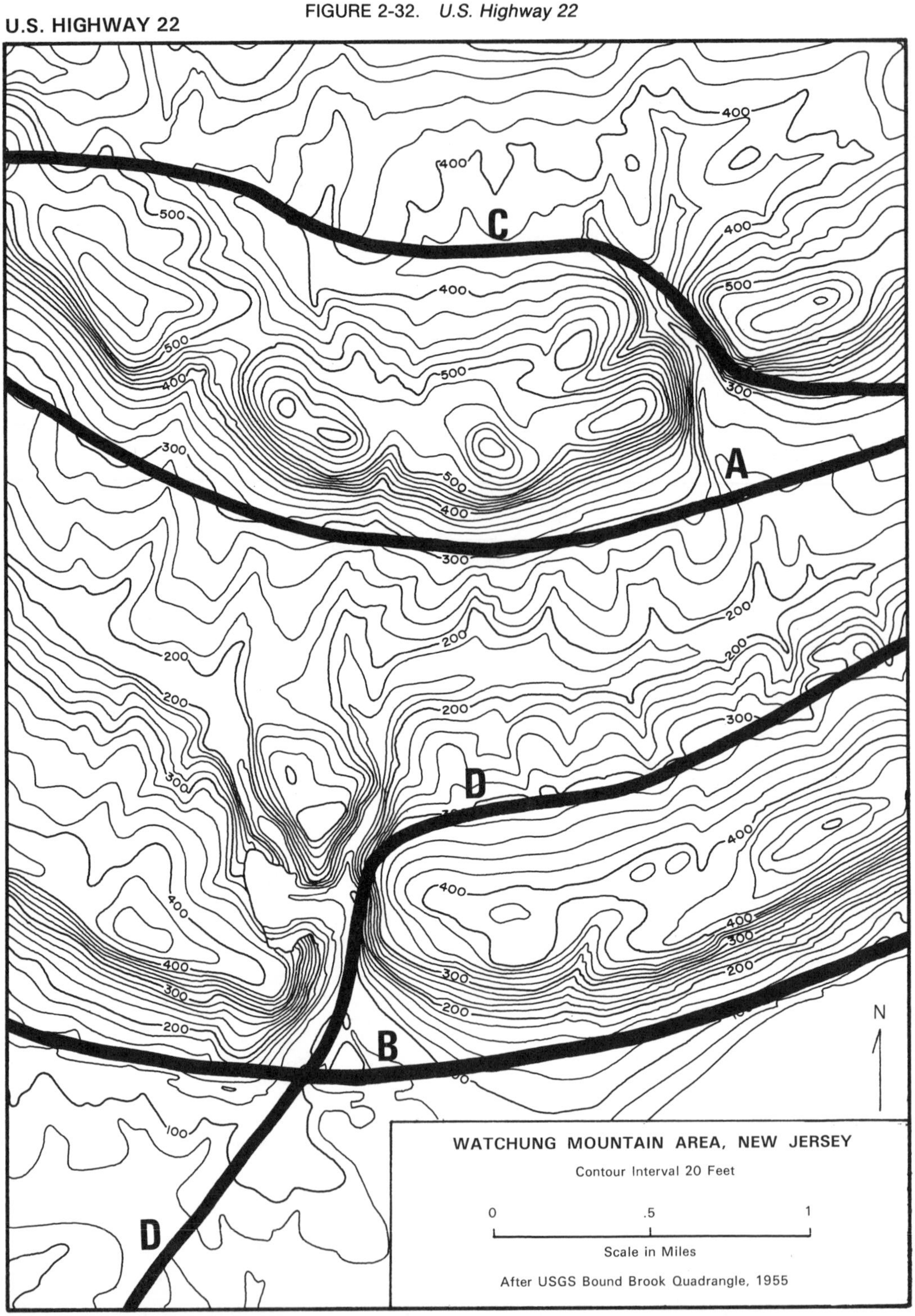
U.S. HIGHWAY 22
C
A
D
B
D
400
500
300
200
100
N
WATCHUNG MOUNTAIN AREA, NEW JERSEY
Contour Interval 20 Feet
0
.5
1
Scale in Miles
After USGS Bound Brook Quadrangle, 1955

FIGURE 2-33. *Urban and Industrial Areas, 1956*

URBAN AND INDUSTRIAL AREAS, 1956

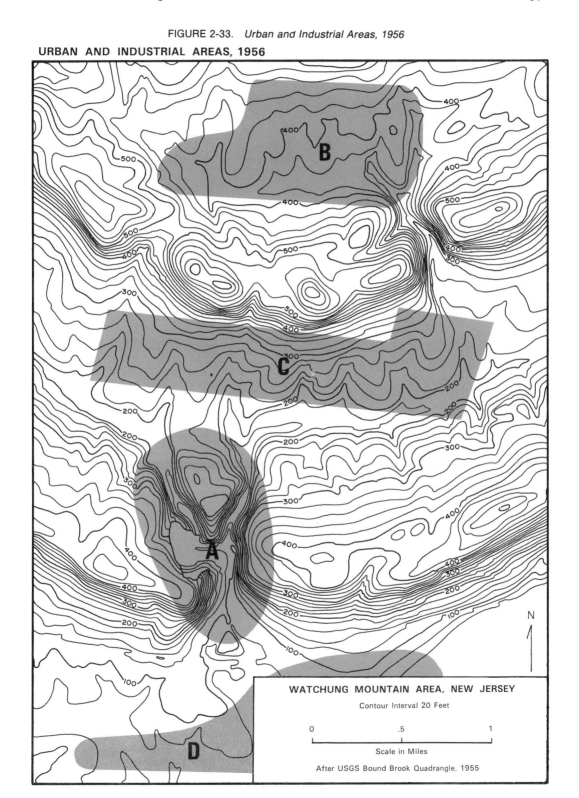

WATCHUNG MOUNTAIN AREA, NEW JERSEY

Contour Interval 20 Feet

0 .5 1

Scale in Miles

After USGS Bound Brook Quadrangle, 1955

PREDICTING 1963 MAJOR NEW HIGHWAY AND
NEW URBAN AND INDUSTRIAL AREAS

Now that you have made and verified your predictions for locations of activities in 1956, you will make two location predictions for 1963 to see if man's responses to the Watchung landscape have changed.

Study Figure 2-34 ("Major New Highways") and Figure 2-35 ("New Urban and Industrial Areas, 1963") and, as before, register your predictions on your work map (Figure 2-29) and verify your choices by consulting Figure 3-9 (page 208). Again, you should be prepared to defend your choices.

FIGURE 2-34. *Major New Highways*

MAJOR NEW HIGHWAY

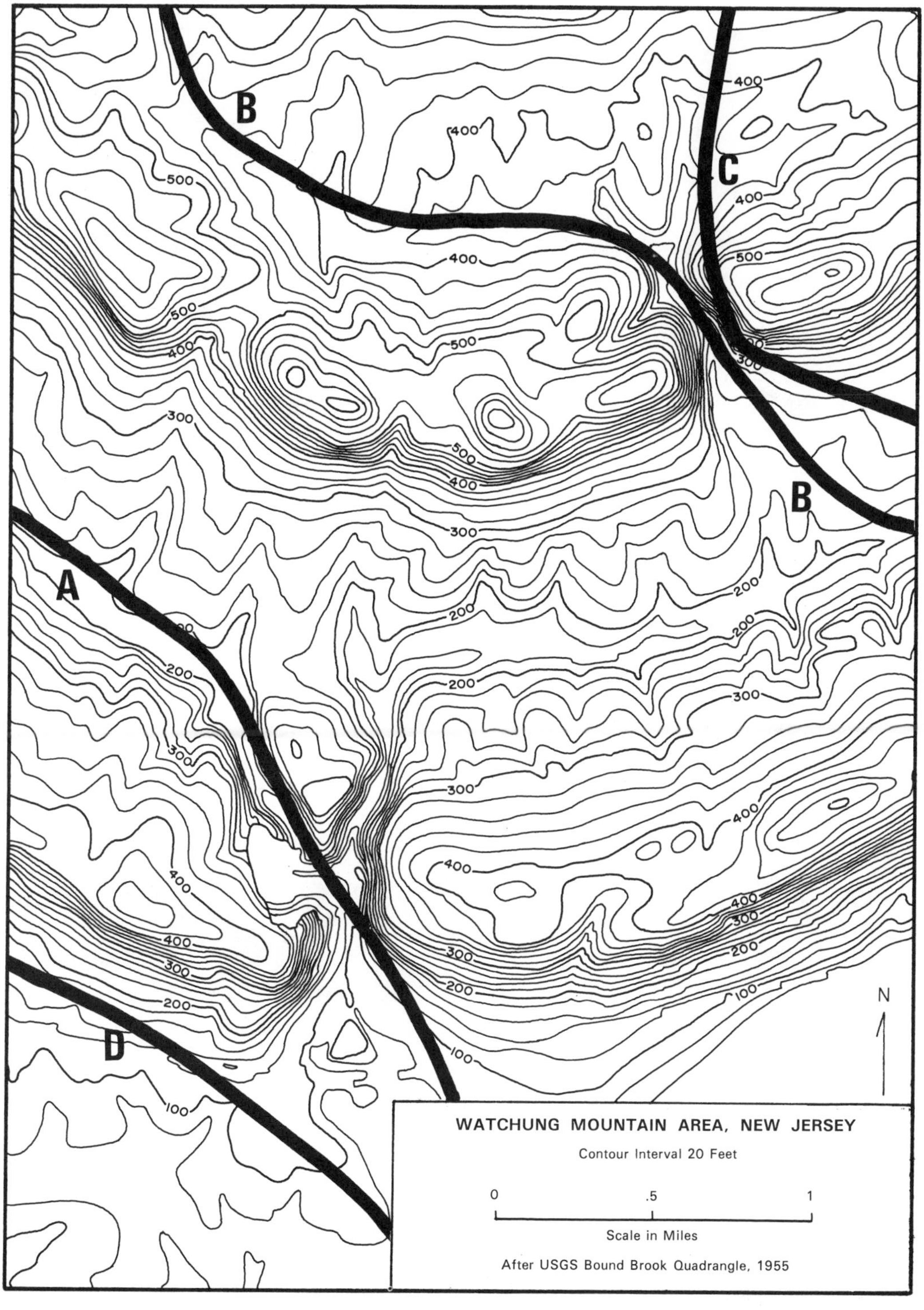
A
B
B
C
D
500
500
500
500
400
400
400
400
400
400
400
300
300
300
300
300
300
200
200
200
200
200
200
100
100
100
N
WATCHUNG MOUNTAIN AREA, NEW JERSEY
Contour Interval 20 Feet
0
.5
1
Scale in Miles
After USGS Bound Brook Quadrangle, 1955

FIGURE 2-35. *New Urban and Industrial Areas, 1963*

NEW URBAN AND INDUSTRIAL AREAS, 1963

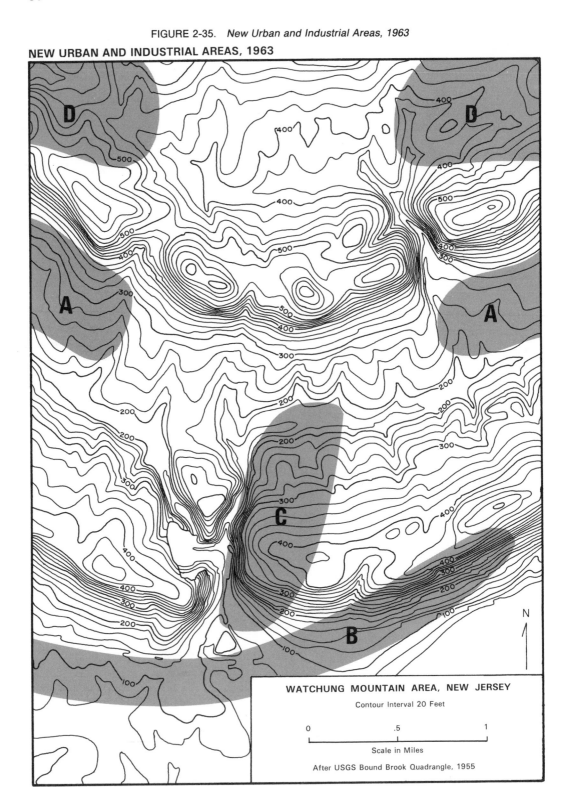

WATCHUNG MOUNTAIN AREA, NEW JERSEY

Contour Interval 20 Feet

0   .5   1

Scale in Miles

After USGS Bound Brook Quadrangle, 1955

ACTIVITY **11**

The Social Context
of Leadership

In this activity, you will investigate the topic of *leadership* in terms of (1) the social situation of the group that affects (2) the group objectives that contribute to the expectations the group has for its leaders and (3) the resulting leadership behavior. To carry out your study, you will read information about two black leaders and their groups and complete Figure 2-36.

The diagram shown in Figure 2-36 illustrates one method — content analysis — that social scientists have devised to interpret social data systematically and objectively. The diagram is just a *model*. It is not the only arrangement possible for pinpointing elements in content analysis, but it does identify important components of leadership behavior. It is a system of categories for classifying materials, using a sociological orientation for studying leadership.

The model can serve as an analytical device, suggesting tentative generalizations and a broader understanding of the subtleties or nuances of leadership.

This particular approach provides a method that is consistent with the theoretical orientation of leadership presented to high school students in the episode. The components of the diagram are as follows:

From the student text and the Instructor's Guide for *Leadership in American Society: A Case Study of Black Leadership*, SRSS Episodes in Social Inquiry Series (Boston: Allyn and Bacon, 1969). Copyright © 1969 by the American Sociological Association. Reprinted with permission. The design team for this episode consisted of James M. Fendrich, Florida State University; Lewis M. Killian, University of Massachusetts; Charles U. Smith, Florida Agricultural and Mechanical University; G. Marion Brady, Brevard County Board of Public Instruction; James J. Mitchell, Florida Agricultural and Mechanical University High School; Edward A. Fernald and Mrs. Nora Nell Jackson, both of the Florida State University High School.

Group or association refers to the supporters or followers of a particular leader. This base enlarges or decreases depending on circumstances and the success of the chosen leader.

Leader or leaders is the person or persons who try to achieve particular or general group objectives by developing plans for action and putting them into effect.

Long-range situational factors refer to a continuing social situation that prolongs or perpetuates problems a particular group would like to see corrected or modified.

Short-range situational factors refer to events that set off immediate action — the things that bring the problem to a head.

General group objectives are the goals a group hopes to achieve. In most cases these general objectives are somewhat idealistic, but they do bind the members of the group together by focusing attention on common concerns.

Specific group objectives are the goals that are expected to be achieved in a particular situation.

FIGURE 2-36. *Situational Components of Leadership Diagram*

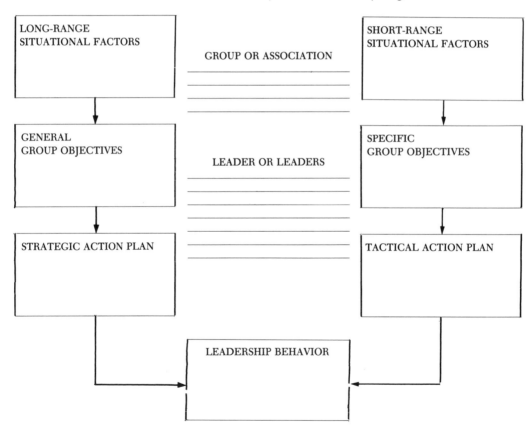

The *strategic action plan* refers to the long-range planning that the leader makes to achieve the *general* group objectives.

The *tactical action plan* refers to the *specific* group objectives — the group's immediate short-range programs and ideas.

Leadership behavior is the action that the leader takes, directed both toward group members and those outside the group to achieve the group's goals.

Below you will find part of the student reading material from an episode lesson, studied by high school students early in the second week of the two-week unit. Analyze the content of this reading and complete the diagram on Figure 2-36 to summarize the situational factors that confronted Martin Luther King, Jr., or Stokely Carmichael, and the organizations they headed.

MARTIN LUTHER KING, JR. (1929–1968)

Martin Luther King, Jr., was born in Atlanta, Georgia, in 1929. His father was a Baptist minister. An excellent student, King went to high school in Atlanta and to Atlanta's Morehouse College. Although at first he had grave doubts about the "intellectual respectability" of a career in the ministry, the president of the college persuaded him to choose the church instead of medicine or law. King received a bachelor of divinity degree from Crozer Theological Seminary in Chester, Pennsylvania, and earned his Ph.D. degree in 1955 at Boston University. It is interesting to note that he turned down several scholarship offers from Morehouse. King's father insisted on paying for his advanced education because he felt that scholarships should be given only to students who had no sources of financial support.

At twenty-seven King became pastor of the Dexter Avenue Baptist Church in Montgomery, Alabama. Little could he know as he assumed his first pastorate that within a short time he would be catapulted into worldwide prominence as leader of the Montgomery bus boycott. Nor could he know that he would be beaten many times, be pelted with rotten eggs in Harlem, be almost fatally stabbed by a mentally ill woman, be made head of the Southern Christian Leadership Conference, be chosen "Man of the Year" in 1963 by Time *magazine, be awarded the Nobel Peace Prize in 1964, and be assassinated while pleading the cause of striking garbage collectors in 1968 in Memphis, Tennessee. The story of Montgomery has been told many times, but it is worth repeating.*

The Montgomery bus boycott has been called the turning point of the black protest movement. It broke through the legalistic boundaries of previous struggles and, for the first time, large numbers of blacks in the local community actively protested. The boycott was a spontaneous confrontation of the white community by a distressed and aroused black community. The movement gave rise to many new tactics — mass meetings, nonviolent techniques, mass boycotts and legal-judiciary measures — tactics that became standard operating procedures for the civil rights movement of the 1960's.

The Montgomery Bus Protest

The Montgomery protest began with an incident on December 1, 1955. That evening Mrs. Rosa Parks boarded the Cleveland Avenue bus, found a seat, and started home after a hard day's work as a seamstress at a downtown department store. At one stop a group of whites boarded the bus. The driver, following Alabama law, told four blacks to stand so that the whites might sit. Mrs. Parks refused. The bus driver summoned the police who arrested her.

The exact reason for her not giving up her seat and thereby being arrested will probably never be known. Her act took courage. During that year five black women and two children had been arrested for disobeying a bus driver. Another bus incident resulted in a black man being shot to death. Louis Lomax has tried to describe why she refused to give up her seat:

> *The truth is that Mrs. Parks was a part of the deepening mood of despair and disillusionment that gripped the American Negro after World War II. She had been an official in the Montgomery NAACP; Mrs. Parks was an alert woman, a dedicated Negro and fully aware of the continuing injustices Negroes all over the nation were enduring. The only way to account for Mrs. Parks is to say she was a part of the times; that, at long last, her cup ran over.[1]*

Word of Mrs. Parks' arrest spread rapidly through the black community. Trouble seemed to be brewing in the poolrooms and bars. Blacks were angry. A few suggested physical reprisals against the bus drivers. To head off violence, the Women's Political Council suggested to E. D. Nixon, head of the local of the Brotherhood of Sleeping Car Porters, that a boycott might be started to let off steam. Mr. Nixon asked the Rev. Ralph D. Abernathy and his assistant Dr. King to arrange a meeting at the Dexter Avenue church. Twenty-four hours after Mrs. Parks' arrest, the largest gathering of local black leaders ever assembled decided to work out a strategy of action.

It was decided to hold the boycott on Monday morning — three days away. The word had to be spread. It was necessary to get black ministers to encourage a boycott of the buses from their pulpits on Sunday. Someone also had the difficult task of mimeographing and distributing printed information on the boycott to Montgomery's fifty thousand blacks. In this situation there were "too many chiefs and not enough Indians," so King accepted the responsibility for the dirty work. The bus boycott was a brilliant success. Monday night, hundreds of blacks met to form an organization to continue the boycott and to plan the strategy. The Montgomery Improvement Association was born, and Dr. King was elected president. In 1962 Lomax stated that Dr. King "was created by the Negro revolt and it could well be that he will be destroyed by it."

Four days after Mrs. Parks' arrest, buses in the black section were without passengers. The bus company had lost an estimated 75 percent of its patronage. The

---

[1] Louis E. Lomax, *The Negro Revolt* (New York: Harper & Brothers, Publishers, 1962), p. 81. Reprinted by permission.

Montgomery Improvement Association (MIA) decided to continue to boycott the buses until city and bus company officials would agree to (1) more courteous treatment of blacks, (2) seating on a "first come, first served" basis, and (3) the employment of black bus drivers on predominantly black runs. The MIA set up car pools to get blacks to work and successfully encouraged blacks not to ride the buses.

From Strife—a Leader and a Philosophy

From the start Montgomery's white leaders expected the movement to collapse. It lasted eleven stormy months. The city police harassed blacks driving cars. Dr. King and other blacks were beaten by whites. The mayor announced his intention to take firm action. An almost forgotten anti-labor law was resurrected and used to indict black leaders. On

Mrs. Rosa Parks is being led up the Montgomery County courthouse steps for trial (March 1956). She had refused to move to the segregated section of a Montgomery city bus in December 1955.

Wide World Photos

November 13, 1956, the U.S. Supreme Court ruled that Alabama's state and local laws requiring bus segregation were unconstitutional. Blacks ended the boycott and by December rode desegregated buses.

As the newly elected president of the MIA, Dr. King had problems. In the early stages, his negotiations with city officials had met with little success. After a breakdown in negotiations the discouraged King offered to resign. Later, on the night of January 30, 1956, his home was bombed while his wife and children were inside. Dr. King rushed home from a mass meeting. After discovering his family was not seriously hurt, he addressed a crowd of angry blacks, of policemen, photographers, and newsmen. He began by saying, "He who lives by the sword shall perish by the sword. . . ."

The bombing helped to create the image of Martin Luther King, but the city officials contributed their part. He and his associates were indicted for conspiracy to obstruct the operation of a business and voluntarily gave themselves up. Dr. King's case was the first when the trials came up. He was found guilty before the reporters and cameramen of the national press.[2] At a mass meeting that night, Dr. King said, "We are not bitter. We are still preaching nonviolence. We are still using the weapon of love."

Lomax aptly describes what happened to Martin Luther King:

Montgomery was the launching pad for Martin Luther King; he soared into orbit before he himself realized what had happened. Once he had a quiet moment to reflect and assess his life, it was too late. He had gained international fame, the applause of the world was ringing in his ears, eighteen million Negroes were calling him "Savior" and world ethicists were comparing him to Gandhi and Thoreau.[3]

King not only led this boycott, but infused the movement with the philosophy of nonviolence — an American adaptation of Gandhi's passive resistance. Two sources inspired this movement. King has written: "Christ furnished the spirit and motivation, while Gandhi furnished the method." King often admonished his followers — "If the streets must run with blood, let it be our blood and not that of our white brothers."

After his success in Montgomery, King symbolized the "New Negro." He organized the Southern Christian Leadership Conference (SCLC) in 1957 to coordinate and execute attacks on segregation. As its president, he led protests in Birmingham, Alabama; Albany, Georgia; and St. Augustine, Florida. In the "March on Washington" in 1963 he delivered the major speech. King stimulated public opinion and worked to secure the passage of the Civil Rights Act of 1964. During that year King received the Nobel Peace Prize as "the first person of the Western world to show that a struggle can be waged without violence."

After the Los Angeles riot of August, 1965, the largest of several insurrections in cities outside the South that summer, King turned his attention to the problems of the

[2] When ordered to pay a fourteen-dollar fine or go to jail, Dr. King chose jail. Thinking that this would only make matters worse, the Commissioner of Public Safety paid Dr. King's fine out of his own pocket.

[3] Louis E. Lomax, *The Negro Revolt* (New York: Harper & Brothers, Publishers, 1962), p. 84. Reprinted by permission.

poverty-stricken northern blacks. In 1966 he rented a run-down flat in southside Chicago. During the summer of 1967 he led unsuccessful marches in favor of open housing in Chicago. In the suburbs of this northern city he and his followers were met with hostility and violence by white people, just as they had been in the South.

In April, 1968, Martin Luther King, Jr., was in Memphis, assisting striking garbage collectors in their struggle over higher wages with the city administration. On April 3 he was assassinated. At the time of his death King had been preparing to lead the largest nonviolent demonstration of his career, the Poor People's March on Washington. This march began the following month, under the leadership of the Rev. Ralph Abernathy, King's successor as the head of SCLC.

SCLC

The Southern Christian Leadership Conference (SCLC), which King founded in 1957, was the first activist civil rights organization to start in the South. It was born in Atlanta with a nucleus of one hundred men. As an interracial organization, SCLC invites ministers and other civil rights workers to participate. Individuals hold membership through its affiliated organizations. SCLC has over one hundred affiliates (churches, civil organizations, etc.) throughout the South and in some northern states. In 1966, it had a full-time staff of more than sixty assisted by many volunteers. Underlying the organization's philosophy are two major guidelines:

1. *SCLC is a nonsectarian coordinating and service agency for local groups seeking full citizenship rights, equality, and the integration of blacks into all aspects of American life.*
2. *Based on a doctrine of Christian love and following a variation of the Gandhian philosophy of nonviolence, it fosters nonviolent resistance to all forms of racial injustice — for example, state and local laws and practices.*

The organization uses a variety of techniques to achieve its goals. It conducts citizenship training and voter registration programs like the "Crusade for the Ballot," which aims to double the black vote in the South. In much of this work it provides not only funds but also staff workers. It organizes and supports forms of nonviolent protest like the boycott, picketing, and marches. For example, it fed, housed, and purchased bus tickets for some of the freedom riders. It also serves as an adviser to local leadership and student civil rights groups.

In the summer of 1968, SCLC organized poor people of all races for the Poor People's March on Washington and took an active role in presenting their arguments for better treatment of the poor at the Republican and Democratic national party conventions.

STOKELY CARMICHAEL (1941–   )

. . . *Carmichael was born in the West Indies, in 1941. When he was eleven, he migrated to Harlem (a black section of New York City) with his family. His father, a carpenter, worked at two and sometimes three jobs to improve the status of his family. Through this hard work the family was able to buy a home in a predominantly white neighborhood.*

Carmichael's adolescence was interesting. In 1952, he entered the elite Bronx High School of Science. There, exposed to the top high school students of New York — the sons and daughters of doctors, dentists, professors, and other successful men — Stokely came in contact with a wide range of political, social, and economic theories. He still kept his old connections in Harlem, however. There he felt he was treated more like a person than a type. Although he liked parts of each world, he lived on the edge of both.

Carmichael led SNCC away from nonviolent protest and championed the development of Black Power.
Wide World Photos

In May of his senior year, Carmichael took part in his first demonstration in Washington, D.C., where he had gone with some white classmates to picket the House Committee on Un-American Activities. From there he went on to a sit-in in Virginia with some blacks he met while picketing. In the fall he enrolled at Howard University in Washington, D.C., but at the same time he continued to participate actively in civil rights groups. In December 1960 he went to Fayette County to help blacks who were being put off their land for trying to register to vote. It was there he met James Forman, the man he would eventually replace as leader of the Student Nonviolent Coordinating Committee (SNCC).

Then came the freedom rides into the South. In Jackson, Mississippi, members of Carmichael's group, confronted by a mob, were arrested and thrown into jail, where some of the freedom riders received rough treatment.

After graduating in June 1964 from Howard University with a major in philosophy, Carmichael spent the summer working on projects in Mississippi, where he helped to form the Mississippi Freedom Democratic Party (MFDP). This group tried to unseat the regular all-white Mississippi state delegation at the 1964 Democratic convention in Atlantic City. The civil rights workers felt the Mississippi delegation was not representative of all the citizens of Mississippi. The Democratic party made a significant compromise but the civil rights workers would have no part of it. All the MFDP won in 1964 was a moral victory and bad press, but its efforts paved the way for the seating of a liberal mixed delegation at the 1968 Democratic convention. In May 1966, Carmichael became head of SNCC, a position he left after one year in order to devote time to his developing interest in a Black Power movement.

Carmichael's ardent championship of the Black Power Movement made him a national figure overnight. This movement . . . emphasizes black achievements and the need of blacks for political, social, and economic independence. . . . However, Carmichael does not see the salvation of blacks in the return to Africa. Whatever gains are to be made will be in the United States and on black terms. Carmichael spells out goals and strategies for black people in a book he published with Charles Hamilton entitled Black Power: The Politics of Liberation in America.

After Brown took over the formal leadership of SNCC, Carmichael made a trip behind the Iron Curtain. In defiance of U.S. passport restrictions, he visited Cuba and Czechoslovakia. While abroad he made speeches denouncing the government of the United States and describing the black community as an exploited colony within the boundaries of the nation. Since his return, he has allied with the Black Panther party, a militant ghetto organization actively seeking the protection and liberation of black Americans.

SNCC

The Student Nonviolent Coordinating Committee (SNCC) was organized in April 1960 at a meeting at Shaw University in Raleigh, North Carolina. Its chief aim was to coordinate the protest work of the many students involved in nonviolent direct action. Its membership is drawn from predominantly black colleges and a large number of predominantly white colleges and universities. In 1966, it had an interracial staff of around seventy-five working out of its Atlanta home office.

SNCC strategy was originally based on both the philosophy and tactics of nonviolence. In its statement of beliefs, love was the central theme. SNCC workers were to love their hostile opposition even while suffering the punishments inflicted on them. The organization wanted to build an interracial democracy that could be made to work in this country. Its idealistic philosophy was not met so kindly by white opposition forces, however, and brutality more often than cooperation was the usual reward.

Already in its short period of existence, SNCC has had to change to meet the needs of a redefined situation. It has become more practical in its approach, no longer emphasizing the importance of loving your enemy. Along with an increased concern with political power, SNCC has discouraged whites from taking an active part in the movement. But even though the goals have changed, the techniques are generally the same. There is still an emphasis on direct action, voter registration, and political and economic participation. In contrast to other civil rights groups, SNCC works mainly to build local leadership instead of national leadership. A number of SNCC's leaders have been jailed because of their activities in the protest movement or their refusal to be drafted into the armed forces. In the late 1960's, SNCC began to react to the frustration of obtaining its goals with more militant activity.

ACTIVITY 12

The Game of Farming

You are to play this game in pairs. Each pair will operate as a single farmer; the members of a pair must agree on the decisions made.

As a farmer moving to western Kansas in 1880, you have selected a 160-acre farm site to homestead. You are thus opening new land to agriculture. You have brought all the necessary farm equipment to the West with you. Since other farmers in the area are also new, there are no experienced farmers to talk with and no farms to visit to find out what crops and what farm methods will succeed in this area. You will therefore have to use your own common sense as a guide on how best to develop your farm.

You must first decide on how you will allocate your money. In addition to the farm equipment, you have $1,500 in cash to start your farm, but you must budget $500 of your $1,500 for the cost of living during the first year. This cost-of-living expense must be set aside each year. You can spend money in $100 units only. The smallest unit of land you can work with is forty acres.

The crops you can plant include wheat, oats, barley, rye, and corn. It costs $100 to raise forty acres of wheat, forty acres of oats, forty acres of barley, or forty acres of rye, but it costs $200 to raise forty acres of corn.

You can also invest your money in beef cattle, dairy cattle, sheep, and hogs. On any forty-acre tract, you may graze from $100 to $400 worth of sheep, beef cattle, or dairy

From Unit 2: "Manufacturing and Agriculture," in *Geography in an Urban Age* (New York: The Macmillan Company, 1969). Copyright © 1969 by the Association of American Geographers. Reprinted with permission. The idea for this activity was formulated by Duane Knos (now of Clark University, Worcester, Massachusetts) in cooperation with the Department of Geography at the University of Kansas.

cattle.   You may mix your investment in sheep, beef cattle, and dairy cattle on a forty-acre tract but only in terms of $100 units, such as $100 in sheep and $300 in beef cattle.   Hogs do not require special land; they can forage on crop or pasture land.   You may invest from $100 to $600 in hogs in $100 units.

You can rent additional land for $100 per forty-acre unit.   If you do not choose to farm all your land, you may rent some of it to hypothetical farmers for $100 per forty-acre unit.   The game assumes that there are numerous individuals in the area from whom or to whom you can rent land.   You need not try to rent from or to other participants.

All costs, such as taxes, seed, labor, supplies, and maintenance, are included in the charges for each of the farming activities.

Record your farming decisions on Figure 2-37 ("1880 Farming Summary").   The second column on the figure is titled "Allocation"; it is the only column you will fill in as you plan your farming activities.   There is a sketch of your 160-acre farm on the right-hand side of the figure.   As you decide how to use each forty-acre square, write the decision or its abbreviation on the diagram, figure the expense, and write that amount in the proper blank in the "Allocation" column.   For example, if you want to plant wheat in one forty-acre area, write wheat in one square and put $100 in the blank next to wheat in the "Allocation" column.   If you want to rent some land, there is another sketch representing land you may rent.   You should record your use of the rented land in the same way you recorded land allocation from your own farm.

The total amount you can spend is the $1,500 recorded as capital at the top of Figure 2-37.   If, after you have made your allocations, you still have cash on hand but no land available, you may invest it in hogs or rent more land.

Once you have made your allocations, you are ready to find out how successful your first year's farming operation has been.   You will receive outcome information from the instructor at this time.   Each type of crop and livestock has a multiplier, a number from zero to five.   For example, if you planted forty acres of corn for $200 and the instructor tells you that the multiplier for corn is two, you will record the two in the "Multiplier" column on Figure 2-37.   Then you will use this number to multiply the amount recorded in the "Allocation" column to figure the "Outcome" for corn.

	Allocation	Multiplier	Outcome
Corn	$200	2	$400

As the instructor gives you the information, you should repeat this operation for each crop or animal you chose to raise.

After you have figured each individual outcome and placed the amount in the "Outcome" column, total this column.   The difference between the "Outcome" total and your initial capital of $1,500 is your net profit or loss for the year 1880.

You are now ready to make your allocations for 1881 on Figure 2-38 ("1881 Farming Summary").   First, record the total of your "Outcome" column from 1880 at the top of Figure 2-38 next to "Capital."   This is the amount of cash you will have to work with for your 1881 farm operation.   Again, you must allocate $500 for cost of living for the

FIGURE 2-37. *1880 Farming Summary*

Year: 1880 .... Capital: $1,500

BUDGET ITEMS	ALLOCATION	MULTIPLIER	OUTCOME
Wheat	$ _____	_____	$ _____
Oats	$ _____	_____	$ _____
Barley	$ _____	_____	$ _____
Rye	$ _____	_____	$ _____
Corn	$ _____	_____	$ _____
Dairy cattle	$ _____	_____	$ _____
Beef cattle	$ _____	_____	$ _____
Sheep	$ _____	_____	$ _____
Hogs	$ _____	_____	$ _____
Cost of living	$ 500	0	$ 0
Rent	$ _____	0	$ 0
Rent income	$ 0	X	$ _____
Total	$ _____		$ _____

Your Farm[c]

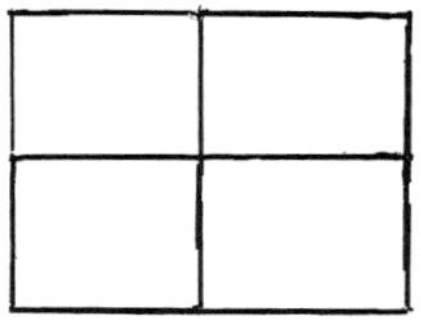

Rented Land

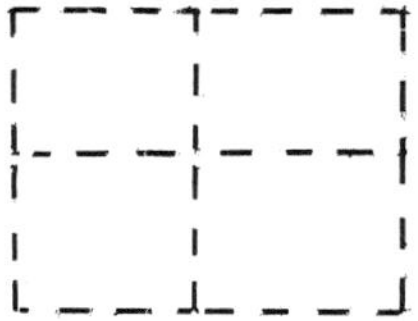

Costs per 40-Acre Unit

Crop
Wheat	$100
Oats	100
Barley	100
Rye	100
Corn	200

Livestock
Dairy cattle (maximum per 40 acres)[a]	400
Beef cattle (maximum per 40 acres)[a]	400
Sheep (maximum per 40 acres)[a]	400
Hogs (maximum per farm)[b] ...	600
Rent	100

[a] Dairy cattle, beef cattle, and sheep investments are in $100 units with a $400 maximum investment per 40-acre unit.
[b] Hogs are a straight cash investment in $100 units with a $600 maximum investment; they do not need allocated land.
[c] Each small square represents 40 acres.

FIGURE 2-38. *1881 Farming Summary*

Year: 1881 .... Capital: $1,500

Your Farm^c

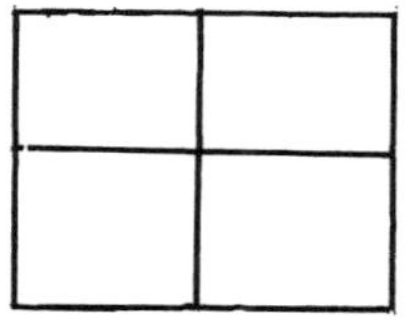

Rented Land

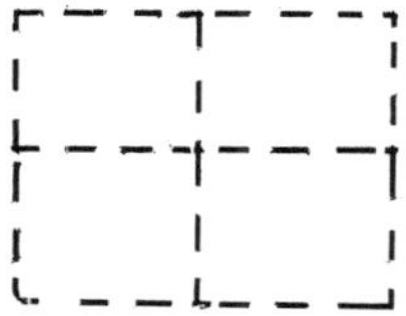

Costs per 40-Acre Unit

Crop
Wheat $100
Oats 100
Barley 100
Rye 100
Corn 200

Livestock
Dairy cattle (maximum per 40 acres)[a] 400
Beef cattle (maximum per 40 acres)[a] 400
Sheep (maximum per 40 acres)[a] 400
Hogs (maximum per farm)[b] ... 600

Rent 100

BUDGET ITEMS	ALLOCATION	MULTIPLIER	OUTCOME
Wheat	$		$
Oats	$		$
Barley	$		$
Rye	$		$
Corn	$		$
Dairy cattle	$		$
Beef cattle	$		$
Sheep	$		$
Hogs	$		$
Cost of living	$ 500	0	0
Rent	$	0	0
Rent income	$	X	$
Total	$	0	

[a] Dairy cattle, beef cattle, and sheep investments are in $100 units with a $400 maximum investment per 40-acre unit.
[b] Hogs are a straight cash investment in $100 units with a $600 maximum investment; they do not need allocated land.
[c] Each small square represents 40 acres.

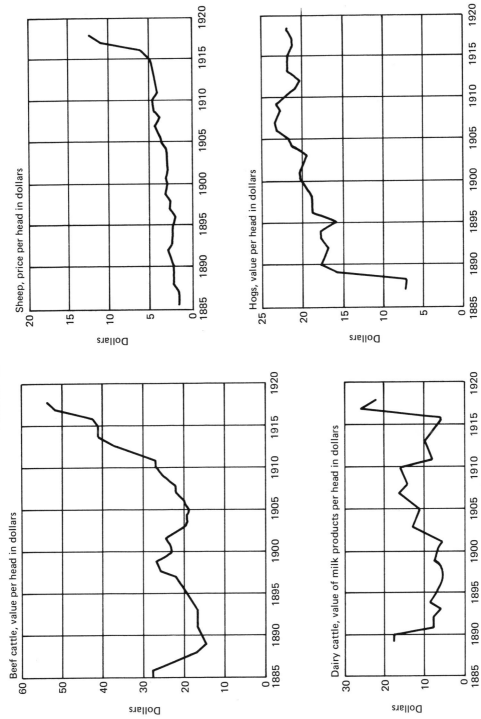

FIGURE 2-39. *Livestock Prices: 1885–1918*

FIGURE 2-40. *1920 Farming Summary*

Your Farm

Rented Land

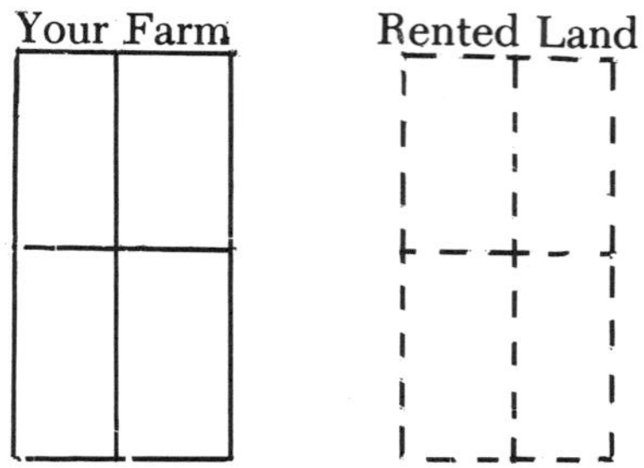

Allocations must be made in 80-acre units, represented by small rectangles.

Costs per 80-Acre Unit

Unirrigated crops
Wheat .... $ 600
Barley 600
Sorghum 600
Irrigated crops
Corn 1,200
Sugar beets 2,000
Alfalfa 1,200
Livestock
Dairy cattle (maximum per 80 acres)[a] 600
Beef cattle (maximum per 80 acres)[a] 600
Sheep (maximum per 80 acres)[a] 600
Hogs (maximum per farm)[b] 600
Rent 800

Year: 1920 .... Capital: $8,500

BUDGET ITEMS	ALLOCATION	MULTIPLIER	OUTCOME
Unirrigated crops			
Wheat	$ ____	____	$ ____
Barley	$ ____	____	$ ____
Sorghum	$ ____	____	$ ____
Irrigated crops			
Corn	$ ____	____	$ ____
Sugar beets	$ ____	____	$ ____
Alfalfa	$ ____	____	$ ____
Livestock			
Dairy cattle	$ ____	____	$ ____
Beef cattle	$ ____	____	$ ____
Sheep	$ ____	____	$ ____
Hogs	$ ____	____	$ ____
Cost of living	$ 2,000	0	0
Payment on indebtedness	$ 1,000	0	0
Labor	$ 600	0	0
Rent	$ ____	0	0
Rent income	$ 0	X	$ ____
Total			$ ____

[a] Dairy cattle, beef cattle, and sheep investments are in $100 units. Livestock may be mixed in units of $100.
[b] Hogs are a straight cash investment in $100 units; they do not need allocated land.

FIGURE 2-41. *1921 Farming Summary*

Year: 1921 .... Capital: $8,500

BUDGET ITEMS	ALLOCATION	MULTIPLIER	OUTCOME
Unirrigated crops			
Wheat			$ ____
Barley			$ ____
Sorghum			$ ____
Irrigated crops			
Corn			$ ____
Sugar beets			$ ____
Alfalfa			$ ____
Livestock			
Dairy cattle			$ ____
Beef cattle			$ ____
Sheep			$ ____
Hogs			$ ____
Cost of living	$ 2,000	0	$ ____ 0
Payment on indebtedness	$ 1,000	0	$ ____ 0
Labor	$ 600	0	$ ____ 0
Rent		0	$ ____ 0
Rent income	$ 0	X	$ ____
Total			$ ____

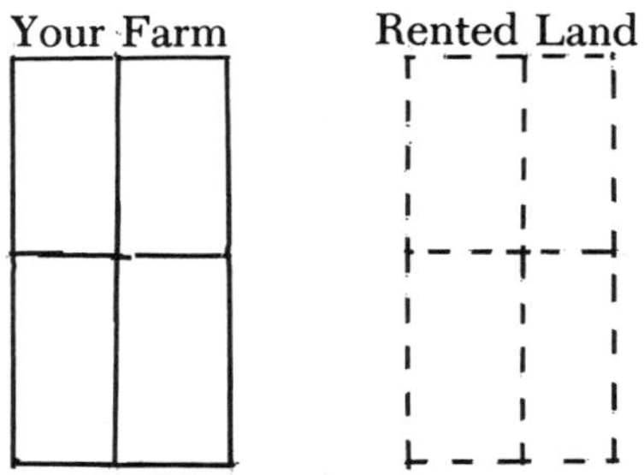

Your Farm   Rented Land

Allocations must be made in 80-acre units, represented by small rectangles.

Costs per 80-Acre Unit

Unirrigated crops	
Wheat	$ 600
Barley	600
Sorghum	600
Irrigated crops	
Corn	1,200
Sugar beets	2,000
Alfalfa	1,200
Livestock	
Dairy cattle (maximum per 80 acres)[a]	600
Beef cattle (maximum per 80 acres)[a]	600
Sheep (maximum per 80 acres)[a]	600
Hogs (maximum per farm)[b]	600
Rent	800

[a] Dairy cattle, beef cattle, and sheep investments are in $100 units. Livestock may be mixed in units of $100.

[b] Hogs are a straight cash investment in $100 units; they do not need allocated land.

year. Base your allocation decisions for 1881 on what you learned during the first year's farming. When you complete your allocations, you will again receive the relevant outcome information from the instructor. The calculation of your net profit or loss for 1881 concludes this round of the game.

The game reopens in 1920. Many changes have taken place since 1881. Changes having the greatest impact on farming in western Kansas include the development of farm equipment (for example, the tractor and the combine) and the building of irrigation systems. New crops, such as alfalfa, sorghum, and sugar beets, have been introduced and adopted by farmers. Also, farmers in 1920 have more knowledge about western Kansas than the homesteaders had. Information about livestock prices from 1885 to 1918 is summarized for you in Figure 2-39.

World War I created such a large demand for agricultural products that prices have been driven to record highs. Many farmers in Settler County have purchased more land and you are no exception. You have bought an additional 160 acres and you now must make mortgage payments. You have also purchased a tractor and other machinery. Your payments for indebtedness on land and machinery amount to $1,000 per year.

The income you have been receiving for agricultural products is high, but your expenditures are also higher than ever. Your living costs have risen to $2,000 per year. You have a greater amount of capital now, however, and you begin the 1920's with $8,500 in cash. Your farm now totals 320 acres and you must hire one laborer. His salary is $600 per year.

Many of your neighbors in Settler County have expanded their operations by renting land. You, too, may rent land at $800 for eighty acres. This fee includes the cost of the additional labor necessary for expanding your operation.

Figure 2-40 ("1920 Farming Summary") shows the cost of production for each crop or livestock choice. You have the option of planting unirrigated wheat, barley, or sorghum; or irrigated sugar beets, alfalfa, or corn. You may irrigate only eighty acres.

Livestock choices include beef cattle, dairy cattle, sheep, and hogs. Notice that you may raise up to $2,400 worth of beef cattle, dairy cattle, or sheep on your 320 acres and that each $600 of investment in livestock will require eighty acres of land. Livestock may be mixed in units of $100. There is a $600 limit to the amount you can invest in hogs.

You are now ready to plan your strategy for "The Game of Farming" for the year 1920 on Figure 2-40. Once you have made your allocations for 1920, your instructor will read the outcomes for that year. Use the multipliers he supplies to compute your outcome for 1920. The result you obtain becomes your capital for 1921.

You may then make your decisions for 1921 on Figure 2-41 ("1921 Farming Summary") and calculate your outcome when the instructor announces the multipliers for 1921.

PART III

Instructor's Guide

ACTIVITY **1**

The Eye of Childhood

I. BACKGROUND

The materials used for this teaching activity are taken from Lessons 12 and 13 in Part 3 of the SRSS sociology course, *Inquiries in Sociology*. The data for analysis consist of four drawings by Ruby, a six-year-old black girl who was attending a recently integrated New Orleans school. The drawings by Ruby appear in the book *Children of Crisis* by Robert Coles.[1]

Prior to being asked to analyze the drawings, high school students have studied the socialization process, examined the institutional structure of society, and considered social class as an aspect of social stratification. At the point in the sociology course where the students study the drawings by Ruby, they are considering race and ethnicity as factors in social stratification; specifically, they are exploring the influence of race on self-image.

II. PARTICIPANT OBJECTIVES

Experience with and analysis of this activity should enable participants:

1.   To examine critically the concepts of race and social class.

[1] Robert Coles, *Children of Crisis* (Boston: Atlantic-Little, Brown and Company, 1967).

2. To make plausible and intelligible associations between race on the one hand and self-image and life chances on the other.
3. To discriminate between the existence of a relationship and its direction of influence.
4. To learn about the need for controlling variables when considering cause-and-effect relationships.
5. *To see one way in which pictures can be used as a source of data for initiating student inquiry.*
6. *To create teaching activities using unintended sources of communication as the basis for inquiry.*
7. *To see how one teaching activity can be used to achieve multiple objectives.*
8. *To be able to assess strengths and weaknesses of teaching activities.*[2]

III. CONDUCTING THE ACTIVITY

Prior to a discussion of this activity, participants should read "Activity 1/The Eye of Childhood" (pages 17–18) and should examine the drawings by Ruby. The initial discussion can follow the sequence of the eight questions presented on pages 17–18 in the reading.

  Analysis of the drawings should reveal important differences between the figures of the white children and the figures of the black children. Ruby's white children are larger than her black children. She rims the sun with black for the Afro-Americans but not for the whites. She places brown under the black children but not under the white children. Her white figures are much more completely formed than her black figures; the latter lack a limb or an ear or other physical features. The difference in shades of color is particularly noticeable in Figures 2-3 and 2-4.

  Question 8 in the participant materials asks: *Is Ruby black or white?* The differences in the drawings and the possible explanations for these differences will probably have revealed that Ruby is black. However, some participants may have concluded that Ruby is white. If so, ask them how they reached this conclusion. They may argue, for example, that the differences in the size of the people and the lack of details in Figures 2-1 and 2-4 indicate that the artist holds a prejudiced view of Afro-Americans. You might ask these participants how they could find out if their conclusion is correct. One way of doing so, of course, would be to obtain drawings from a six-year-old white girl who was in the same situation as Ruby was.

  After it is established that Ruby is indeed black, ask the participants: *How could Ruby have acquired her view of race and self?* [High school students studying the SRSS sociology course are expected to recall some of the studies on socialization presented in Part 1 of the course when considering this question.] Of course, there is no information in the drawings to give us an answer to this question. Participants can speculate, however,

[2] Numbers one to four are content objectives; five through eight are pedagogical objectives.

about the ways in which a young child learns such things. They might hypothesize that Ruby learned about race and self when the mob screamed at her at the school. In what other ways might whites have conveyed their feelings toward her and influenced her perceptions? How might her parents have passed on to her a feeling that Afro-Americans are inferior? Why would they have taught her such a thing? One explanation might be that they need to warn her of the dangers of doing things which are unacceptable to whites and which might bring retaliation. The perceptiveness of very young children to the unspoken attitudes and feelings around them cannot be overlooked. Chance remarks by parents or neighbors, the manner in which a storekeeper addresses her father, and the way her mother holds her when in the presence of whites are examples of cues to which Ruby and other young children, both black and white, respond. Even the young child may come to see that blacks hold "inferior" jobs and have less prestige and less money than whites.

Throughout this discussion it has been assumed that the drawings demonstrate the influence of ethnicity and prejudice on Ruby's self-image. This assumption, however, is only part of the explanation of the pictures. Some participants may have suggested other factors that account for Ruby's drawings. The experience Ruby was going through, the influence of a white investigator on her artwork, her own unique personality, her age, her family background — all are possible explanations for her low self-image.

Now ask the participants to suggest several hypotheses, using an independent variable other than race, which might further explain Ruby's low self-image or which might even explain the apparent relationship between minority group membership and low self-esteem. One hypothesis that will likely be suggested is that there is a relationship between poverty and low self-esteem. (If the participants do not suggest the hypothesis, you can introduce it into the discussion.) It might even be argued that it is poverty rather than race that causes low self-esteem. After the hypothesis relating poverty and low self-esteem has been articulated, ask the participants to develop a research procedure for testing the hypothesis. In creating the research design, participants must understand, of course, that they are dealing with two independent variables (race and poverty), one of which must be controlled or held constant if they are to assess the effects of the other. For example, race could be held constant and the income level of the sample varied to assess the effects of income on self-image. Even if a positive relationship between income and self-image were to emerge (the higher the income, the better the self-image), participants cannot assume that racial differences play *no* part in the development of one's self-image.

IV. REFLECTIONS ON THE LEARNING AND TEACHING

In developing a teaching activity such as this one, our aims are neither single nor simple. We want to help participants discover certain seminal ideas and the conceptual framework through which they are expressed. And we seek to do it more effectively than customary, conventional strategies permit. Now that participants have experienced the activity, we pause to ask two questions: (1) What matters of sociological content have been learned? and (2) What has been learned about effective teaching strategies?

A. Analysis of Learning Outcomes

1. *What meanings have been attached to the concepts of self-image, social differentiation, race, and social class?*

For an adequate understanding of the Ruby materials, participants must have discovered and come to understand the way in which such concepts as those enumerated in the question above help to order and illuminate the data — the contrasting ways in which Ruby depicted her schoolmates.

A central concept to be understood is that of self-image or identity. The teaching activity focuses on the unexpressed question: *Who am I?* It is a question that everyone faces — and one that he answers with varying degrees of satisfaction and accuracy. For members of minority groups considered inferior by majority group people, it is a particularly difficult question. Studies show that some black children as young as three years of age are not only aware of color but tend to depreciate their own color.

Ruby apparently "sees" two categories of people: whites and blacks. It is doubtful that she could articulate the differences her pictures reveal. There is a wholeness and brightness of body, spirit, and environment characterizing the whites that is absent in the pictures of the black boy and girl. We see in these drawings, then, a form of social differentiation.

There are, of course, many forms of social differentiation — differentiation by age, sex, income, religion, power, and the like. In this case the differentiation is by race, a biologically rooted concept. But the chief significance of race lies in the social meanings attached to it. Indeed, in human affairs, we can think of race as a rather unimportant biological fact but as an enormously important social fiction. As a biological concept, "race" signifies a breeding population transmitting distinctive biological traits from one generation to another. As a social concept, race carries connotations of superiority and inferiority (as in the term "Aryan race," misused and misunderstood by the Nazis). In U.S. society, it implies differences in opportunity and rewards. It points to differing life chances. And such differences in life chances are what we infer from Ruby's drawings.

Class, another important concept, was defined by the German sociologist Max Weber as a category of persons characterized by the same life chances. People of one class tend to belong to the same categories of occupation, education, and income. Race caste is class carried to the *n*th degree — in the past, an immutable fixing of life chances. But while life chances are similar for all people of a given category, they differ between classes. Thus both race and class point to social differentiation.

2. *What relationships have been discovered between the following social phenomena: race and self-image, race and class, and race and poverty? What has been learned about the* direction *of such relationships?*

In analyzing Ruby's drawings, the inference is made that Ruby sees two categories of people: whites and blacks. The inference is also made that race and class are linked with deprivation-privilege. This apparent linkage raises yet another question: What causal connection, if any, is there between race and privilege or race and deprivation?

That two concepts are linked — or, more accurately, that the social phenomena they summarize are linked — does not automatically reveal a causal connection. We must ask two additional questions: (1) Are there variables other than race, perhaps more important ones, that vary with degree of deprivation-privilege? Or is there some third factor — for example, some genetic trait — that accounts both for racial characteristics and degree of deprivation? and (2) What is the direction of the causal relationship?

If a given outcome — poverty, for example — can be brought about by a number of influences (illiteracy, poor health, discriminatory treatment), somehow we must eliminate the effect of all but one influence if we are to determine the extent to which it is related to poverty. Consider a prosaic example. A man comes to a physician complaining of pervasive fatigue. It turns out that he has been working hard, for long hours over several years. To what do we attribute his run-down condition? To attribute it to work may be an impetuous judgment. As it turns out, he is also a hard drinker and a heavy smoker. What then causes his exhaustion? If the doctor instructs him to stop smoking, we can then discover (other things being equal) whether hard drinking and hard work, in combination, are linked with exhaustion. But to assess the linkage of hard work with fatigue, we would have to eliminate the influence of *both* the drinking and the smoking.

So also with the case of Ruby. The extent of connectedness between race and deprivation will be unanswerable until we control (eliminate the influence of) factors other than race that might affect one's life chances: poverty, religion, education achieved, sex, age, and the like.

To discover that two factors vary concomitantly still leaves us short of another objective. Have participants learned to discriminate between the *existence* of a relationship and its *direction* (the direction of the flow of influence)? If, for example, race and deprivation are linked as in Table 3-1, what causes what? Does race cause deprivation? Or does deprivation cause race?

TABLE 3-1.

	Privilege	Deprivation
White	All our observations fall in upper left	
Black		and lower right cells

Such questions may seem absurd, but there are parallels that suggest the uncertainty we often experience with regard to the direction of causal influence. Consider, for example, the notion that criminal behavior is the cause of a social reaction that entails punishment. But is it not possible that retaliatory responses cause criminal behavior? Indeed, we know that the stigmatizing of an offender often narrows the range of possible legitimate behaviors, thus driving the offender once again into illicit activity. And we know, too, that the societal reaction that we call imprisonment is an institutionalized means of training the amateur delinquent in the skills and values of criminal conduct. Thus when we link the two concepts, crime and punishment, it is not at all clear which way the causal influence flows.

What shall we say of Ruby's case? We establish the fact that this child discriminates between two categories, blacks and whites (even though she may be unaware of the way in which she discerns and describes them). Second, we infer from her drawings that the concept *race* is linked with privilege-deprivation. Third, we are probably disposed to say that race causes deprivation. It would not seem to make sense to assert that deprivation causes race.

But, of course, that is the point. Concomitant variation leaves the *direction* of influence unspecified. And there are always two possibilities. In this instance, it turns out to be quite plausible that deprivation is a cause of race. (We are thinking of race in its significant sense, as a social fiction.) Deprivation (stemming from discriminatory behavior) limits human development and so stunts aspiration and achievement as to produce the traits that define an inferior race. This is perhaps the most devastating instance of the self-fulfilling prophecy. As Liza Doolittle says, with Shaw's usual perception, "The difference between a lady and a flower girl is not how she behaves, but how she's treated." [3] So we create race as we create crime, war, delinquency, and poverty: by carving the image of our prejudices in the rock of social institutions.

3. *How do we institutionalize discriminatory treatment of people like Ruby?*
At the time she made the drawings, Ruby was only six years old. Thus the circle of her "teachers" was necessarily limited: her family and her age peers in the neighborhood and at school. The process of learning how one's social world operates — including where one stands in the pecking order — is called socialization. Ruby's socialization includes the acquiring of a deprecatory self-image.

We create and re-create our worlds as we define our situations. People define situations as real if the consequences are real. Therefore, reality is inevitably a social construction.

Thus there are two more fundamental insights to be gained from analyzing the pictures drawn by Ruby. First, a person is a creation, an endless creation worked out in fruitful interchange among men. Second, what men construct is not necessarily constructive! The fruit of the tree of knowledge — it might better be called the tree of beliefs — has consequences for good *and* evil. In the creation of a human being like

[3] George Bernard Shaw, "Pygmalion," in *The Complete Plays of George Bernard Shaw* (London: Constable and Company, Ltd., 1931), p. 746.

Ruby, we have the capability of producing a person who betrays her potential. She has learned that she is less worthy and has been taught to respond in ways that will confirm the false stereotype of racial inferiority.

B. Analysis of Teaching Strategies

The following questions and brief discussions may be useful as participants analyze the teaching strategy used in this activity.

1. *What data serve as the basis for inquiry?*

    One way of viewing an activity is to focus on the kind of data around which the inquiry is structured. In this case, the data consist of four drawings by a six-year-old black girl who was attending a recently integrated New Orleans school. In contrast to data gathered for the purpose of testing a stated hypothesis, these pictures were secured for a reason other than their use in this teaching activity. Thus the pictures can be viewed as a source of unintended communication, unintended in the sense that they provide data that allow us to achieve a stated educational objective that was not a part of the original study.

2. *How structured is the inquiry?*

    The inquiry is relatively unstructured since participants are simply presented with the data (four drawings) and asked to analyze them using personal experience and knowledge. [With the high school student, some of the knowledge has been acquired through a study of previous parts of the SRSS course.] The inquiry is structured to the extent that the thinking is restricted by the questions asked about the four drawings.

3. *How might the direction and nature of the inquiry be affected if participants were simply given the four drawings and asked what they think the pictures (data) illustrate?*

    Although we have no data to help us answer this question, the participants may benefit from speculating about how the inquiry might have been different if guiding questions had not been included. Can the objectives for this activity be achieved without the guiding questions? How do the questions make the experience different from an experience that has no such guidelines?

4. *What levels of analysis are exhibited in the sequence of activities in which the participants engaged?*

    Another way of viewing an activity is to focus on the sequence of events presented. Participants in this demonstration should see that the lesson moves from *description* (simple statements of fact about the drawings) to *analysis* (why Ruby feels the way she does and what is implied by these feelings) to a *search for further explanations* of the facts discovered (variables other than race that might account for the low self-image of minority group members). Thus, as participants proceed through the lesson, the level of thinking required moves from simple description to the higher intellectual processes.

5. *What different types of educational objectives does this activity achieve?*

An interesting aspect of this activity is its effectiveness in achieving multiple objectives. As was mentioned previously, the content of the activity focuses on the question *Who am I?* — a particularly difficult question for minority group members to answer. The first objective of this lesson is to demonstrate that it is indeed true that members of minority groups find it difficult to develop a positive self-image. Thus, through an analysis of the drawings, students discover on their own a problem worth pursuing. The lesson then goes on to consider causes and implications, calling upon the group's personal experiences and acquired knowledge to provide insight into why this problem exists. Finally, the group identifies factors other than race that might account for Ruby's low self-image. Thus, skill objectives are also achieved — skill in identifying and stating a hypothesis and skill in developing a research design to test the hypothesis developed.

Other types of outcomes may be in the affective domain. You should be sensitive to any affective outcomes of the demonstration that participants may express.

V. APPLICATION

Participants might be asked to engage in some of the following activities in order to apply the knowledge and skills gained from experiencing and analyzing this activity:

1. Develop a teaching activity using an unintended source of communication as the data around which an activity is structured.
2. Locate several different types of data useful in developing a concept selected by participants.
3. Locate several different types of data to develop further one or more of the concepts considered in this activity.
4. Create a teaching activity that is effective in achieving multiple objectives.

ACTIVITY 2

Metfab

I. BACKGROUND

This activity is based on the Metfab simulation exercise in Unit 2, "Manufacturing and Agriculture," from the HSGP course *Geography in an Urban Age.* The materials for the activity consist of written information, tables, and maps which enable high school students to use the technique of role playing in making group decisions about where to locate a new manufacturing plant called "Metfab."

Prior to becoming involved in the exercise, high school students have learned that decisions about factory locations can be influenced by a variety of site and situation factors, such as accessibility to raw materials, markets, labor, and transportation. In addition, they are familiar with the part manufacturing plays in influencing the standard of living in the United States.

II. PARTICIPANT OBJECTIVES

Experience with and analysis of this activity should enable participants:

1. To examine the importance of least cost and maximum profit considerations as influences on manufacturing location decisions.

2. To discuss some of the intangible and noneconomic factors that influence the decision-making process in locating a manufacturing plant.
3. To analyze the way in which small-group dynamics influence the decision-making process.
4. To explore the importance of the Metfab activity in terms of attitudinal changes toward geography, manufacturing, decision-making, other students, group activity, and school.
5. *To use simulations effectively.*
6. *To discuss the inherent advantages and disadvantages of simulations as teaching devices.*
7. *To evaluate decision-making simulations in terms of problem, choice, data influencing choice, and role conflict.*
8. *To develop new simulation activities.*[1]

III. CONDUCTING THE ACTIVITY

The Metfab activity uses the technique of role playing to demonstrate that location decision-making is a complex process involving many factors. In this simulation exercise, participants form management teams that are responsible for making the decisions necessary to locate Metfab, a metal fabrication company that makes large containers for agricultural and industrial chemical companies. Groups of five participants each use written information, tables, and a map to help them arrive at their decisions. Each team uses the same materials. However, different personal and group reactions to the information presented may result in different but equally favorable locational choices. Discussion of these different choices stimulates participant interest and emphasizes that there is no single correct answer.

The estimated teaching time for the activity is fifty minutes, which includes time for participants to read the background information and their role descriptions (see pages 22–27). Although each participant does not read all the role descriptions, you will find it helpful to do so. The following information on how to conduct the activity has been divided into three sections: Introduction, Group Work, and Summary.

Introduction

You can introduce participants to the location-decision exercise by indicating that most manufacturers consider good locational decisions very important in determining the success of their business. Therefore, they try to make the most rational decisions they can, based on current and expected conditions.

[1] Numbers one to four are content objectives; five through eight are pedagogical objectives.

Explain that participants will assume roles and operate as management teams to consider some of the factors that influence the location of one type of manufacturing plant. Each team of five people will make a location decision for the imaginary factory.

You can follow these introductory remarks by asking the participants to form into groups of five and to read the introduction to "Activity 2/Metfab" on pages 19–20. Each person on a management team should then select a different role based on the limited information provided to this point. The roles are designed so that all participants will complete their work at approximately the same time; however, different roles place somewhat different demands on the participants.

If you cannot divide the class evenly by five, you can assign four participants to a management team and omit one role. Since the president is instructed to chair the meeting of his management team and to help his group arrive at their decision, his role is the only one which cannot be omitted. In assuming their roles, participants may use any knowledge they have about the problem. However, no additional research should be done.

You should point out that much of the data contained in the role descriptions are fictitious. That the data are fictitious, however, does not affect the validity of the concepts involved in making factory-location decisions nor does it affect the development of the abilities that are the major objectives of the exercise. You can also tell the class that you will serve as research consultant. This will give you the opportunity to be accessible to each group.

Group Work

Each participant should be instructed to spend about ten minutes studying his role as outlined in "Role Descriptions" (pages 22–27). He should analyze his data and decide which city or cities he feels would make the best location for Metfab. In addition, he should be able to defend his viewpoint. Then, under the leadership of the president, the members of the team should debate the relative merits of their preferences in order to reach a group decision on the best location for the company. The team meeting should take approximately twenty minutes.

Summary

After the management teams have made their decisions, bring the class back together for discussion. Ask each team to state its choice of city, to challenge the choices of other groups, to defend their own location choices, and to make brief mention of the reasons for their group decision. However, discussion about the actual decision should be kept to a minimum.

IV. REFLECTIONS ON THE LEARNING AND TEACHING

Now that participants have experienced the activity, two issues can be examined: (1) What skills, attitudes, and geographical concepts have been learned, deepened, or extended? and (2) What has been learned about effective teaching strategies?

A. *Analysis of Learning Outcomes*

Briefly, the objectives of the Metfab activity are increased understanding of the various factors that influence factory-location choices, improved thinking and group process skills, and positive attitudes toward the activity. As participants mention various learning outcomes, your questioning should bring out their meaning and value as social studies objectives. You should help participants clarify the worthwhile objectives they think can be achieved by this simulation. If participants do not cite specific learning examples, the following questions might be used for a more detailed analysis.

1. *What is the importance of least cost and maximum profit considerations as influences on manufacturing-location decisions?*
    Participants should recognize that such factors as market, shipping costs, availability of transportation and raw materials, labor, climate, and financial considerations are among the criteria to be assessed when making factory-location decisions. Participants should also realize that the factory-location decisions they have just made relate to a special case. The types and relative importance of the various factors to be considered in choosing a location may be expected to vary with the type of manufacturing, the region, or the political system under consideration.

2. *What are some of the intangible and noneconomic factors that influence the decision-making process in locating a manufacturing plant?*
    Participants will probably mention subjective influences that vary from individual to individual, such as personal interests or preferences. The likes and dislikes of individuals with regard to environmental considerations, recreational activities, and nearness to relatives may influence the locational decision as much or more than objective or economic considerations.
    In addition to being influenced by personal interests, an individual or group may place particular emphasis on different factors or different combinations of factors. For example, one group may have felt that an economic factor such as accessibility to a large potential market was of top priority in making the location decision. Another group may have felt that the availability of an adequate supply of labor was the most important factor to consider. Still another group might have considered noneconomic factors, such as air pollution, to be of ultimate importance in influencing their decision.

3. *How did small group dynamics influence the decision-making process in each management team?*

Participants may suggest that the kinds of interaction within each group — who talked most frequently, who supported whom, who was most analytical and logical, who blocked the discussion most often, who was most willing to consider several options before making a final choice, etc. — had great influence on the final decision.

Many simulation exercises provide opportunities for group interaction and it is likely that the ability to work in a group improves with practice. One learning outcome that can accrue from a group situation is the growing awareness of how different people use different kinds of reasoning when examining alternative solutions.

4. *Can attitudes be affected by this activity?*

Participants may feel that the Metfab activity can succeed in developing positive attitudes toward subjects such as geography, manufacturing, decision-making, other people, and school. Certain attitudes such as increased tolerance for complexity, awareness that convincing others is a difficult task, and increased respect for the opinions of others might be affected by participation in the activity.

In the high school setting, positive attitudes toward school experiences may result from the high degree of student involvement. Teachers usually consider interested students a fortunate by-product of teaching, yet a good case can be made that the development of positive student attitudes toward school or a school situation should be a conscious educational objective. As students mature and begin to make more of their own decisions, their view of their school experiences is likely to become crucial in making future educational choices.

B. Analysis of Teaching Strategies

There are many ways to analyze the teaching strategies that are part of an educational simulation. In this analysis, the major elements of educational simulation are explored. Discussion should elicit the presences in the simulation of the following five elements: first, a problem that has several plausible solutions; second, specific solutions that players are to consider; third, variables that influence the choices under consideration; fourth, data relevant to each variable; and fifth, role descriptions that present information and initiate conflict about the problem.

In the following material, you will find a question about each element which may be useful in helping participants discover or clarify the characteristic. Material for discussion is also included so that participants can analyze the simulation strategy in which they were involved.

1. *What was the problem or issue that was the focus of the simulation?*

This simulation exercise is based upon the problem of selecting the best location for a manufacturing company's production facilities.

Educational simulations contain a problem or issue that requires a decision. The problem can be of immediate concern to high school students, such as cheating on tests, using drugs, or planning a class trip, or it can be of broader social concern, such as problems of interest to social scientists, historians, political scientists, or military men.

The success of a simulation depends not so much on the subject matter as it does on the basic conflict that is built into the situation. Competition or disagreement provides motivation for participating and for learning. Without disagreement, players would have little reason to defend the choices they make. Reasons for interaction and discussion exist because of the need to defend the decisions. A simulation exercise of this type is self-generating because student groups can function effectively with minimal teacher intervention.

2. *Did the developer of this simulation limit plausible solutions? If so, how did he simplify the choices?*

The decision-making process was simplified by limiting choices to eight metropolitan areas: New York, Cincinnati, Atlanta, Houston, Los Angeles, Pittsburgh, Detroit, and New Orleans.

Crucial to any simulation problem is the variety of choices available to the decision-maker. In real life, people face many problems that have no clearly defined alternatives from which to make a choice. In fact, most significant problems are sufficiently complex that alternatives are not readily identifiable. In simulations, however, choices must be limited to a workable number.

Thus, in analyzing an educational simulation, you need to determine whether the simulation has a simplified problem situation with clearly defined choices, or whether it is necessary for players to first distinguish and clarify the choices that seem to be available. A simulation is probably less complex for high school students when clear-cut alternative solutions to the problem are indicated.

Thus far in the discussion, two important elements of the Metfab activity have been identified:

1. Defining a problem with several plausible solutions.
2. Limiting the plausible solutions.

These elements can be diagrammed as in Table 3-2.

TABLE 3-2.

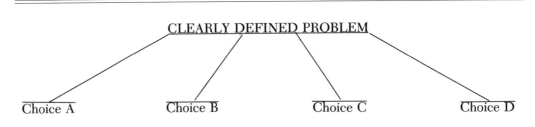

3. *In this factory-location simulation exercise, what variables were selected as influences on the location decision? Which variables would be classified as objective and which would be classified as subjective?*

Objective variables selected for consideration were market factors (such as total existing market, anticipated share of the market, and potential future market) and cost factors (such as raw materials, labor, taxes, interest rates, and shipping charges to buyers). Some of the subjective variables chosen were the location of family relatives and personal climatic preferences. Another subjective element, not specified as a variable, was the relative importance different people attached to any one of the objective factors.

It must be kept in mind that all objective and subjective influences on a decision cannot be included in a simulation exercise. A simulation is a simplified representation of reality. When considering or devising a simulation, one must be particularly alert to the variables, for it is the variables that determine the viewpoint from which the participants will consider the problem. *In other words, the objective and subjective variables selected to remain in the simplified process or problem should relate to the educational objectives of the simulation.*

4. *What types of data are presented in relation to each variable?*

In the Metfab activity, data in the form of role descriptions, tables, and a map are provided as part of the written information. For example, data about raw-materials locations (steel making and copper refining companies) are given on a map. For the product shipping costs variable, a table showing the product shipping cost for each city is included. Personal variables, such as nearness to relatives and fondness for skiing, are included in the written descriptions of the roles of the president and production manager.

In examining a simulation exercise, questions sometimes arise about how accurate the data must be in order for the simulation to work. At times, data for some of the variables influencing the decision need to be fictitious, for it might be the case that real data indicate that one choice is superior to all other choices. Such a situation would create little likelihood of disagreement among members of the group. In a group decision-making simulation, it may be necessary to manipulate data to generate disagreement. Participants may argue that making decisions based on incomplete data is unfair. However, they should be aware that there are many risks involved in decision-making, and the possibility of incomplete data is one such risk.

Working with oversimplified and fictitious data is not always easy for teachers to do. However, when the educational objectives of a simulation exercise are kept in mind, accurate information is not as important as understanding the variables influencing the decision. Therefore, if the success of a simulation exercise depends upon data manipulation, the teacher must be willing to do such manipulation. However, data modification should be kept within reason; otherwise, the plausibility of the simulation will come into question. Students should be informed when data are modified.

Two additional elements of the Metfab simulation have now been identified:

1. Selecting relevant variables which influence choices.
2. Collecting data about each variable.

TABLE 3-3.

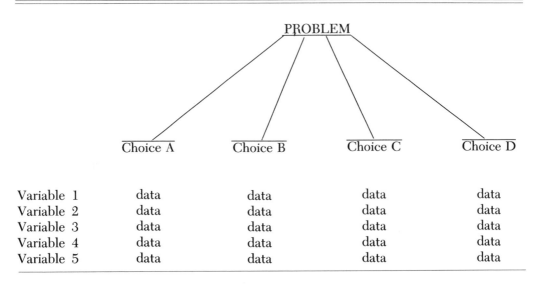

	Choice A	Choice B	Choice C	Choice D
Variable 1	data	data	data	data
Variable 2	data	data	data	data
Variable 3	data	data	data	data
Variable 4	data	data	data	data
Variable 5	data	data	data	data

Thus, the simulation model diagram can be extended as shown in Table 3-3.

5. *For the factory-location simulation exercise, identify some of the variables assigned to each role other than the president's.*

The sales manager was given an interest in the total available market and in finished-product shipping costs for each city. The production manager was assigned a concern for raw materials, shipping costs, and labor productivity. The personnel manager had to consider labor costs and availability. The treasurer was assigned such factors as corporate taxes, available bank deposits, and interest rates.

The way in which information about the problem and the variables is presented in order to create conflict is another element of an educational simulation. In many simulation exercises, roles are used to perform this function. Since roles are carried out in a group context, the kind of group making the decision should be described. If the problem is deciding on what should be produced on a farm, choices may be made by members of the farm family. If the problem is deciding on what to do about inflation, the choice makers may be presidential advisers or persons representing particular economic interests, such as labor, business, or the aged.

In the educational simulation discussed here, there are two occasions when participants must make choices, that is, when role conflict comes into play. The first time is when the individual must make a decision based on the objective and subjective factors built into his role. It is possible that different students, in assuming the same role, will reach different conclusions about the problem.

The second time a choice occurs is when the team makes its decision. Each participant must move from the knowledge he has acquired about his role to learning about other variables from other group members. Role conflict must be resolved in order to reach a group consensus.

The completed diagram for decision-making simulations like the Metfab activity is displayed in Table 3-4. The diagram shows how a role, such as A, can be planned to incorporate the study of a limited number of variables that influence the choice to be made. Data provided about each of the variables have positive, negative, or neutral implications for each choice. For example, the president was assigned a role that contained information about the following variables: anticipated share of the market (variable 1), long-range market prospects (variable 2), and family personal preference (variable 3). In terms of anticipated share of the market, the data about Pittsburgh were positive, Atlanta positive, New York neutral, and New Orleans negative. In terms of family preference, New Orleans was positive, New York negative, Atlanta neutral, and Houston positive.

In addition, Role A is most positive about Choices A and D, Role B is most positive about Choices B and C, and Role C is most positive about Choice C. For example, the

TABLE 3-4.

PROBLEM

		Choice A	Choice B	Choice C	Choice D
Role A	Variable 1	positive	positive	neutral	negative
	Variable 2	negative	neutral	positive	positive
	Variable 3	positive	negative	neutral	positive
Role B	Variable 4	positive	positive	neutral	negative
	Variable 5	negative	neutral	positive	positive
	Variable 6	negative	positive	positive	neutral
Role C	Variable 7	negative	neutral	positive	positive
	Variable 8	negative	positive	positive	neutral
	Variable 9	positive	negative	negative	neutral
Role D	Variable 10	etc.	etc.	etc.	etc.
etc.	etc.				

president was probably most positive about Atlanta, whereas the production manager was most positive about New York.

You may wish to conclude the discussion of the analysis by asking participants the following question:

What appear to be some of the major advantages and disadvantages of simulation exercises?

Those who support the use of simulations in the high school classroom tend to focus on the positive attitudinal responses of students. Additional affective outcomes are discussed in other parts of this book. Those who favor simulations also believe that a more lasting understanding of principles is achieved and that students learn thinking and group-process skills. One disadvantage of simulations is the greater amount of time required for the teaching of the generalizations that are built into the simulation. To teach these generalizations directly is usually quicker, although students often do not retain the generalizations as long. A second possible disadvantage is the apparent disorganization of the classroom, which could lead a teacher into difficulties with his administrators. Finally, the large amount of teacher preparation necessary may be considered a disadvantage. However, it is up to an individual teacher to assess the appropriateness of a teaching strategy according to his own situation.

V. APPLICATION

Participants might be asked to engage in some of the following activities in order to apply the knowledge and skills gained from experiencing and analyzing this activity:

1. Compare another simulation to the Metfab activity. In what ways is the new simulation similar to and different from the factory-location simulation with respect to:
   a. the problem requiring a decision?
   b. the use of clearly designated choices?
   c. the variables that seem to influence student decisions?
   d. the data presented to students?
   e. the use of roles?
2. Teach a simulation activity of their choice and analyze the experience in terms of what students seem to be learning with respect to:
   a. concepts and generalizations.
   b. intellectual abilities or skills.
   c. attitudes about school experiences, themselves, and fellow students.
3. Construct a simulation activity using the model developed in the Metfab activity. Participants could build their simulation around any problem of interest to them.

ACTIVITY 3

Occupational Prestige
Rating Questionnaire

I. BACKGROUND

This activity is the first lesson in the SRSS episode *Class and Race in the United States.* No advance preparation or special knowledge is required of high school students since the activity consists basically of completing the Occupational Prestige Rating Questionnaire and analyzing the results.

II. PARTICIPANT OBJECTIVES

Experience with and analysis of this activity should enable participants:

1. To view occupational prestige as a criterion of social stratification.
2. To identify other criteria of stratification.
3. To classify criteria as objective or subjective.
4. To examine the criteria which the participants believe are the most significant indicators of social class.
5. To begin to form hypotheses about the relationship of various criteria of stratification to social class structure.
6. *To develop techniques for engaging high school students in problem-solving by using their ideas and judgments as data sources.*

7. *To develop skill in treating subjective factors (criteria) as empirical data in the classroom.*[1]

III. CONDUCTING THE ACTIVITY

There are two ways in which this activity can be started: you can administer the Occupational Prestige Rating Questionnaire in advance of class analysis so the data can be tabulated, or you can administer the questionnaire on the day of the discussion and not tabulate the results.

Advance Preparation Option [2]

The advantage of using this option is that the participants themselves will create a set of empirical data derived from their subjective judgments about occupational prestige.

A day or so before you begin this activity, have the participants complete the Occupational Prestige Rating Questionnaire (see page 29). This activity will take about fifteen minutes. It will require about an hour for you (or a participant or a small committee) to tally the results.

Review with the participants the instructions printed at the top of the questionnaire. They are to rate each occupation on a scale that ranges from one to five — from poor to excellent — according to how much social prestige they believe each occupation has. Ask them to work quickly, to record their first impressions, to keep silent about their decisions, and to rate *all* the occupations. Even if participants should ask what is meant by "social standing" or "prestige," do not discuss it with them. Tell them to use their intuition and to rate the occupations according to what they think the terms "social standing" or "prestige" mean.

You can determine the results of the survey by compiling the answers from the individual questionnaires on a blank worksheet. Using a simple tally system ($\mid\mid\mid\mid\mid$), proceed as follows:

1. For each occupation, tally the number of responses received for each adjective.
2. For each occupation, multiply the tally received for each adjective by the number that appears above the name of each adjective. "Good," for example, is in box four; it constitutes a factor of four. If six participants rated artist "good," the total would be twenty-four for that box; that is, $6 \times 4 = 24$.
3. For each occupation, add the totals for each of the five adjectives to obtain a total prestige score for that occupation.
4. Rank order the occupations based on the total prestige score of each.

[1] Numbers one to five are content objectives; six and seven are pedagogical objectives.

[2] From the Instructor's Guide for *Class and Race in the United States* (Boston: Allyn and Bacon, 1972). Copyright © 1972 American Sociological Association. Reprinted with permission.

No Advance Preparation Option

In this option, administer the questionnaire as described in the first option but do not tally the results or rank order the twenty occupations. Rather, ask participants to speculate on how the occupations would probably be ranked and proceed with the discussion when the participants have agreed among themselves that occupations can be ranked in accordance with perceived levels of prestige.

The advantage of using this option is that you will save time by not tabulating the results of the questionnaire.

Discussing the Activity [3]

To begin the discussion (whichever option you have chosen), ask participants to respond to the following question: *What are some of the things you considered when you rated the occupations on the basis of high or low social prestige?*

If more prompting is needed to get them involved, you could ask: *What are the things that people think of when deciding "who is really who" in a society?* If necessary, you might have to explain that you want them to brainstorm for a few minutes, sorting through the criteria that people use when classifying other people, thereby separating the "winners" from the "losers." You can expect that the participants will have some intuitive knowledge of the conventional criteria of stratification. (The term stratification, borrowed from geology, implies that layers of social classes are analogous to layers in geological formations. But, of course, social "layers" are divided according to differences in power, prestige, property, and the like, with people at the top having the most and people at the bottom having the least.)

List responses on the chalkboard as they are given. If the discussion lags, you might mention one or two of the criteria listed below.

Various criteria for stratification have been considered important from time to time and from place to place. The major ones are as follows:[4]

Authority

Power (political, economic, military)

Ownership of property, relation to the means of production, control over land (the feudal estates)

Income — amount, type, and sources

Consumption patterns and style of life

[3] Adapted from the Instructor's Guide for *Class and Race in the United States* (Boston: Allyn and Bacon, 1972). Copyright © 1972 American Sociological Association. Reprinted with permission.

[4] From *Human Behavior: An Inventory of Scientific Findings* by Bernard Berelson and Gary A. Steiner (New York: Harcourt Brace Jovanovich, 1964), p. 454. Copyright © 1964, by Harcourt Brace Jovanovich, Inc. and reprinted with their permission.

Occupation or skill, and achievement in it
Education, learning, wisdom
Divinity, "control" over the supernatural
Altruism, public service, morality
Place in "high society," kinship connections, ancestry (i.e., inherited position)
Associated ties and connections
Ethnic status, religion, race

[If this activity were being taught in a high school class and the students were to suggest *race* as a criterion, it is suggested that the teacher ask the class to suspend consideration of this factor until the second week of the episode when *race* would be dealt with as one variable affecting *class*, rather than the basis for it. You can point this out to your participants if the need should arise.]

CLASSIFYING THE CRITERIA

We suggest that you allow the participants about ten minutes to discuss their ideas about the criteria of social stratification and that you do not begin to evaluate their suggestions until everyone has had a chance to contribute. Then together you can begin to classify the criteria and to eliminate some of them according to the procedure that follows.

Ask participants to classify as objective or subjective the criteria they have suggested. *Objective measures* include such things as income, property, education, or power — characteristics that can be measured or quantified. *Subjective measures* involve less measurable, more directly psychological considerations, such as occupational prestige, a person's style (or personality), behavior, attitudes, background, dress — the elements that tend to affect decisions about where people fit into the class structure.

In order to describe the structure of stratification, participants should agree as to which criteria are objective and which are subjective. You can guide them to a consensus on the objectivity or the subjectivity of each criterion, and then label them accordingly on the chalkboard.

After the responses have been classified as subjective or objective, ask: *Which criteria are the most important for determining stratification?* The object of this question is to help reduce the number of criteria by eliminating the less important ones. Participants will probably recognize that the three most commonly used criteria are *occupational prestige*, *education*, and *income*. The last two can be readily measured objectively, and, although the first involves subjective judgments, it can be examined empirically. [These are the three principal variables considered by high school students in the SRSS episode.]

IV. REFLECTIONS ON THE LEARNING AND TEACHING

A. *Analysis of Learning Outcomes*

A reasonably successful treatment of this activity would result in getting some answers, however tentative, to a number of questions. For example: *Do people commonly differentiate between occupations, according them more or less prestige? If so, is there any agreement in the way people rank occupations?*

The first question is readily handled: people do indeed assign different degrees of prestige to various occupations. And if the experience of participants resembles national findings, they will discover that there is marked agreement about which occupations rank higher and which rank lower. (Cross-national studies show that occupational rankings by Japanese, Russians, Germans, Frenchmen, and Englishmen are remarkably similar to those of national U.S. samples.)

A third question is now posed: *What measures are implicitly — or explicitly — used in ranking occupations?* Participants will doubtless hit upon two commonly used objective measures: level of education achieved and amount of annual income. Other measures of occupational standing typically go along with education and income. For example, there is the blue collar–white collar dichotomy, or participants may have noted that we discriminate levels of prestige depending on whether the occupation entails manipulation of *symbols* or dealing with *things*.

If the inquiry is pushed far enough, participants will recognize that an index of occupational rank that is useful today may not be useful tomorrow. A genuinely progressive tax scheme might reduce the variation in usable income, simultaneously reducing its effectiveness as an indicator of occupational standing. Or the extension of education to ever more persons and for longer periods of time could make level of schooling achieved a less effective indicator of occupational prestige.

A fourth question has not been explicitly posed, but it may have emerged as a variety of cues to occupational standing were considered. *What are the standards or criteria by which some occupations are judged superior — or inferior — to others?* Participants will recognize that at times a person's position is *ascribed* to him on the basis of family-linked traits, whereas at other times it is *achieved* by his own efforts. Thus a person who comes from a long line of physicians has a family background providing lore, acquaintances, learning, and wealth that eases his entry into medicine. On the other hand, the plumber's son who becomes a physician must depend more on his personal achievements. Sometimes occupations have been ascribed on the basis of sex: women are nurses, elementary school teachers, lower-echelon librarians, and the like. But the engineer, the priest, and the surgeon have been typically males. Occupational rank has been ascribed, also, on the basis of race, religion, and nationality. Thus two important standards are at work in assessing occupational standing: *ascription* and *achievement*.[5]

[5] Actually, while these two standards or criteria for according standing are separable analytically, they work jointly in any specific case.

Central to this activity is the answer to a fifth question: *What is the link between position in the labor force — the rank order of one's occupation — and stratification?* It will be understood that occupational prestige is being used as one of the simplest indicators of stratification. One might wish to use a more objective measure of class, or stratification, such as income. But it is not always easy to discover income, whereas, even at very young ages, people have notions of occupational prestige. Furthermore, occupational prestige is itself a measure of social class — a family's place in the stratification system — so participants are using one index of stratification to discover others. And finally, when one chooses criteria of social importance, one is actually revealing the value system of his society. A person who judges social class on the basis of the size of the family dwelling, for instance, is tacitly assuming that in his society the more important a family is, the larger its house will tend to be.

Finally, one might note the almost inevitable ethical question: *On what grounds is it just to reward one man more and another less?* Are not the occupations of plumber and drayman as worthy as those of teacher and physician? And if indeed these last two occupations require more time and education, is this not more privilege than penalty, and thus not justifying larger rewards? One would hope, then, that participants would discover significant affective as well as intellectual issues entailed in the analysis of differences in occupational prestige.

B. Analysis of Teaching Strategies

An assessment of how well this activity contributes to the attainment of the pedagogical objectives can be made by considering several questions.

The first question explores the teaching techniques used to initiate the activity: *How can an instructor engage participants in the consideration of a topic through the use of their own ideas and knowledge?* Several different teaching techniques are employed in this activity. As the springboard for a two-week unit that is to consider specific concepts and generalizations about social class (with race considered as a variable of social class), it is important for the instructor to involve participants in active inquiry at the same time that he is beginning to shape the instructional sequence around the data presented in the curriculum materials. In this particular activity, many data related to stratification are already known in an elementary way to participants; the task is to help them organize and study these facts in more depth. The focus of the discussion is on the ranking of occupations, data that participants have supplied by completing the questionnaire.

The activity begins with the instructor providing an example of how to get a class to brainstorm. As participants supply the criteria by which they assign prestige to different occupations, the instructor records the different suggestions and asks questions to help the participants sharpen their criteria or to help them identify other factors. However, the instructor is cautioned not to pass judgment on the offerings that the participants make but to consider each offering equally, deferring examination of the adequacy of the criteria until later in the activity.

When participants have supplied the factors they regard as criteria for stratification, they are asked to classify the items into categories of objective and subjective criteria. As participants reflect on each criterion, they should begin to sharpen or develop an ability to discriminate between those items which can be measured empirically and those which are matters of subjective judgment. But here again the instructor should be hesitant about supplying correct judgments and should rely instead on probing the ideas that the participants suggest or on stimulating the group to reflect upon what has been said.

Another question relates to helping participants develop skills for treating subjective factors as empirical data in the classroom: *How can empirical inquiry into a complex social topic be initiated using data based on the subjective judgments of the participants?* The importance of this question lies in the realization that opinions of people are facts; that is, it is a fact that more people will assign higher prestige to the occupation of physician than they will to the occupation of shoeshine stand attendant. Thus, subjective judgments of the participants become empirical evidence in the study of stratification.

The problems of extending the interest established by the springboard activity include considering the teaching-learning strategy of the curriculum unit and providing participants with the opportunity to reflect on the value dimensions of stratification. The SRSS episode provides opportunity for examination of the value issues in its full two-week high school treatment. In a single short session this reflection can only be started.

In terms of cognitive processes, the activity is limited to a few rather low-level steps. Once the existence of a problem has been established (that people in U.S. society are stratified and this idea is not universally accepted), the instructor should initiate an inductive sequence of problem solving. The task is to stimulate the participants into establishing preliminary hypotheses about the relationships between the structure of stratification and the factors that they have identified as determinants of or closely related to occupational prestige. Although the instructor is encouraged to keep the discussion open and to avoid guiding it toward closure, in order to begin to test and evaluate their hypotheses it is necessary that participants work toward consensus on the relative importance of the criteria they have identified. This will probably involve consideration of the value standards that the participants may hold concerning the "appropriateness" of different criteria. However, the examination should be made in such a way that conflicting standards will be clearly defined as such. It is not necessary at this point in the activity to try to settle disputes over which value standard is "best"; the point of the discussion is to identify which criteria predominate in a system of social differentiation.

[In the SRSS episode, when high school students reach consensus on the major criteria of social stratification, they begin to examine empirical data about occupational prestige, level of education, and family income to test their ideas about the relationship between these factors and the structure of stratification.]

V. APPLICATION

The information that follows may be helpful in extending the concepts and teaching strategies developed in this activity to other instructional situations.

What good questions were raised by participants in the discussion, extending the inquiry beyond the limits of the data and their immediate analysis? One hopes that good questions emerged which carried the inquiry beyond the nominal boundaries of the enterprise. For example, someone may have raised the question: *Why is it that some kinds of work are more highly valued than others? Why is the physician more rewarded than the mason?* One answer to this question has been that those occupations most essential for sustaining the social order are the ones most highly rewarded. But how does one assess indispensability? Does the persistence of our social system depend on the generously rewarded services of Johnny Carson, Tom Jones, or Barbra Streisand? And does the winner of the Irish Sweepstakes receive handsome payment because of his functional indispensability? And when we think of cities hoisted on their own heaps of solid waste, is the physician filling a role more indispensable than that of the sanitation department truckman?

Another explanation has it that society best rewards those who invest most in developing their occupational skills. Thus the time and money put into a medical education justifies the prestige, power, and pelf enjoyed by the practicing physician. Although we can find disparities between size of income and length of occupational preparation (the public school teacher might be a case in point), in general it is true that occupational prestige and income vary directly with length and cost of education.

Perhaps some participants observed that a person's occupational standing need not necessarily be the same as that attached to his educational status, income, or ethnic status. That is to say, standings along these various scales may not be consistent. And depending on degree of status consistency, other things may follow. (One early study of status consistency reported that persons with more consistent standings tended to favor the Republican party, whereas those with low status consistency inclined toward the Democratic party.) In any case, it would be worthwhile to consider the implications of varying degrees of status consistency.

One pedagogic technique in the activity that is not treated in the short demonstration session is that of replication of experiments. There were two nationwide studies of occupational prestige on which the replication in the episode is based. The first study was designed by two sociologists, C. C. North and P. J. Hatt, and was conducted in 1947 by the staff of the National Opinion Research Center (NORC) at The University of Chicago.[6]

In this study, a national sample of more than three thousand adults in the United States was asked to rate ninety occupations (selected to represent the entire range of occupations) according to the following categories of prestige: excellent standing, good standing, average standing, somewhat below-average standing, and poor standing. After the interview data were tabulated, the responses for each occupation were added together, averaged, and converted into an occupational prestige score. They were then rank ordered. The results of the study closely matched what sociologists expected. Generally, the professional occupations tended to be ranked near the top of the prestige

---

[6] The study is described in Albert J. Reiss, Jr., et al., *Occupations and Social Status* (New York: Free Press of Glencoe, 1961).

hierarchy, whereas the so-called "unskilled" occupations were ranked near the bottom.

The second study was done sixteen years later, in 1963, when NORC repeated the 1947 study.[7] The same procedure was followed and the same occupations were considered. Even the sample of persons to be interviewed was drawn in the same way, although in 1963 only 651 persons were interviewed. The smaller sample was shown to be just as reliable as the larger one. The results of the later study compared with the earlier study showed a correlation of .99, which means that the rankings were almost identical. (A perfect correlation — if the results from the two studies had been exactly the same — would have been a correlation of $+1.0$.)

You could consider the idea of replicating experiments by posing the question: *Why should replication of scientific experiments be employed in classroom inquiry?* One answer lies in the positive value of engaging students in scientific inquiry processes using their own ideas and knowledge as input and comparing the outcome with prior research evidence. Your participants may think of other answers.

---

[7] Robert W. Hodge, Paul M. Siegel, and Peter H. Rossi, "Occupational Prestige in the United States, 1925–63," *American Journal of Sociology*, Vol. LXX (November 1964).

ACTIVITY 4

Hunger

I. BACKGROUND

"Hunger" is adapted from "Manufacturing and Agriculture," Unit 2 of the HSGP course *Geography in an Urban Age*. Prior to participating in this activity, high school students have studied the nature, distribution, and importance of manufacturing in the United States. "Hunger" begins the agriculture section of the unit and introduces students to the problem of mass hunger throughout the world. The hunger activity is followed by studying worldwide distribution of a variety of agricultural commodities, examining the problems faced by farmers throughout the world, and returning to the problem of hunger to reexamine possible solutions.

II. PARTICIPANT OBJECTIVES

Experience with and analysis of this activity should enable participants:

1. To discuss the major physical, social, and economic characteristics of areas in the world where mass hunger is prevalent.
2. To hypothesize relationships among mapped variables.
3. To offer and defend possible solutions to the problem of mass hunger.

4. *To develop a teaching activity based on an interesting topic which will lead to discussion, analysis, and possible resolution of a problem.*
5. *To engage high school students in the study of problems derived from activities based on an interesting topic.*
6. *To explain the advantages and disadvantages of using teaching strategies based on interesting topics.*[1]

III. CONDUCTING THE ACTIVITY

Participants should read "Activity 4/Hunger" (pages 30–38) before you conduct the activity in class.

There are three major parts to this activity. First, participants will engage in a short, general discussion to hypothesize about causes of hunger. Following the general discussion, small groups will analyze and discuss one or two of the causes of the hunger problem, and, in addition, should formulate possible solutions to the problem. The total group then will reassemble to examine potential solutions in terms of their desirability, effectiveness, and practicality in solving the problem of hunger.

You might want to open the general discussion on hunger in the world by noting that we all have seen disturbing pictures of people in areas where malnutrition is a serious problem. Further, we are probably aware of the large proportion of the world's people that goes hungry each day. In addition we know that there seem to be too many people in some areas of the world for the land to support.

After this brief introduction, you might pose the following question: *What are some major characteristics of persistent-hunger areas in the world?*

Characteristics participants are likely to mention might include high population density, high infant mortality, high incidence of disease, high death rates, low per capita income, lack of capital, low literacy rates, little modern industry, unfavorable climate, and primitive farming methods. Participants might also mention migration generated by population pressures, land tenure systems that restrict the amount of land available for crop agriculture, and inefficient distribution systems for supplying needed social resources and amenities, such as adequate housing, waste disposal, medical services, and schools.

You can suggest that the class explore further one or two of these variables, such as population density and primitive farming methods, in relation to mass hunger. Divide the class into discussion groups of four or five participants and ask each group to explore two related hypotheses:

1. *Population density is positively related to mass hunger.*
2. *Poor farming methods are positively related to mass hunger.*

Based upon their discussions and the material they have read, participants should be able

---

[1] Numbers one to three are content objectives; four to six are pedagogical objectives.

to refine or modify the hypotheses. The groups should also consider possible solutions to the problem of hunger.

After the groups have completed their tasks, call the class together to examine the small group conclusions. You can expect several outcomes from the small group discussions. For example, by comparing the information in Figure 2-7 (map of well-fed and poorly fed countries) with that in Figure 2-8 (population map), participants can hypothesize a positive relationship between population density and hunger areas. They may note, however, that some hunger areas in Africa and Latin America have sparse population, whereas some well-fed areas, especially in Europe and in the northeastern United States, are densely settled. Thus in some areas the hypothesis holds; in other areas it does not.

By relating Figure 2-9 (map of approximate cropland area) to Figure 2-7, participants should see that every hunger area seems to have available cropland. It is likely that the farming methods used in these lands are poor compared with methods used in well-fed areas. The participant reading material verifies this relationship. Therefore, it is valid to hypothesize that the problem of hunger is related to existing farming methods in a country.

After this discussion, have each group present its possible solutions to the problem of hunger. Several solutions, such as the following, may be suggested:

1. Increase mechanization of agriculture in hunger areas.
2. Open new agricultural lands.
3. Initiate population control measures in hunger areas.
4. Improve education and health services in acute hunger areas.
5. Supplement natural food supplies with synthetic nutrients.

Encourage participants to discuss the advantages and disadvantages of each solution presented.

IV. REFLECTIONS ON THE LEARNING AND TEACHING

Participants can now analyze some of the outcomes from the hunger activity. As the discussion develops, you will want to focus on both the cognitive and affective aspects of the hunger activity as well as the teaching strategy used to develop the activity. A number of questions might be posed for discussion.

A. Analysis of Learning Outcomes

How might one's perception of the problem of world hunger be affected as a result of participating in this activity?
It is likely that at least some of the participants' preconceptions of the problem of

hunger will be modified as a result of studying and discussing the data provided in this activity. A significant geographic learning would be the recognition of the areal relationships of the hunger problem to other areal problems common to developing countries, such as poor health with the attendant debilitation of individuals which results in low work productivity. In addition, one might reflect upon the small amount of time that is left for activities other than producing enough food for subsistence, or upon how people in hunger areas might work long hours for an income that provides only the bare necessities for survival. There is little or no time for creative and imaginative pursuits; life in hunger areas is fraught with stinting, hardship, and frustration.

Another important learning is that each problem attendant to hunger has areal expressions which are not only internal to each hunger area but which produce interaction patterns peculiar to the condition — a widening ripple effect can occur. For example, poor yields in one section of India can cause migration to more fortunate regions within the country, placing pressures upon the available resources in these new regions. In addition, external problems can ensue: emergency measures to provide foreign aid to the suffering nation could cause changes in foreign-aid policies, both for the recipient country and for the giving country.

B. Analysis of Teaching Strategies

How were the various data about hunger presented? What skills were developed in analyzing the data?

Participants studied maps, read and interpreted a table and a drawing, and drew conclusions from a reading. They also made simple map comparisons to associate the location of poorly fed areas with other factors such as population distribution and available cropland. These data helped participants test the validity of the two related hypotheses about the relationship between hunger and factors such as population density and farming methods. Thus, the participants modified or confirmed the hypotheses by data analysis.

How effective is an activity of this kind in the high school classroom?

The effectiveness of an activity depends on several things. First, if students already have a thorough understanding of the subject at hand — in this case, the problem of hunger — then the activity's usefulness might be considerably lessened. Second, the ways in which the data — the maps, drawing, table, and reading material — are presented are important when considering effectiveness. Students with low reading levels may not perform as well as those with better reading skills, but map and chart reading plus effective pictures can assist in maintaining interest and in ensuring learning. Third, initial class interest in the topic should contribute to the success of the activity in the classroom.

You can raise the idea at this point of using an interesting topic as a springboard for discussion in the classroom. Participants are probably aware that posing a topic of high student interest in the classroom, if managed properly, will motivate student discussion and analysis. Such topics will vary depending on current social problems. At present such topics as ecological imbalance, widespread drug abuse, controversy over sex education, campus unrest, and American involvement in Southeast Asia would probably initiate discussion in most classes. With the current emphasis on population pressures and efficient resource allocation and management, hunger is also a topic that is likely to stimulate student discussion.

What are some advantages and disadvantages of using an interesting topic approach with high school students?

Initial interest and involvement by students in a subject is desirable only if it leads them to contribute their ideas in a discussion, ask important questions, and seek new information to clarify and to support their ideas.

Of course it is possible that interesting topics will generate discussion only for the sake of argument. Students may take positions and hold to them by expounding personal views that have little factual basis. Participants should be able to offer various observations on how to deal effectively with the problems of personal bias, prejudice, and poorly documented evidence that they will encounter in the high school classroom.

Often in the heated discussion of a controversial or interesting topic, students are challenged in their positions. One can help high school students learn how to deal with inconsistencies by encouraging them to examine new data sources and rethink their positions. If an interesting topic is raised and discussed without hypothesis formulation, data analysis, or hypothesis modification, the interesting topic has little value other than generating a "rap" session.

Participants should be aware that the interesting-topic approach can be over-worked. If high school students are discussing pollution in English, science, and social studies classes, they may become saturated and even bored. The interesting-topic strategy should be used judiciously and coordinated with other subject areas whenever possible.

Assuming the interesting-topic approach initially captures student interest, what subsequent plans or strategies should be made to take advantage of the interest?

The teacher may wish students to pursue a single facet of the topic or to continue with a deeper analysis of several aspects of the topic in order to extend the initial interest. For example, in the HSGP "Manufacturing and Agriculture" unit, the hunger activity introduces the study of agriculture. Depending on the topic, students can be directed to study further specific aspects of agriculture or problems common to developing countries.

Is there a model or sequence of events in the hunger activity that can be extracted for use with other topics?

Participants may offer several interpretations of the teaching model for this activity. One possible sequence is as follows.

Interesting-Topic Teaching Sequence

1. Raise an interesting or controversial question or topic. Question students to elicit their present knowledge of the topic. Accept all student responses, including misconceptions, but lead students toward the formulation of tentative hypotheses.

2. Provide more data on the topic under discussion. (In the hunger activity, they consisted of the reading on hunger, along with the maps, a table, and a drawing.) Based on the new data inputs, guide students toward a modification of both the hypotheses and the opinions they have formed.
3. Raise a question about possible solutions to the problem. Ask students to work on preparing solutions.
4. Discuss the possible solutions or resolutions of the problem. Stress interchange along with justification of the position taken on the solution.
5. Subsequent activities or lessons should capitalize upon and follow up the initial discussion on the interesting topic or problem and provide in-depth analysis for students.

V. APPLICATION

In order to extend and apply their understanding of how to use an interesting-topic strategy in the classroom, participants might prepare one or both of the following topics:

1. Participants might develop a lesson using the model or sequence for interesting topics discussed above. Participants should base their lesson on a subject area of their choice. Questions to raise about the developed lesson might include:
   a. In what context would the lesson be used?
   b. What material would be used to provide data for analysis?
   c. What is the teaching sequence or strategy of the lesson?
   d. What problems might be encountered in using the lesson?
2. Participants might prepare some suggestions for developing interdisciplinary approaches to interesting topics or subjects to avoid the kind of overlap that contributes to possible loss of student interest.

ACTIVITY 5

Dilemma of the Tribes

I. BACKGROUND

The SRSS episode *Simulating Social Conflict* is the source of the materials for this teaching demonstration. In this episode, high school students study social conflict by playing two versions of the simulation game "Dilemma of the Tribes" and three versions of the simulation game "Resources and Arms." After a brief reading which introduces them to the idea of simulation and to the use of such a technique for exploring social conflict (and its opposite, cooperation), students play the two versions of "Dilemma of the Tribes."

II. PARTICIPANT OBJECTIVES

Experience with and analysis of this activity should enable participants:

1. To add depth to a common-sense understanding of the concepts of *conflict* and *cooperation* (and perhaps, by contrast, *rivalry* and *competition*).
2. To discover how *process* (a form of social interaction called conflict) gives rise to *structure* (a crystallizing of roles as two tribal representatives come to define their relationship as one of collaborators or enemies).
3. To become aware of the part communication plays in reaching definitions of a situation.

4. To gain insight into why people or groups of people behave as they do in situations of potential conflict.
5. *To illustrate the use of gaming as a teaching technique.*
6. *To show how learning (awareness of strategy) develops through participation rather than through instruction.*[1]

III. CONDUCTING THE ACTIVITY[2]

On the day you begin the activity,[3] have participants read "Activity 5/Dilemma of the Tribes" (pages 39–40). This simulation is fashioned after the game called "Prisoners' Dilemma" which is famous in game-theory literature. "Dilemma of the Tribes" is a game that simulates the interaction of two tribes, the Golos and the Mantas, in the African state of Equatoria that has recently become independent. Each tribe desires to protect its own interests. In the game, most participants will act as chiefs of the two tribes. They are seated in pairs and each pair plays twenty "rounds" of the game. In every round, each player must choose either to be cooperative (A) or to be belligerent (B). The scoring system is not explained to the participants so that they will not be able to analyze it in advance and determine playing strategies. You are to explain it just before play begins. Participants will play two versions of the game.

Two characteristic conditions of this game place the players in a dilemma: (1) the two players (chiefs of the two tribes) must decide *simultaneously* on their stances toward each other, and (2) the consequences of their choices are strictly defined by the rules of the game.

Each player's total score for the twenty rounds is determined by his actions and those of his opponent. An explanation of four situations that can develop in the game and their corresponding scores follows:

Situations	*Score for Each*
1. Both chiefs decide to be cooperative (A). The consequence is that each tribe is moderately rewarded through a cooperative sharing of power.	G scores $+1$ M scores $+1$
2. The Golo chief wants his tribe to dominate and takes a belligerent stance (B). The Manta chief takes a cooperative stance (A). In this combination of choices, the Golos gain power while the Mantas lose power.	G scores $+5$ M scores -5

---

[1] Numbers one to four are content objectives; five and six are pedagogical objectives.

[2] Adapted from the Instructor's Guide for *Simulating Social Conflict* (Boston: Allyn and Bacon, 1971). Copyright © 1971 American Sociological Association. Reprinted with permission.

[3] Before you start the activity, you will need to make two copies of the scoring sheet (see page 145) for each participant, make the referee scoring cards (see page 141), and have available for use a watch with a second hand and several colored pencils.

3. The situation in Number 2 is reversed — the Manta chief is   G scores −5
    belligerent (B) and the Golo chief is cooperative (A). The   M scores +5
    consequences are the same in reverse.
4. Both chiefs try to be belligerent (B). They fight each other to a   G scores −1
    standstill and both are somewhat disadvantaged by the costs in   M scores −1
    suffering and resources.

      It is clear that if, in any round, one chief tries to put his tribe in a dominant position while the other is cooperative (thus scoring +5 and −5, respectively), the latter is likely to retaliate on the next round. If this happens, and both continue to be belligerent, each will get a score of −1 in each round — despite the fact that if both were cooperative, they could each get positive, though moderate, gains of +1.

      The essence of the dilemma is to try for maximum gain (+5) and perhaps fail or to trust the other chief to be cooperative and thus achieve a small positive reward (+1).

      When the players begin the game, they have no clear concept of the potential for either conflict or cooperation. As the game progresses, they begin to see these possibilities. This realization is an important part of the learning experience and should not be revealed in any way. As a safety measure, we suggest the following "DO'S" and "DON'T'S":

DON'T   use the word "opponent" or "partner" when referring to the other player. These words may be taken to indicate conflict and cooperation, respectively.

   DO   use terms such as "the other player in your pair" or simply "the other player." These expressions may be awkward, but they are neutral.

DON'T   speak of "beating" the other player or "winning the game."

   DO   emphasize that it is one's own *individual score* that is important and that it is rated against a fixed scale or against the rest of the class, not against the other player in a pair.

      By stressing individual goals, a neutral and individual orientation is established. With this orientation the participant himself begins to generate the elements of either conflict or cooperation.

Conducting the Simulation

ARRANGING THE CLASSROOM

The players will be seated in pairs, back to back with an aisle between them. (If you do not have movable seats in the room, the members of the pair should be across the aisle from each other, both sitting sideways in their seats so that they are back to back.) A referee will be in charge of a row of either three or four pairs (six or eight players). Those who cannot participate because the seating arrangement would be clumsy or because there is an odd number of participants will be observers.

The referees you select should be competent participants since they will help you conduct the simulation game. Make for each referee one small (3" × 5") scoring card. This scoring card should be similar to the sample below. The referees will use these cards for reference as they pass through their aisles and assign the scores. Give these scoring cards to the referees on the day the game is played. Also, supply each referee with a colored pencil, which he will use to enter the scores on the score sheets of his players as he passes through the aisle. This will prevent the players from changing their answers.

PLAYING VERSION 1

On the day of play, determine the number of participants present and arrange them into the proper number of pairs, referees, and observers. As you choose the pairs, try *not* to choose two persons who are already established friends or enemies.

After the class is properly arranged, you can begin the instructions for "Dilemma of the Tribes: Version 1." Remind the participants that there will be twenty rounds of play[4] and that they have an option of being either cooperative (A) or belligerent (B) in each round. Each player should try to make the highest score he can. *Make sure each player understands that his score will depend on what both he and the other player in his pair do.* Tell participants you will pass out score sheets in a few minutes; then outline what is going to happen:

1. At the beginning of each round you, the instructor, will say, "Round ———" (number of the round).

[4] In the interest of saving time in this activity, you might choose to play only fifteen rounds in Version 1 of the game and ten or fifteen rounds in Version 2.

TABLE 3-5. *Sample Referee Scoring Card*

REFEREE SCORING CARD

(Other Player)

		(A)		(B)	
	A	+1	(+1)	−5	(+5)
One Player					
	B	+5	(−5)	−1	(−1)

2. Each player has five seconds to write an "A" or a "B" in the "Move" column on his score sheet. (Detailed scoring instructions appear below.)
3. After each round the referees will write in colored pencil each player's score on the player's score sheet.
4. No player may erase an "A" or "B" or a score in order to change it.
5. After every five rounds, the player totals his score.
6. At no time may players talk or gesture to each other.

DESCRIBING THE SCORING RULES

The best way to help participants understand the scoring is to draw Table 3-6 on the board. Then explain each possible score that "you" can receive. For example, if "you" choose "A" and the "other player" chooses "B," then "you" get −5, as indicated in the upper right-hand cell (square). Be sure to explain all four possible scores that "you" can receive.
    Next enter in the table all the possible scores the "other player" could receive. *Place each score in parentheses in order to set each one apart from the scores that "you" could receive.* When you have completed your table, it should look like Table 3-7.
    You should explain that if both players choose "A," then "you" get +1 and the "other player" also gets +1. A similar explanation should be given for each cell of the table.
    Participants should now be able to enter the same information on a scoring list. Put Table 3-8 on the board.

TABLE 3-6.
(Other Player)

	(A)	(B)
You A	+1	−5
You B	+5	−1

TABLE 3-7.
(Other Player)

	(A)		(B)	
You A	+1	(+1)	−5	(+5)
You B	+5	(−5)	−1	(−1)

TABLE 3-8. *Scoring List*

Moves		Scores	
Players		Players	
G	M	G	M
A	A		

_____   Total Scores

Ask what each player's score would be if both players choose "A." Ask similar questions about the possible combinations of "BB," "AB," and "BA," so that as participants give the answers the complete scoring list is filled in on the board. Then ask the participants to total each player's score. Enter the totals on the board. Answer any questions about the scoring system.

BEGINNING THE GAME

Now pass out the "Dilemma of the Tribes Scoring Sheet" to each player to examine (see sample on page 145). Point out exactly where each player is to place his choice for each round and where he is to write in his running scores.

Emphasize again that there must be no talking or other communication such as nods or gestures. The members of a pair must not communicate with each other or with members of other pairs.

Observers should feel free to watch the players, but they should not discuss their moves.

Play begins when you, the instructor, say "Round One." Each player then writes down an "A" or a "B" in the first of the twenty "Move" blanks provided on the scoring sheet. Then the referees inspect the moves of each pair in turn. Each referee should carry his scoring card in his hand for ready reference. The referee writes with colored pencil each player's score for that round on the player's score sheet.

As the game progresses, the player may figure out whether the other player has chosen "A" or "B." Thus, in the above example, if a player chose "A" and got -5, he would know that the other player had chosen "B." *Do not suggest this possibility.* Say nothing about the play.

The decision to write "A" or "B" is final. After the referees have finished scoring the fifth round, give the players a few minutes to add their scores up to that point, so that they can see how they are doing. At the end of every five plays, they should total their scores, keeping a running overall total in the boxes. This should discourage careless play.

At the end of the simulation have each referee collect the score sheets of the players he has monitored and hand them to you so that you can determine the five players who made the highest scores.

PLAYING VERSION 2

After the game, announce the names of those with the five highest scores and begin preparation for playing Version 2. In Version 2, the persons who acted in the roles of referees and players in Version 1 will act in the same roles again. Do not alternate players, referees, and observers, but no players who were paired together for Version 1 should be paired together for Version 2.

Version 2 differs from Version 1 in only one detail: The players are allowed to communicate with each other for forty-five seconds at four points — before the start of the game and after rounds 5, 10, and 15. If a student served as an observer during Version 1, he can help you time the communication periods during this game. You or the observer should give a warning after thirty seconds.

Distribute additional copies of the "Dilemma of the Tribes Scoring Sheet" to the players and play through Version 2 of the game. After the game has ended, collect the scoring sheets as before and announce the names of the five players who made the highest scores on this version of the game.

The expected outcome of this second version of "Dilemma of the Tribes" is that communication will encourage the pairs to adopt an "AA" strategy — one in which both players of a pair choose a cooperative stance. However, it is also expected that some players may defect from this stance on the last move in the hope of gaining a +5 advantage over the other person.

IV. REFLECTIONS ON THE LEARNING AND TEACHING

A. *Analysis of Learning Outcomes*

An effective analysis of man's dealings with others entails the use of concepts — abstract terms that distill a wealth of concrete experience. Clearly "Dilemma of the Tribes" requires us to ask: *What do we mean by conflict and cooperation? How do we discriminate between these concepts and two others, rivalry and competition?*

FIGURE 3-1. *Dilemma of the Tribes Scoring Sheet*

First Name _____ Last Name _____

(Circle) Version 1 2

Other Player's Last Name _____

Referee's Last Name _____

SCORING CHART:

		(Other Player)	
		(A)	(B)
A	+1 (+1)	−5 (+5)	
You			
B	+5 (−5)	−1 (−1)	

SCORING SUMMARY:

A(A) . . . . . +1 each
B(B) . . . . . −1 each
A(B) . . . . . −5 (+5 for Other Player)
B(A) . . . . . +5 (−5 for Other Player)

Highest Score Possible = +100
Lowest Score Possible = −100

ROUND	MOVE	SCORE
1.		
2.		
3.		
4.		
5.		

Score
So Far

ROUND	MOVE	SCORE
6.		
7.		
8.		
9.		
10.		

Score
So Far

ROUND	MOVE	SCORE
11.		
12.		
13.		
14.		
15.		

Score
So Far

ROUND	MOVE	SCORE
16.		
17.		
18.		
19.		
20.		

TOTAL
SCORE

As participants engage in this simulation, they will discover that conflict emerges as a form of human interaction only as the rules of the game develop. When a player says to himself: "Oh, so *that's* how you're going to play!" he is, in effect, formulating a rule to govern his conduct toward another. Such rules imply a reciprocity in human relationships: if you do that, then I shall do thus-and-such — and can be expected to do so. Hence rules and reciprocity are important connotations of the concept of conflict (as they are in other modes of human interaction).

Common-sense usage makes "conflict" a destructive relationship in which one party (either a person or a group) seeks to vanquish the other. But as a process, participants will note, conflict works toward its own elimination. Given a degree of equality in the power of contending parties — and this is the case in this activity — conflict is a way of working through antipathies to some less costly solution. Conflict, then, may be seen as a positive process through which the costs of cupidity are reduced. It is the route to cooperation.

The customary use of the word "cooperation" is less misleading than is the case in the use of the word "conflict." Cooperation means collaborative effort in achieving common goals. Representatives of the Golos and the Mantas share the objective of maximizing gains and cutting losses. We can distinguish both modes of interaction (conflict and cooperation) from competition by pointing out that competition is a process in which contending parties are motivated by *like*, not *common*, aims. Thus two merchants have like objectives in seeking to increase their profits. But with a limited market, one's gain must be the other's loss. On the other hand, the goals of peaceful coexistence, civic improvement, and reducing external danger are common ones, and their achievement by one party enhances the other's welfare.

Competition can be distinguished from conflict in another way. The former is a three-way relationship: *A* versus *B* in competing for *C*'s favor (merchant versus merchant seeking the buyer). But the latter is a two-way relationship in which *A* and *B* seek to reduce the threat represented by the other.

Rivalry, on the other hand, is a variation on the conflict theme. As we see it in sports, it is a publicly sponsored form of conflict thought to promote the general welfare. Health, fair play, and patriotic sentiments are the common social justifications for various forms of rivalry.

A second learning outcome is achieved if participants can answer this question: *How do social structures emerge?* The notion of structure is probably so common that we may miss both its general implications and its specific bearing on "Dilemma of the Tribes." Buildings, symphonies, and sentences have structures. Indeed, the elements of our worlds are discernible, and dealing with them is possible only to the extent that they take on some structure. What is common to structures is some systematic — nonrandom — arrangement of parts. So it is with social structures, in which the parts that are arranged are human relationships. When, to meet basic social requirements, we arrange such parts in a fairly fixed fashion, we call them institutions.

Social arrangements do not emerge automatically, however, for they imply the process of arranging. The child, the GI in basic training, the new employee — all go through a process of arranging their relationships with others. The emerging set of relationships is a social structure.   Process gives rise to structure.   In this activity, participants have the opportunity to see such a structure emerge through the process of conflict.

Furthermore, participants will be able to answer the question: *What difference does communication make?*   What difference does it make that in the first version, players deal silently with one another, whereas a second version allows them to communicate briefly with one another at four points?

John Dewey once suggested that it is no accident that the words communication, community, communion, and communal have common etymological roots.   A sense of common cause, or of community, is impossible without communication.   In the first version of the game, the Golos and the Mantas can communicate only remotely and inferentially through the intervention of the referee.   Obstacles to communication are impediments to community.   On the other hand, the communication built into Version 2 promotes a clear understanding of what is mutually advantageous and opens paths to its achievement.

Conflict takes on myriad forms across the spectrum of human relationships.   To unravel its implications as a concept, to see it as a structure-creating process, and to understand the effects of communication on conflict is to deepen our grasp of social reality.

B.   Analysis of Teaching Strategies

Two pedagogic outcomes (numbers five and six) are suggested in the "Participant Objectives" for this activity.   A third broad avenue of inquiry can be derived from an application of these two objectives.

Consideration of gaming as a teaching technique affords participants the opportunity of examining ways in which specific aspects of social reality can be isolated for study. One method of studying complex problems in the social sciences is to use a model — a scheme whereby essential elements of a social system are abstracted and manipulated.   In "Dilemma of the Tribes," participants work with a simplified model of a conflict situation. They should be able to derive three learnings about models from this activity:

1.   If the *essential* dimensions of reality are built into the model, it helps one to understand reality.
2.   If one *participates* in a simulation based upon a good model, one can *experience* reality to a degree.
3.   A good model may reveal scientific truths *previously unknown* if the roles are played out under new conditions.

These three principles apply to most scientific inquiry.   An understanding of them might help participants gain new insights into inductive approaches to teaching.

Analysis of "Dilemma of the Tribes" also provides participants with the opportunity of assessing the manner in which classroom behavior is shaped by role expectations and by patterns of teacher-student interaction.   The school socialization process usually results in a pattern of behavior in which students try to find out what the teacher expects (rather than endeavor to learn as much as possible) and the teacher takes pains to conceal specific data that will be included in the "test" (rather than facilitate student learning). Simulations can improve student performance by altering conventional patterns of teacher-student interaction. If participants are asked to look at the instructor's role in this activity and to consider in particular the importance of neutrality in conducting the game, it should become apparent to them that neutral, nondirective, slow-to-closure teacher behaviors will lead to channeling student inquiry toward mastery of the learnings. In this activity, the instructor's neutrality makes it possible for learning about conflict and cooperation to unfold in the course of participating in the game. Thus, teacher behavior can lead to encouraging independent inquiry and to discouraging dependency on teacher approval.

Participants should also become aware that student involvement is an important ingredient in improved performance. Simulations, by their very structure, encourage participation and involvement. Students find this method of learning more enjoyable than methods in which they are passive recipients of information.

Evaluating teaching performance in simulation games is easier in one respect than assessing the effectiveness of teacher behavior in other methods of instruction. If you have time and want to make a broader application of the first two objectives, you might ask: *How does the use of gaming contribute to more effective teaching?*

To answer this question, it is helpful to look at the concept of "teacher effectiveness" as it is used in educational evaluation, where teacher effectiveness is judged on the basis of change in student attitudes or in learning achievement. Typically, research on effectiveness involves observation to ensure control of teacher behavior and measurement of gain in student achievement. The nature of the role of the leader in a simulation game results in consistent behavior; in effect, the role helps control teaching performance. This degree of control contributes to the assumption that what the leader *does* in the role prescribed by the game affects in a positive way what participants derive from the experience.

V. APPLICATION

Extension of the concepts and teaching strategies from this activity may be aided by the following suggestions.

Participants might identify situations in which the parties in conflict would turn to forms of antagonistic cooperation. Such situations could range from global issues between "super powers" to issues between two persons. The object then would be to consider the appropriateness of the simulation developed in "Dilemma of the Tribes" for the situations that the participants have defined.

Situations that participants regard as too complex for the "Dilemma of the Tribes" simulation could become the focus for the development of new and appropriate simulation games by the participants.

School Districts
for Millersburg

I. BACKGROUND

This learning activity has been abstracted from "Political Geography," Unit 4 of the HSGP course *Geography in an Urban Age.* In this unit, which deals with the interplay between geography and politics, territorial expressions of political decisions are examined in five learning activities so that high school students will better understand the territorial system in which politics take place. In the "Millersburg" activity, students are faced with the specific problem of locating six new high schools and determining the boundaries of the districts to be served by each school.

II. PARTICIPANT OBJECTIVES

Experience with and analysis of this activity should enable participants:

1. To identify and analyze the factors that influence school location and districting decisions.
2. To discuss the concept of region in relation to a school district.
3. To identify and understand the attitudinal outcomes that result from simulation experiences like Millersburg.

4. To identify and discuss the group process and intellectual skill objectives that will result from participating in the Millersburg activity.
5. *To construct a simulation of the Millersburg type for use in their own classrooms.*[1]

III.   CONDUCTING THE ACTIVITY

The suggested procedures outlined in this section represent one approach to conveying the ideas about this simulation exercise.   There are certainly other imaginative and worthwhile approaches.   You can use this approach if it meets the needs of your participants or you can rearrange and substitute materials or procedures as your interests and insights dictate.   Allow about one hour for the simulation and another hour for the analysis of the activity.

In advance of teaching the Millersburg activity, you will want to read the participant materials for the exercise (pages 41–49).   You will also need to reproduce enough acetate maps from the master (Figure 3-2) for each discussion group to have a map.   In addition, you will need grease pencils for each group and an overhead projector.

Initiate the Millersburg activity by asking the participants to read about the hypothetical city of Millersburg (pages 41–42).   This reading discusses Millersburg's growth, examines the ethnic and racial background of the population, and describes some of the physical characteristics of the city.   A problem is presented: Millersburg is about to redistrict its high schools.

The reading informs participants that there are currently more than 12,000 students of high school age in Millersburg, and that the number is expected to increase. The existing high schools in the city are old, unsafe, and scheduled to be phased out of use. Six new high schools are to be built and participants must decide where they are to be situated and what the district boundaries should be for each school.   Four maps of Millersburg (pages 44–47) give participants information about industrial and commercial zones, family income areas, ethnic composition of the population, population density, transportation facilities, and locations of elementary schools.

When the participants have completed the reading, divide your class into groups of four.   Give each group an acetate map (made from the master on page 154) and a grease pencil.   The map should be used to register each group's redistricting decisions.   In addition, each group should record the rationale for reaching its decisions.

As this activity is used in the high school classroom, a teacher has the option of assigning to students the roles outlined on pages 43, 48–49.   These roles, if adhered to, provide useful insights into a wide spectrum of citizens' political views.   So that members of your class can experience and compare both alternatives of this option, we suggest that you permit half the groups to make the redistricting decisions without being assigned roles and half to make the decisions after being assigned the roles.   (There is one role for each

[1] Numbers one to four are content objectives; five is a pedagogical objective.

member of each group.)   After allocating the roles to half your groups, give the participants a minute or two to read the role descriptions (pages 43, 48–49).

Allow about twenty minutes for the groups to arrive at their decisions and then call the class back together.   Ask one member of each group to come forward, in turn, and, by using the overhead projector, share his group's redistricting decision and the rationale behind it.   During these presentations, the class should pretend that it is a group of concerned Millersburg citizens.   If the decisions seem unsound, they should feel free to raise questions or to take issue with the spokesmen.

When the group decisions have been shared and the citizens have had the opportunity to react to them, end the simulation.   Indicate to the class that when high school students engage in this activity, a series of questions is used at this point to focus attention on what has been learned.

IV. REFLECTIONS ON THE LEARNING AND TEACHING

A. Analysis of Learning Outcomes

To focus participants' attention on the content of this activity, you may wish to ask questions of the following type:

1.   *What kinds of things would high school students know, feel, or be able to do at the conclusion of this experience that they would have been unable to do at the beginning?*

It is likely that participants will emphasize knowledge outcomes of the simulation. There are indeed several important concepts and generalizations that should be grasped, the most obvious of which are the social and economic factors that influence decisions of this nature.   Considerations of accessibility to the schools, integration and social isolation of specific racial and ethnic groups, and least cost factors regarding student transportation are influential in the decision-making process.

At another level of abstraction, one of the core concepts of geography is exemplified.   To determine the districts to be served by each high school, participants are presented with maps showing specific types of regions, i.e., economic, racial, and ethnic. In order to develop new regions, they must select new criteria.   For example, the regions of the city presented on the Millersburg maps are differentiated from each other and are internally homogeneous according to some social or economic criterion.   The new regions (the school districts) are likely to be socially and economically heterogeneous in order to achieve social and economic balance.   These newly created school districts may be functionally homogeneous, however.   That is, they will probably contain almost equally balanced representations of a variety of social and economic groups and may *function* to provide equal educational opportunities.

The six regions created by the participants can be considered functional subregions in the larger region of Millersburg.   The city is in itself a region, whose boundaries delimit its corporate control over a specific area.

2.   *What attitudinal or skill learnings are likely to result from the Millersburg activity?*

It was the intent of the developer of the activity that high school students participating in "Millersburg" would develop more positive attitudes about the study of urban problems and would develop more empathy with civic decision-makers as a result of this experience.   It was also anticipated that students would become more proficient in the skills of making group decisions.

B.   Analysis of Teaching Strategies

This part of the analysis should focus the participants' attention on the structure of the simulation itself.   If your class has participated in "Activity 2/Metfab," it will be useful to compare the two simulations.   The simulation model exemplified by "Millersburg" is similar in many ways to the "Metfab" model, but it is also different in several important aspects.   If a participant is interested in using simulation as a major teaching strategy, knowledge of both models will enable him to achieve greater variety in the learning experiences he develops for his high school students.

Several general characteristics of simulations are identifiable in the Millersburg activity.   First, a problem or issue is posed that allows for different solutions.   Second, variables are presented that will influence the choice of solutions. Third, data or information in one form or another related to the variables are provided.   Fourth, roles of decision-makers who are faced with the problem may be delineated.

Questions of the following type may be useful in analyzing the simulation model exemplified in the Millersburg activity and in helping participants design a similar activity of their own.

1.   *Simulation activities focus on a problem or an issue requiring a decision.   Can you identify the problem involved in the Millersburg activity?*

Participants will recall that they were asked to locate six new high schools and determine the boundaries of each school's district.   If your class has participated in the Metfab activity, you may wish to ask at this point: *How are the problems posed in these two activities different in terms of inherent interest?*

Clearly there is a difference in the degree of interest or relevance inherent in the two problems.   Manufacturing location decisions might inspire little interest among high school students.   The success of the Metfab activity depends heavily on the conflict generated in the prepared roles of the decision-makers.   In contrast, "Millersburg" is centered on a currently debated social issue.   Conflict is guaranteed as soon as the problem is posed, for conflict is inherent in the nature of the issue.

2.   *What are the alternative solutions available to the decision-makers in the Millersburg activity?*

In many educational simulations, specified choices are provided for the decision-makers.   In the Metfab activity, for example, the alternatives for the location of the factory are limited to eight cities. In "Millersburg," there is no limit to the number of solutions. The problem is open ended except for the constraints imposed by the boundaries of the city and the need to establish six districts.

3. *In the Millersburg activity, what factors influence the school location and redistricting decisions? Which factors would you classify as objective and which would you classify as subjective?*

Objective factors likely to be mentioned are equalized school enrollment; projections of the influence of city growth on school location; ethnic, racial, and income balance; busing costs; and school accessibility.

Some factors may not have been considered by all the groups and some groups may have found additional factors. The construction of the Millersburg activity avoids specific designation of factors to be considered; the factors are descriptive rather than quantitative.

Subjective influences on the decisions will probably be more apparent to those participants who assumed one of the citizen roles. For example, the aristocratic orientation of William Kent, the intense cultural pride of LeRoy Washington, or the fiscal conservatism of Frank Sarma are all factors that influence decisions in reality.

Consideration of these subjective influences provides an easy transition into analyzing the use of the role profiles. To get at this dimension of the simulation model, you might ask:

4. *Are the role profiles that some of you were given necessary for this simulation? Would the learning outcomes for participants who assumed the roles be different from the outcomes for those who played no role? What would these differences be?*

It should be evident that the role profiles are not necessary in this simulation. The structure of the simulation is based on information that is generally already known and is not dependent on the facts outlined in the role descriptions. In a decision-making situation that requires knowledge which high school students are unlikely to possess, role descriptions would, of course, then serve the function of providing basic data.

It is likely that there will be different learning outcomes for those who were assigned roles and for those who were not assigned roles. Participants who assumed the roles of certain Millersburg citizens may have gained an appreciation of the range of political and social views one would encounter in a real community. Participants who made the decisions without the knowledge of the role descriptions may have found that the simulation helped them formulate or crystallize their own views regarding this social issue. Articulation of personal views is less likely to occur when a student must assume another identity.

In summary, the simulation model exemplified in the Millersburg activity includes the following components:

1. Selection of a currently debated, controversial social problem which necessitates a decision.

FIGURE 3-2.   *Transparency Master, Millersburg*

MILLERSBURG

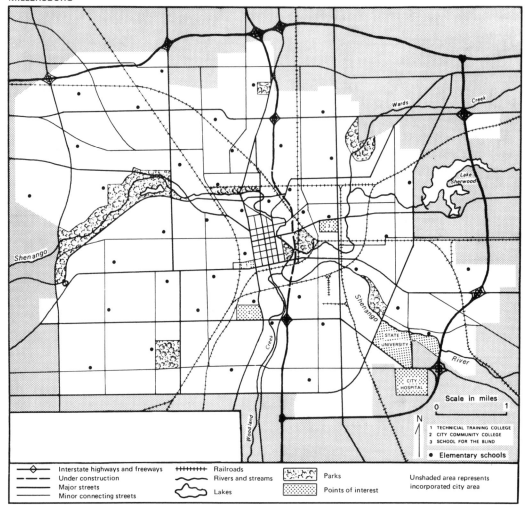

Scale in miles

N

1 TECHNICIAL TRAINING COLLEGE
2 CITY COMMUNITY COLLEGE
3 SCHOOL FOR THE BLIND
• Elementary schools

Interstate highways and freeways	Railroads	Parks
Under construction	Rivers and streams	Points of interest
Major streets	Lakes	Unshaded area represents
Minor connecting streets		incorporated city area

2. Recognition that although alternative solutions to the problem are discernible, they should be left unspecified.
3. Incorporation of nonquantifiable information on objective and subjective factors that will influence the decision.
4. Determination of the learning advantages and disadvantages of including role profiles in the decision-making.

V.   APPLICATION

The following suggestions for activities may be useful in extending your participants' understanding of simulations or of the concept of region:

1. Construct a simulation activity of the type represented by the Millersburg activity. The issue of locating a low-income housing development in a city might be the basis for such an activity.
2. Find the boundaries of your school district and try to determine the criteria used in delineating them. In what ways does this area represent a region?

ACTIVITY 7

Settling Accounts

I. BACKGROUND

This activity is an excerpt from the SRSS episode *Social Change: The Case of Rural China*. Prior to this exercise in the episode, high school students have examined social change as a general concept, have read a brief summary of the historical setting of the Chinese revolution, and have read an extract from Chapter 3 of the short story *The Hurricane* about land reform in the village of Tungmao. In addition, students have been cautioned to be aware of possible biases in the original source material (*The Hurricane*) and have been asked to speculate on the picture of land reform that might have been given by someone unsympathetic to the Communist approach. They then listen to a fifteen-minute dramatization of Chapter 5 of *The Hurricane* — a struggle meeting between peasants and landlords — called "Settling Accounts."

II. PARTICIPANT OBJECTIVES

Experience with and analysis of this activity should enable participants:

1. To become familiar with certain concepts central to the activity: social movement, leadership (formal and informal), social control, and social change.

2. To gain some sense of the coercive influence of the group — quite apart from the use of violence to gain objectives.
3. To grasp the meaning of social change in this Chinese village and for mainland China as a whole.
4. *To develop skill in using audio recordings as instructional media.*
5. *To reflect on radical means of effecting social change.*[1]

III. CONDUCTING THE ACTIVITY

In advance of your class session, participants should read the brief introduction to the activity and the story about land reform in Tungmao (pages 50–53).

In this activity, you will play the record "Settling Accounts" (included at the back of this book) to illustrate the use of audio media as a teaching strategy for initiating discussion on social control and social change. (A transcript of the recording is on pages 161–68). Before you play the record, however, you first should make certain that the context of the struggle meeting is understood. You might ask some of the following questions to see if participants have sufficient background for an understanding of how social change was effected in China.

1. *What are some general ideas about social change in China that are important?* Participants should be aware of some of the following ideas:
    a. Any major change encounters obstacles from custom, old values, and old power holders.
    b. Before planned social change could be introduced, the Chinese Communists had to break up the traditional social organization in the villages and build a new organization that would respond to their leadership. They had to *mobilize* the peasantry.
    c. The disorder and the seriousness of problems in the Chinese countryside led the leaders to choose measures more drastic than most Americans would consider necessary in our society.

2. *What were some of the specific problems that the Communists faced in their efforts to initiate land reform in the villages?*
    a. How to rid the landlords of their power. They have held power in Tungmao for a long time and obviously have the most land to lose in land reform.
    b. How to win the support of, or at least how not to antagonize, the rich and middle-class peasants who are more or less satisfied and may not want radical change.
    c. How to overcome the poor peasants' fear of the landlord and mobilize them into action. They are accustomed to landlord domination, and they are not sure who

---

[1] Numbers one to three are content objectives; four and five are pedagogical objectives.

the outsiders like Team Leader Hsiao are. They fear the landlords might regain power and take revenge.

3. *What problems had to be solved to bring about confrontations with the landlords?*
    a. In order to encourage and mobilize the peasantry, Team Leader Hsiao had to organize the poor peasants to work together. Only in unity would they find the strength necessary to challenge the power of the landlord.
    b. Poor peasants might be reluctant to take this role in land reform because of fear, personal ties to landlords and rich peasants, or acceptance of traditional relationships.
    c. Given the seriousness of the conditions in Tungmao Village — the plight of the poor peasants and the arbitrary power of the landlords — a peaceful solution seemed unlikely.

After the initial discussion, play the fifteen-minute recording. In this activity, participants should be listening for indicators of (1) changes in the social relationships among the residents of Tungmao and (2) changes within the village structure. Participants may find the situation amusing at first but they should come to realize the importance of the struggle meeting as the play goes along. The characters on the record appear in the following order (write them on the chalkboard):

NARRATOR
OLD SUN, the carter, a man about fifty years old
CHAIRMAN KUO (gwoh), chairman of the Peasants Association
GOODMAN TU (du), the landlord
BIG LI (lee), Goodman Tu's bodyguard
MRS. PAI (bah-ee), a peasant's wife, the only female main character
Other peasants of Tungmao Village

After the discussion of the changes in social relationships and in village structure that the participants have identified, you can ask participants to reflect on the concept of struggle meetings in the context of contemporary U.S. society. Try to elicit a discussion of the value issues underlying radical forms of planned social change.

IV. REFLECTIONS ON THE LEARNING AND TEACHING

A. *Analysis of Learning Outcomes*

The learnings to be gleaned from this activity hinge on an understanding of several terms — social movement and social change. The reorganization of Chinese life in the years immediately after the takeover of the government of mainland China by the Communists is an interesting example of a government-directed social movement. We might ask: *What does one think of when he thinks of social change?*

ACTIVITY 7/Settling Accounts

If one thinks of the suffrage movement, the civil rights movement, and the women's liberation movement, he sees in each of them a planned and organized attempt to alter prevailing patterns of human relationships. This means that certain roles must be redefined. The suffrage and women's liberation movements would redefine the woman's role and, therefore, relationships with men, employers, governors, and others. The civil rights movement would, of course, redefine the black's role and black-white relationships.

Much social change (which consists in the redefinition of roles and relationships that social movements seek to achieve) is unplanned. For example, the vast development of metropolitan areas in our country, the decline of the number of farmers in the labor force, the decline in birth rates, the secularization of religion — these are momentous changes but not consciously contrived ones. Much social change is like this, moving silently and inexorably like subsurface currents. Social movements, however, represent consciously contrived efforts to reshape man's social world.

We are accustomed to social movements that are effected by private, voluntary groups. In this activity, however, we see a social movement confronting a problem so vast that no centralized government, much less private organization, could promote reform by conventional means, for the territory of rural China is too vast and too heavily populated. Thus, using Communist party members as an inciting and organizing cadre, the government fostered a social movement among the peasants to take power from the landlords and redistribute the land. Here, then, is a sweeping reorganization of the most populous country in the world, carried through by methods that represent almost a new social invention.

What are the kinds and sources of authority suggested in the struggle meeting experience? What means of social control are touched on, directly or indirectly, in the activity? Authority has its source, Max Weber once said, in immemorial tradition, in rational-legal judgments, and in the special powers of the charismatic leader. In this material, we find the authority of leaders rooted in tradition (traditionally Goodman Tu and Han Number Six had great power to control others' destinies). We also have authority based on law (Hsiao and Little Wang are backed by the People's Government.) If we introduce Mao (unmentioned in this selection), we would have a charismatic leader, one who is accorded virtually supernatural authority.

These sources of authority point to differing modes of social control — by which we mean the ways the group exerts its influence over individuals. This influence is obvious when enraged peasants, aided by government representatives, punish the landlord Goodman Tu. But the obvious effects of threatened violence tend to mask the more subtle ways in which group influence is exerted. Participants need to consider the question: *What are the ordinary, largely unnoticed ways in which the authority of the group is felt?*

What we call custom is one mechanism of social control through which groups control individual behavior. Customary ways are especially reinforced by isolation, and isolation by illiteracy. (In Tungmao, eighty percent of the peasants could not read or write.) Thus, to the extent that they were cut off from outside change-inducing influences, customary patterns of life were sustained. The peasant could not break through the crust of custom. Of course, this is precisely why the government felt it necessary to send out their specially trained change agents.

Linked with custom is religion, with its mandates for appropriate behavior, and superimposed on both custom and religion is the agency of law which, in groups more complex than Tungmao, becomes the obvious agency of social control. The effect of such mechanisms of control are registered in the person when he feels guilt, humiliation, shame, or embarrassment. These are, as it were, socially induced signals telling the person to conform. They act as a first control over deviant behavior. The second line of social defense, summoned when deviance offends beyond the ordinary, is legal punishment.

What does social change mean in this particular village and for mainland China as a whole? In Tungmao, change is seen at several levels: interpersonal, economic, and political. Great gaps in political and economic power are reduced. As a result, there is an equity in personal relationships not hitherto obtaining. The right of command and the duty of deference are redefined. Authority hitherto residing in the landowner role is now located in the decisions of the peasants' meetings. It is to such collective decisions that one must now defer, not to the economically powerful.

For China as a whole there are, we may infer, changed power relationships between the landlords and peasants. The power of the landlords was destroyed, while that of most peasants, especially those who cooperated with the Communist Party, was increased through the organization of the Peasants Association. This reallocation of power was paralleled by a reallocation of property — and both point to a changing social structure in the People's Republic of China.

B. Analysis of Teaching Strategies

What techniques help make effective use of audio (records or tapes) curriculum materials? To derive maximum effect from audio media materials, the instructor should ensure first that participants are aware of the instructional context of the recording and second, that the participants have an analytic task in mind as they listen. In short, the listener should know what the record is supposed to contribute to the instructional sequence. In this activity, the instructor questioned participants to see if they knew the purpose of the struggle meeting in the larger land reform plan of the Chinese government. (Because of the brevity of the participant materials, participants in this demonstration may have required some additional background information as suggested in the section on "Conducting the Activity.")

The next step is to establish a common objective for analyzing the content of the record. Then after presenting the audio material, one should follow up on how well the participants "heard" what they were supposed to hear. In this activity, participants were to listen for indicators that revealed (1) how social relationships among the village people had changed, and (2) how the social structure in the village had been changed.

How can an instructor lead into a consideration of the value issues related to radical forms of planned social change? One method of getting students to examine value issues is to have them apply contrasting value positions to a common situation. In asking the participants to think about the concept of struggle meetings in the context of contemporary U.S. society, the instructor can demonstrate the technique of contrasting value positions. The discussion might examine such points as the following.

Why is it so hard to imagine anything like a struggle meeting in the United States? Where would the resistances to the possibility come from? Would these resistances be personal or institutional? What kinds of court cases would immediately be initiated if the United States Department of Agriculture tried to carry through a program of crop limitation or soil conservation on a similar basis?

Participants will probably realize that the most fundamental constitutional rights of U.S. citizens would be violated. This provides a good opportunity to compare how the ideological value systems of the Communist regime and of the United States government affect relationships between citizens and government officials.

V. APPLICATION

The suggestions that follow may be useful in extending the concepts and teaching strategies developed in this activity to other teaching situations.

An activity that analyzes literary material would provide an excellent opportunity to use some of the conceptual and pedagogical elements of this activity. Participants might select a novel or another form of literary work and analyze it in terms of how social change is portrayed. They might also consider how such works might be treated in the high school social studies class. The following books might be analyzed:

The Grapes of Wrath by John Steinbeck
The Autobiography of Malcolm X by Malcolm X and Alex Haley
The Greening of America by Charles A. Reich

Literary works might also be analyzed in terms of the social values that the authors bring forth or examine. The suggestions given in Activity 11, "The Social Context of Leadership" (pages 85–94), for applying the techniques of content analysis to other forms of social studies investigations are relevant also to this inquiry.

TRANSCRIPT OF RECORD, "Settling Accounts"

A STRUGGLE MEETING

CHARACTERS:

Narrator

From the Instructor's Guide for *Social Change: The Case of Rural China*, SRSS Episodes in Social Inquiry Series (Boston: Allyn and Bacon, 1971). Copyright © 1971 American Sociological Association. Reprinted by permission. The script is based on Chou Li-po's novel, *The Hurricane* (Peking: Foreign Language Press, 1955).

Old Sun
Chairman Kuo (pronounced gwoh)
Mrs. Pai (pronounced bah-ee)
Goodman Tu (pronounced du)
Big Li (pronounced lee)
Peasants

NARRATOR. Tenants and laborers of Tungmao Village, members of the Peasants Association, were coming out of their huts once again to meet at the temple and discuss the next step in land reform. The meeting was made particularly urgent by the recent news that Han Number Six, the most evil of the landlords, had just escaped from the village. They were anxious that the actual reform should begin, taking land and possessions away from the landowners and distributing them among the peasants in accordance with the plan of the government in Peking. But the process had been slow and deliberate. For some it had seemed far too slow.

(*Voices of peasants gathering together. As they settle, one voice is dominant.*)

OLD SUN. Chairman Kuo, may I speak?

CHAIRMAN KUO. I hear Old Sun, the carter.

OLD SUN. Chairman Kuo, we have been talking and talking for weeks now. But when are we going to take action?

CHAIRMAN KUO. Old Sun, it is the wish of our government. . . .

OLD SUN. To be thorough and just, yes, and that's good. But let me say something. Half the peasants stay away from our meetings. Do you know why? They say we talk but do nothing. And all the while the landlords keep stewing in their fat. We must act!

PEASANTS. He's right. Let's get the landlords. No more playing around. Let's begin tonight.

OLD SUN. You will see, Comrade Kuo. I suggest we go to the home of Goodman Tu this very evening and have it out with him.

PEASANTS. Yes, yes. To Goodman Tu's. Before he runs like Han Number Six. Let's beat Goodman Tu.

CHAIRMAN KUO. Hold on. We'll go to Goodman Tu and struggle against him. But the Party forbids the beating of landlords. (*pause*) All right, let us leave immediately.

NARRATOR. The peasants were happy. Singing and shouting they began to walk together across the village to the house of Goodman Tu. Along the way other peasants joined them, anxious to see the actual reform begin. Goodman Tu, meanwhile, pacing up and down in his big house had called in his bodyguard, Big Li, for protection and comfort.

GOODMAN TU. Are the jewels hidden? Good. And the cloth? You've covered the grain in the cellar? We can't take a chance on anything.

BIG LI. Everything of value is out of sight, Master Tu.

GOODMAN TU. How does my coat look? I've put patches all over it to make me look like a poor man. Pretty clever, eh? You've hidden all the gold behind the wall? How about the kettles?

BIG LI. Buried in the orchard, Master.

GOODMAN TU. So Han has run away has he? That's all we need to get the peasants yapping at our ankles. I've read the law of these Communists. They'll have Han strung up by his toes for this. The fool. Well, I've got nothing to fear. They won't find a thing here of value. All of it is hidden away. I'm not afraid.

BIG LI. No, Master Tu.

GOODMAN TU. Don't interrupt. Can't you see I'm trembling with fear? Listen to my wife and daughter in there. Crying since dawn. And for what? For fear these dogs will come strip us of everything, take our goods and land. And you. I know you. You'll take to your heels, once those peasants come clawing at our walls.

BIG LI. They wouldn't dare enter this place.

GOODMAN TU. Oh they wouldn't, huh? They'll come crashing along like stampeding sheep. . . . What's that? I heard shouts in the distance.

BIG LI. It's nothing, Master Tu.

GOODMAN TU. There, I heard it again.

BIG LI. The peasants are meeting again; that's what you heard.

GOODMAN TU. To decide what to do about Han, no doubt. Well, I've got nothing to worry about. This peasants' reform is bound to pass over and things will keep on like before. Then I can stop sweating and get some sleep. There! I heard it again. What's that noise?

BIG LI. There are many lights in the distance, Master. The peasants are walking this way by the looks of it.

GOODMAN TU. How many?

BIG LI. I would say a hundred at least. Master, they're marching straight for your house! Here they come!

GOODMAN TU. Quick, get the whip! Lock the door! You've whipped them before, so now do your stuff.

BIG LI. Too many for my whip. I'm going.

GOODMAN TU. Then get the dogs, bring me my dogs. Hey there, where are you running off to? Come back here, you coward. I knew you would take to your heels. . . . Oh merciful Buddha, show them how poor and what a good man I am.

PEASANTS. Goodman Tu! Open up your door to the peasants of Tungmao! You're at our mercy now. Your bodyguard has run away. Open up.

GOODMAN TU. (*hesitantly calling out*) What do you want with me?

CHAIRMAN KUO. We have come to settle our grievances with you.

PEASANTS. Open up! Drag him into the yard! Break down the door!

CHAIRMAN KUO. Open your door, Goodman Tu.

NARRATOR. The peasants waited for the door to open. When they heard the latch lift, they came forward a little, eager to meet their longstanding enemy face to face. But instead of Goodman Tu appearing, three growling watchdogs were let into the yard, gnashing and clawing at the peasants' throats.

(*Sounds of dogs, the peasants yelling, "Watch out, the dogs," "Help, Help!" "He's let his dogs loose"*)

PEASANTS. Kill them! Kill the dogs, then we'll kill Goodman Tu! Hang the dogs on his gate.

NARRATOR. The peasants, with clubs and forks which they had in hand, killed the dogs and hanged their bodies on Goodman Tu's gate.   Then they crowded close, beating on the door, demanding Tu's life in return for this insult.   The door was crushed and the peasants rushed into the house.   Chairman Kuo managed to step in front of them, holding up his hands to quiet them.

CHAIRMAN KUO.   Comrades, we must not beat the landlords!   Quiet, please, everybody. Goodman Tu is at our mercy. (*The peasants quiet down, grumbling*)   Goodman Tu, come out of hiding.   You have no choice.   You know who we are.   You're not a stupid man.   You know the rules of the land reform.   We are here to settle accounts with you. . . .   Soon as all is quiet, any man or woman who has suffered by your hand may step forward and speak against Goodman Tu. (*There is a pause*)

GOODMAN TU.   Good friends, why do you bother me?   I am only a good man who. . . .

CHAIRMAN KUO.   Silence!   Your turn will come. . . .   Will no one step forward? Comrades, do not be afraid. . . .

OLD SUN.   Goodman Tu, you know me, Old Sun, the carter.   Once I tried farming on my own.   But I got very sick, and you came, pretending to want to help me.   Then, when I got well again, I discovered that you had forged a deed to everything I owned, and I was left with nothing.   And if that wasn't enough, you took every picul of grain I had harvested, just so you could feed your fat horses.

GOODMAN TU.   That's a lie.   I've been kind to the peasants.

MRS. PAI.   Kind!   Listen to the stupid fox!   Whose dogs were those let loose just now in the yard?   Goodman Tu, I know you're not used to hearing women speak up boldly to you.   But I accuse you to your face.   One day my husband asked you for a loan.   You said you couldn't give it to him.   How about a fifty percent interest?   You said no.   Eighty percent?   Still no. (*To the crowd*) Not until he got 100 percent interest did this scoundrel agree to loan the money.   And we had to take it, for it was winter, and so cold that if we hadn't bought clothes with the money, we would have died of the cold!

GOODMAN TU.   These are lies.

PEASANT ONE.   Shut up you pig!   You took a coat right off my back once, all because I didn't bow my head when I passed you.   You're going to get beaten, and I'm the one to do it!

CHAIRMAN KUO.   Hold on.   Remember, the law forbids the beating of landlords.

PEASANT TWO.   What about the well?   Remember?   We peasants sweated like horses digging that well outside your gate.   But when we were done, you beat us back, saying it was your well.   Any man who wanted to use it had to work for you for nothing, three days a month. (*Spits*)

GOODMAN TU.   These are lies, lies!

PEASANT THREE.   How many acres of land has he stolen from us, can anyone tell me?   He is an evil man.

PEASANT ONE.   Don't worry, we'll get everything he owns.

PEASANTS.   Yah, yah.   Let's get even.   Han may have gotten away, but not Goodman Tu.

MRS. PAI.   Why are you sweating so much, Goodman Tu?   Are you afraid?   Well, you should be, for you have the burden of a black heart to carry.

(*Appropriate reactions of the crowd, as the Narrator's voice comes in, close*)

NARRATOR.   Every peasant who had a grievance spoke up.   Goodman Tu stared at the floor, thinking that his one chance would be to convince the peasants that he wasn't as evil or rich as they thought. Finally it was his turn to speak, and he turned to face the peasants, blinking as if tears were in his eyes.

GOODMAN TU. Friends, you are too hard on me. You say you want my land, my money, my goods. What you see, you are welcome to. You accuse me of being evil. Have I ever broken down your doors like this and come crashing into your homes? Do you hear that crying? (*Appropriate sounds*) My wife and daughter are flooding out their tears because of you. You accuse me of many things. But you must realize that I worked harder than any of you. Yet I am not rich. Look around. If I had gold and expensive jewelry, I would gladly give them to you. But now, I beg of you, let me alone, for you have caused me great trouble. Please, my good friends, take what you can find, but let me alone. You have bothered me enough. And besides, you're messing up my house.

NARRATOR. Some peasants were taken aback by this. They edged toward the door believing he was sincere. But as Goodman Tu turned from the crowd, Old Sun spotted something and he leapt forward angrily, yanking at the gown which Tu was wearing.

OLD SUN. Look here! Look at this, comrades! Poor, is he? He's got patches on the outside, but inside it is lined with silk. He's a liar! Look, over here, he's put ashes over his table to fool us. How much else have you hidden, eh, Goodman Tu?

GOODMAN TU. There is nothing else, leave me alone.

OLD SUN. Are we going to let him get away? Look around you and see where he's hidden things.

(*Peasants respond to Old Sun's discovery*)

GOODMAN TU. Get out of my house.

OLD SUN. Back away, you hunk of fat. Look there, a brick is loose in the wall. Tear it out, one of you. Tear open the wall.

(*Appropriate sounds*)

Well, look at the gold. Oh, he's a poor man, all right! Where have you hidden the rest, Goodman Tu?

GOODMAN TU. There is nothing else, leave me alone, I tell you.

OLD SUN. Friends, don't listen to him. Get your picks and shovels. We'll shove the lies right back into his damned face!

(*Great uproar among the peasants*)

NARRATOR. The peasants, angered once again, quickly dug up the cellar and the orchard, finding clothes here, silver lanterns there, and grain hidden elsewhere. Mats were thrown back. Every possible hiding place was torn up and the goods were brought in and dumped at the feet of Goodman Tu, who by this time was frightened to death. Within an hour the mansion was dug apart, top to bottom, and the peasants gathered once again, hatred glaring in their eyes.

CHAIRMAN KUO. You know the penalty for resisting us, Goodman Tu?

GOODMAN TU. I have read your laws.

PEASANTS. Whip him! Beat him like a dog! Death is too good for him!

CHAIRMAN KUO. Do you confess your evil?

GOODMAN TU. Have pity on me!

MRS. PAI. Listen to him, begging us for pity!

OLD SUN. Someone hand me that stick.

CHAIRMAN KUO. It is against the law to. . . .

OLD SUN. Oh, I won't beat him. I just want to play with him a little. You remember, Goodman Tu, how you made me kneel in your stable for two whole days, because a colt died and you thought it was my fault? Well, now it's your turn. Get down on your knees.

GOODMAN TU. I can't. I'm too weak.

OLD SUN. Too fat, you mean. Get down!

GOODMAN TU. Friends, I will confess everything. Only let me stand.

OLD SUN. On your knees! There, that's better. Now, how much land do you own?

GOODMAN TU. One hundred acres.

(*Sounds of a stick cracking on the floor. Goodman Tu cries out in fear*)

OLD SUN. How much?

GOODMAN TU. One hundred and twenty acres.

OLD SUN. Is that all? What else have you hidden?

GOODMAN TU. Nothing else.

(*Sound of the stick again*)

Well, a few other things, perhaps.

OLD SUN. Where are they? Where is the rest?

GOODMAN TU. Please, I will tell everything, only let me up.

OLD SUN. Comrades, what shall we do with him?

PEASANTS. Keep him on his knees. Beat him, he's on his knees. Death is too good for him. Kill him, kill the landlord!

CHAIRMAN KUO. Hold on, everyone. Quiet please. Peasant comrades, we must be just, even to the landlords. We will get everything he owns, be assured of that. . . . Goodman Tu, do you confess your guilt?

GOODMAN TU. In the name of Buddha, don't strike!

CHAIRMAN KUO. Answer me! Do you confess your guilt?

GOODMAN TU. I confess.

CHAIRMAN KUO. It will be better for you if you do not resist. Many landlords have already been put to death. You will not be hurt if you obey us. One week from tonight you must come to the temple, where everything you own will be distributed among the peasants. You will learn then what your share will be. You will be an equal like every other man in the village. An equal: no better, and no worse. Do you agree?

GOODMAN TU. Please, my legs!

CHAIRMAN KUO. Do you agree?

GOODMAN TU. I must agree.

CHAIRMAN KUO. Goodman Tu, for the life you have lived, let us see you bow down before the peasants of Tungmao, until your forehead touches the floor. Bow deeply. Show that you honor the Revolution.

PEASANTS. Bow! Bow! Bow down before the peasants of Tungmao! . . .

(*Fade out as Narrator's voice takes over*)

NARRATOR. As Goodman Tu bowed, they laughed and shouted at the humiliated landlord. Then they left the house of Goodman Tu, happy and proud, for the first of the landlords of their village had been defeated. The rest would follow. In fact, three days later Han was found, tried, and put to death for having killed more than eight peasants, and for resisting the Revolution. When word came of Han's execution, Goodman Tu knew that there was nothing for him to do but comply with the wishes of the peasants. He came to the temple the following week, where a complete distribution of all the lands and goods of his and Han's was made. Though it burned him like fire to do it, he quietly accepted his share, like any other peasant. Then, a month later, as the peasants held another meeting of the Peasants Association, Chairman Kuo made an announcement.

CHAIRMAN KUO. Comrades, tonight I have received an application from Goodman Tu who wishes to become a member of the Peasants Association. He is outside the door, waiting for us. What shall we do about it?

MRS. PAI. Don't let him in! We may have gotten his land, but we can't change his heart. He'll always want to be rich again. You can never trust a landlord.

OLD SUN. Chairman Kuo, I disagree. I think we should accept him.

MRS. PAI. No man can wear jewelry all his life and then give it up, just like that. Besides, he'd ruin our meetings. Keep him out.

OLD SUN. How can he ruin them? He has no power now. His bodyguard ran off. His cellar has been emptied. His animals are scattered around the village. His land is gone. I have suffered as much as anyone under him, but I say, give him a chance. Besides, the Party says so.

PEASANTS (*murmuring, mixed reactions*). A landlord, sitting here with us? Not while I have anything to say about it. No, wait a minute, maybe he's right.

OLD SUN. We have nothing to be afraid of. The peasants are now in control. The landlords will never threaten us again. Look at Tu. He shares his house with former tenants. He wears a patched coat now, and with no silk on the inside. Even his wife has begun to mix with the wives of poor peasants. He is a man now. I think he should be admitted.

MRS. PAI. Old Sun, I will agree with you, only on the condition we keep an eye on Goodman Tu. It's true, he works in the fields with the rest of us, but he still hates to get his fingers dirty.

CHAIRMAN KUO. Then are we agreed?

(*Appropriate reaction*)

Let Goodman Tu enter.

(*Noise as Goodman Tu enters*)

Goodman Tu, you have applied for admission into our association. In what spirit do you come to us?

GOODMAN TU. Chairman Kuo, I must be honest. I have no other choice. If I am to live among you in Tungmao, I will do the best I can. There is no stopping the Revolution, and therefore I submit to it.

CHAIRMAN KUO. Then we accept your application. With these conditions however: First, we have the right to investigate your property any time we wish. Secondly, every three months you must bring to us a written report of the progress in your attitude towards the peasants, in giving up the thoughts and ways of a former landlord. If these reports are not satisfactory, we have the right to press you to mend your ways. Do you agree? And do you understand?

GOODMAN TU. I agree, Chairman Kuo.

CHAIRMAN KUO.   Then be seated.   Comrade peasants, make room for our newest member, Goodman Tu, who shall sit among us from now on.   Now, to continue our business.   Tonight we have finished the distribution of Han's estate.   The tenants south of the village are to receive their allocations, and we will begin by calling out the names. . . .

(His voice diminishes, as the Narrator's takes over)

NARRATOR.   And thus the struggle against one landlord is completed, in one village of many thousand villages, as the peasants' Revolution of China proceeded towards its goal: land reform.

ACTIVITY **8**

Culture Change: A Trend toward Uniformity

I. BACKGROUND

"Culture Change: A Trend toward Uniformity" is the final activity in "Cultural Geography," Unit 3 of the HSGP course *Geography in an Urban Age*. It illustrates the accelerating rate at which ideas are becoming diffused and exchanged around the world.

In the "Cultural Geography" unit as taught in the high school, activities prior to this final one focus on the concepts of cultural diffusion, cultural relativity, and geographic region. In this exercise, high school students analyze a series of photographs in an attempt to reach conclusions about the cultural characteristics of cities.

II. PARTICIPANT OBJECTIVES

Experience with and analysis of this activity should enable participants:

1. To discuss ways in which different cultures are becoming similar.
2. To explain the increasing similarity of commercial aspects of cultures around the world, considering decreasing time-distance from place to place as one explanation.

169

3. To discuss aspects of a culture that are most susceptible and least susceptible to rapid change.
4. *To become familiar with inquiry procedures illustrated in this activity.*
5. *To devise an activity using the inquiry process illustrated in the cultural change activity.*
6. *To discuss the advantages and disadvantages of using this inquiry procedure.*[1]

III. CONDUCTING THE ACTIVITY

There are two major parts in this exercise, each of which should take about twenty minutes. The first part consists of viewing and discussing seven photographs which depict traditional architecture in various cities throughout the world. Participants are to locate the scenes regionally from cultural clues presented in the photographs. The second part includes a set of photographs of downtown sections of modern cities, which participants are also to locate regionally.

Following these activities, you will analyze the learning outcomes and teaching strategies of the exercise.

To begin the exercise, direct the participants to page 55 and ask them to study the photographs of the various cities shown in Figures 2-14 through 2-20. Tell the participants to look for clues that will help them identify the country and the continent in which each photograph was taken and to record their conclusions alongside the figure numbers.

When participants have completed their guesses, discuss the photographs in terms of the major cultural clues that helped them identify the location of each city. A brief discussion of each photograph should center on participants' reasons for associating specific cultural clues with particular parts of the world. You may want to use a wall map of the world to pinpoint the locations of the cities.

As you tell your group the name of each city, the following information may help you answer questions:

Figure 2-14: Thailand (Asia). City of Bangkok. All the buildings in this scene are religious buildings (Buddhist temples, pagodas) and are distinctly Oriental. Most of the people in the picture are native Thais but are wearing Western-style clothes.

Figure 2-15: Belgium (Europe). City of Bruges. Of special interest is the stairstep profile of the gables — a fairly common sight in the past in parts of northwestern Europe.

Figure 2-16: Chad (Africa). City of Korbol (approximately 10° N lat., 15° E long., about two hundred twenty-five miles southeast of Fort-Lamy, Chad). Styles of buildings vary widely in Africa, although these building materials (woven rushes, thatch, and mud) are widespread. Thus, the buildings in this picture are "new," yet the style is very old. Cities in Chad would have looked very similar to this two hundred years ago.

[1] Numbers one to three are content objectives; four through six are pedagogical objectives.

Figure 2-17: England (Europe). Street scene in town of York. The buildings are either old or new but constructed in old styles. Note the narrowness of the street and the style of architecture. Obviously, the streets were built prior to the automobile. English identification can be made from the sign to the left "United Friendly Insurance Co. Ltd." or by the "bobby" (policeman) farther up the street.

Figure 2-18: Yemen (Asia). City of San'ā. This capital city is surrounded by a mud brick wall containing seven wooden gates that are still closed nightly. (The walled city was once a very common feature of much of the world.) One dominant feature of any Muslim city is the mosque. Many of the flat-roofed buildings are two or three stories high, a height rather unusual for buildings constructed out of mud bricks. This is practical here because there is very little rain. There is no evidence of modern influences. Presumably this city would have looked much the same three hundred years ago.

Figure 2-19: United States (North America). A residential street in St. Louis. The scene is in the older part of the city, not far from the central business district. The buildings shown on the far side of the street probably date from the late nineteenth century. In their height and sidewalk frontage, these buildings are more or less representative of much housing built in larger American cities a half century or more ago.

Figure 2-20: Soviet Union (Asia). A scene from the city of Yakutsk in Siberia. The picture illustrates both the old and the new. In the foreground are the older, traditional one-story wooden houses with their distinctive window shutters and framing. This part of the city is nearly all wood. The new buildings in the back are of stone or brick, painted various pastel shades, and appear to be four or five stories high.

Most participants will do quite well on this part of the activity. Ask them to state and discuss a few generalizations that helped them locate the photographs accurately. They may mention some of the following things:

1. Residential areas in older parts of cities generally tend to look different in distant countries, illustrating cultural differences.
2. Houses of worship (churches, mosques, temples, shrines) still tend to look different in different culture regions. Religious buildings are often the best clues for matching a city with its culture region.
3. It is possible to locate cities by using the concept of culture region.
4. It is possible to determine the location of cities by using cultural clues.

The second part of the exercise involves looking at six photographs showing scenes of downtown sections of cities. Direct participants to study Figures 2-21 through 2-26 (pages 62–67). Tell the participants that they are again to look for clues that will help them identify the country and the continent for each city.

Before you reveal the locations of the pictures, tally the guesses per photograph for each continent. This tally will be used to answer one of the questions raised in the discussion of the teaching strategy.

Participants should discuss the cultural clues that helped them locate the cities.

Some of the scenes show nothing that is particularly distinctive, so do not belabor the search for clues. You will want to give the name of each city shown in the photographs.

Information that may help in answering participants' questions about the six photographs follows:

Figure 2-21: Tokyo, Japan (Asia). All you can say about this picture is that you are in a modern, industrial city. You could be almost anywhere — a large American or European or Australian city. Certainly, the freeways and office buildings are not distinctive. Some of the residential areas (right-hand side of photograph) would give clues if we had a closer view.

Figure 2-22: São Paulo, Brazil (South America). Again, there is nothing distinctly Brazilian in this view. All we know is that we are in the middle of a big, modern city that appears to be growing rapidly. The church steeple suggests that it is a Christian country. Only a few houses, at lower right, have "typically Mediterranean," gently sloping red-tile roofs. A few of the signs are in Portuguese.

Figure 2-23: Ulan Bator, Mongolian Republic (Asia). Twenty years ago the capital of Mongolian Republic, Ulan Bator, was described as "a huddle of one-story shacks." Now, from this distance, it looks like any modern city located in a semiarid environment. The round buildings in the foreground are not gasoline tanks but "yurts" or "gers," the collapsible "tent" homes of nomads.

Figure 2-24: Boston, Massachusetts, United States (North America). Those who know the local geography of Boston might recognize the city (that is, the Charles River at the right, the bay in the foreground) but otherwise this is just another modern city. An occasional church suggests a country with a large Christian population.

Figure 2-25: Kinshasa (formerly Leopoldville), Zaïre, formerly the Democratic Republic of the Congo (Africa). There is nothing particularly African about this scene, unless you know that the river is the Congo River and that the green in the distance is tropical rain forest. Although nearly all the inhabitants of the city today are Congolese, Kinshasa (like many African cities) was built by Europeans — in this case, the Belgians. The modern, multistoried buildings can be found in almost any city of the world.

Figure 2-26: Suburb of London, England (Europe). Except for the church, which identifies the area as Christian, the scene could be anyplace in the world where modern buildings are found.

Ask participants receiving the highest scores how they arrived at their correct answers. They may admit to luck. The exercise is a difficult one because the cities look so similar.

You might extend the class discussion to include the temporal dimension by asking participants how pictures of the downtown areas of American cities today would compare with pictures of the same areas taken a hundred years ago. Would there be more cultural clues in the earlier pictures?

Again, ask the participants to state and discuss a few generalizations about what they learned from this second set of photographs. You might expect such ideas as the following:

1. It is difficult to distinguish the modern downtown sections of large cities around the world.
2. Modern apartment complexes tend to look much the same all over the world today.
3. Cities all over the world are becoming more similar at an increasing rate.

IV. REFLECTIONS ON THE LEARNING AND TEACHING

This activity about culture changes not only helps participants develop concepts related to similarities and differences in cities around the world, but it also illustrates a teaching technique useful for increasing student awareness that misconceptions can lead to inaccurate generalizations.

A. *Analysis of Learning Outcomes*

1. *After experiencing this activity, do participants have an understanding of the concept of cultural diffusion?*

    Simply stated, cultural diffusion is a process of movement of ideas from a point of origin to other areas on the earth's surface. This diffusion of ideas forms a pattern that can be analyzed in terms of carriers and barriers.

    The manner in which an idea is carried depends on whether it moves from those who know to those who don't know (expansion diffusion), or whether the carrier moves and establishes the idea in a new location (relocation diffusion). An example of expansion diffusion would be the spread of the Christian religion in its early days or the spread of a rumor as people pass it from one to another. Figure 3-3 illustrates the expansion diffusion idea. An example of relocation diffusion (diagrammed in Figure 3-4) would be the movement of missionaries to new areas (i.e., Hawaii) or the expansion of British culture during the nineteenth century.

    Barriers will influence both the rate at which things move and the type of pattern that results. Barriers may be physical (mountains, water, desert) or cultural (linguistic, religious, political) and may be classified as impenetrable or permeable. Very strong cultural traits or impassable swamps are examples of impenetrable barriers that stop the diffusion of ideas. Permeable barriers can slow down the movement of ideas, thus creating differential rates of diffusion.[2]

2. *Can participants make plausible and intelligent associations between cultural diffusion and characteristics of cities around the world?*

[2] For further information on this topic, see Peter R. Gould, *Spatial Diffusion*, Resource Paper No. 4, Commission on College Geography (Washington, D.C.: Association of American Geographers, 1969).

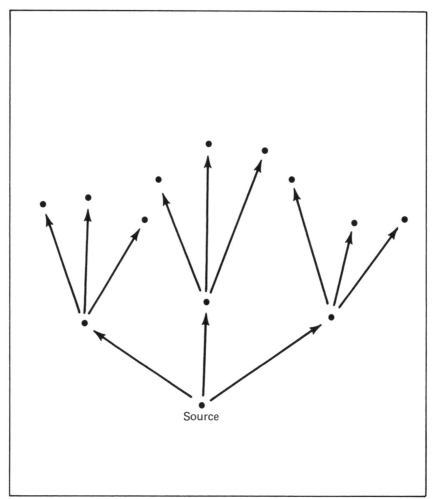

Many of the factors that influence the increasing similarity of cities are economic and technological. Further, as areas become more industrialized, manufacturing and associated support activities concentrate in urban areas. Consequently, as functions of cities become more similar, forms of cities also tend to become more alike. For example, increasing population and demand for space in cities has resulted in similar types of buildings and similar architectural styles. The increasing use of automobiles has led to similar developments in arterial access to city core areas in some cities around the world, i.e., freeway access to city centers, depressed roadbeds, and complex interchanges.

Participants may give other examples of how cities are becoming more uniform. They might suggest that more affluent dwellers concentrate in highrise apartments in the urban core of a city or in suburban areas. Also, highrise, low-income, and middle-income apartment complexes may be evident. Older residential areas near the center of the city

FIGURE 3-4. *Relocation Diffusion*

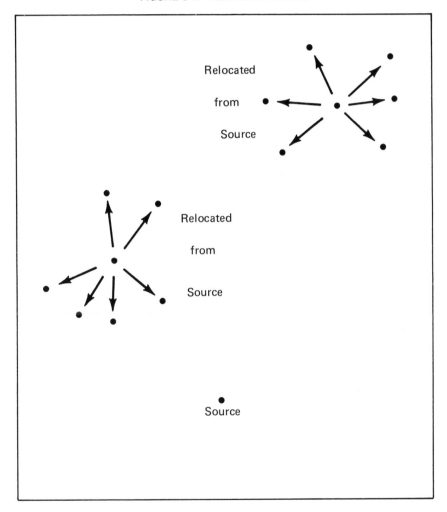

are occupied by low-income people and are often removed to provide room for highrise apartments or office buildings. Not only are the distributions of land uses becoming similar in cities, but actual structures are often duplicated in various cities. Examples of like structures would be hotels, motels, drive-in restaurants, and office buildings.

3. *Do participants understand which urban characteristics illustrate resistance to change and which indicate acceptance of new ideas?*
     From their study of this activity, participants should realize that the central business district of the city will change more rapidly than the residential areas. Such changes would be a function of movement of ideas and accessibility. That is, business services are concentrated in the urban core and reflect technological advances, management demands, and increasing competition for prime commercial space. Different countries engaged in similar economic functions using similar technological processes will develop similar industrial and business sections. However, if the cultures are different, entertainment, religious, and residential areas will be distinctive.

B. Analysis of Teaching Strategies

After the participants have analyzed learning outcomes, you can direct their attention to the teaching procedures used in the exercise. The following questions can help guide the discussion.

1. *What teaching strategies underlie the use of pictures in the activity?*
     Participants should be aware that photographs serve as the basic data for the exercise rather than as illustrations of the text. The pictures provide data that would be difficult, if not impossible, to find in written material. Photographs are an efficient way of presenting information and are particularly advantageous for use with high school students who have low-level reading skills.
     Participants may state that they had to classify pictures in terms of certain categories, in this case, allocating cities to different continents and countries. This strategy requires using picture interpretation skills to yield data on which to base classifying judgments.

2. *What process did you use to decide about each photograph? Did this process lead you to derive general conclusions about each set of pictures?*
     To assign a photograph to a particular continent, it is necessary to identify specific characteristics that match those variables used as a basis for classification. For example, in Figures 2-14 to 2-20, various cultural characteristics, such as architecture and dress, were identified. These were then matched with personal conceptions of how people construct buildings and how they dress in various continents. An inference was drawn and the photograph was assigned a location. Further, as inferences were made about each photograph, a body of experience was accumulated that supported generalizations about the whole set of photographs.
     For example, participants may have made inferences about the first group of

photographs by using the assumption that "cities are easily identified by cultural clues." Obviously, this idea does not hold in the analysis of the second set of photographs.

In the second set of photographs, the variety of detail and obvious differences that characterized the first set were lacking. Consequently, participants had less evidence on which to base inferences. They had to rely more on their past ideas about cities, with the result that their inferences may not have been as accurate.

If participants will reflect on the reasoning that guided them in their attempts to infer the location of the photographs, they will probably realize that they associated modern cities with Western cultures. When a person can discern nothing more about a photograph than that it shows a modern city, he probably will associate the photograph with those areas of the world he thinks have modern cities, in this case, countries in the Western world. Does the tally of choices for the second set of photographs support this hypothesis?

3. *What revised generalization would lead to a more accurate identification of the second set of photos?*

An example of a revised generalization might be "Large modern cities are found in all parts of the world," or "Cities around the world are becoming more alike, especially in the downtown sections," or "The location of many large modern cities cannot be readily determined by cultural clues."

Suggest that participants summarize the process they have just experienced. As the discussion proceeds, you can construct on the chalkboard a diagram of an inquiry technique similar to that found in Figure 3-5.

In Figure 3-5, the first box ("Identify Stereotype or Generalization to Be Examined") is the first generalization that may have guided participants' thinking. For example, they may have believed that cities could be identified by cultural clues, thus inferring that large modern cities are found mainly in Western Europe and Anglo-America. This mind-set, or expectation, would influence participants' thinking in attempting to locate the cities.

Now refer to the second box in Figure 3-5 ("Structure Problem That Reinforces Set"). In the culture change activity, participants probably identified the first set of photographs with considerable accuracy. Perhaps this success helped reinforce the mind-set that cities could be identified by cultural clues.

The third box in Figure 3-5 is entitled "Introduce Data That Challenge Set." Participants were asked to locate the second set of photographs. Because of previous success, the participants probably expected to encounter little difficulty locating the second set of photographs. However, it is likely that they completed the second section with less accuracy. Participants then attempted to reason why locating the photographs became more difficult.

At this point, the participants probably realized that whatever led them to successful hypotheses for locating the cities in Figures 2-14 to 2-20 did not apply to the photographs in Figures 2-21 to 2-26. They were forced to search for new ideas to guide their thinking.

The fourth box in Figure 3-5 ("Restructure the Generalization") refers to the new generalization participants may have derived in their discussion of the second set of pictures. The participants were asked to state a new generalization, such as "Cities around the world are becoming more alike, especially in downtown sections."

FIGURE 3-5. *Inquiry Technique (Modeled After* Culture Change: A Trend Toward Uniformity)

IDENTIFY STEREOTYPE OR
GENERALIZATION TO BE EXAMINED
e.g., Large modern cities are found mainly in
Western Europe and Anglo-America.

STRUCTURE PROBLEM THAT
REINFORCES SET
e.g., Participants found that they were accurate
in their reaction to the first set of photographs.

INTRODUCE DATA THAT
CHALLENGE SET
e.g., The second set of photographs could not be
easily identified by cultural clues.

RESTRUCTURE THE
GENERALIZATION
e.g., Cities around the world are becoming more
alike, especially in downtown sections.

4. *What are the advantages and disadvantages of this inquiry technique?*
      Participants may cite some of the following advantages of this type of teaching strategy: It will help high school students understand that they have certain values and will help them identify their biases or prejudices. This, in turn, should increase student awareness of the tentativeness of hypotheses or inferences and of the need to check all data before arriving at conclusions that seem certain. High school students may learn more effectively because they are learning on their own. They may also become more critical or questioning of learning experiences.
      The following are some disadvantages of this inquiry method which participants

might mention: High school students could react in a negative way if this teaching technique were used too often, since its success depends on an element of surprise. Needed materials might be difficult to find and it might take more time for research and data collection than a teacher would wish to give. Further, some participants may feel that the time spent in class with this type of activity may not be justified. For certain school situations, the noise level and movement of students may be considered undesirable.

V. APPLICATION

To help participants consider ways of using this inquiry technique in their teaching, you may wish to use the following suggestions:

1. Ask participants to identify topics that could provide a basis for developing a lesson using the inquiry process demonstrated.

    An example of introducing a topic might be the following: Two men meet and reminisce about their war experiences. One man describes his life in a World War II prison camp. He talks about the small allotment of rice at meals, the brutal treatment from the guards, the inferior housing and clothing. When the conversation is completed, the man talking is identified as a Japanese who was describing conditions in an Allied prison camp.

    If high school students were asked to identify the historical situation, they would probably say that the man talking was a prisoner of the Japanese forces during World War II. The anecdote could be used to introduce a study of World War II, the topic of war in general, or a study of students' attitudes about war.

    Participants may suggest examples based on other historical or social science possibilities, such as relationships among race, income, crime, or education.

2. Devise and/or teach a short activity using the following data and the inquiry process developed in "Culture Change."

    Read aloud the following excerpt, dealing with the topic of war:

    One does not often speak or read of the war in reality, of its blood and filth, of mutilated flesh, and other revolting things. This restraint is necessary, but it ought to be recognized that the war is not presented when one writes of debates in Congress, of flanking movements, of retreats and advances . . . of divisions doing this and brigades doing that. In the sense of full realism war cannot be discussed. The human mind will not stand for it. For the very word "war" the realist would have to substitute some such term as "organized murder" or "human slaughterhouse." In drama as distinguished from melodrama murder often occurs offstage. In most historical accounts, especially military narratives, the war is offstage in that its stench and hideousness do not appear.

    Of course it is not suggested that the generation of the sixties had any copyright on blundering. It is not that democracy was at fault. After all . . . war has not become chronic on these shores, as it has in some nations where politics of force is the rule. One can at least say that the [war] was exceptional; that may be the best thing that can be said about it. A fuller measure of democracy would probably have prevented the war or at least have mitigated its abuses. To overlook many decades of American democracy and take the [war] period as its test, would be to give an unfair appraisal.[3]

This quotation could be a newspaper or television account of a Vietnam war protest which might have occurred in Washington, D.C., or in any other major city in the United States. In fact, however, the quotation is a view of the Civil War written in 1940. If high school students were given this quotation without being told its source, they might guess that it describes events in the United States within the past decade.

Another quotation that participants might use in an activity illustrating the inquiry process developed in "Culture Change" can be found in Volume IV, "1930–1940," of the Time-Life series, *This Fabulous Century*, on pages 25–26. If high school students were given this description of the breaking up of the Bonus March on Washington during the 1930's, without being told its source, they might think it an account of a recent protest or civil disorder. If this quotation is used, participants should be sure to delete the names General Douglas MacArthur and Dwight D. Eisenhower, as well as the references to "cavalry" and "sabers," since these provide clues to the era of the account.

[3] J. G. Randall, "The Blundering Generation," *The Mississippi Valley Historical Review*, Volume 27, Number 1 (June 1940), pp. 3–4, 6–11, 13–16. Cited in Kenyon C. Cramer, *The Causes of War* (Glenview, Ill.: Scott, Foresman and Company, 1965), pp. 90–91.

ACTIVITY 9

The Decision-Maker

I. BACKGROUND

The materials used for this teaching activity are taken from Lessons 7, 8, and 9 in Part 2 of the SRSS sociology course, *Inquiries in Sociology.* Prior to engaging in this activity, high school students have studied the socialization process, and they have examined the institutions of the family, education, and religion. In the interest of clarity, each institution was treated separately, but since institutions are not separate and autonomous in actuality, this activity was designed to consider the problem of institutional interrelationships.

II. PARTICIPANT OBJECTIVES

Experience with and analysis of this activity should enable participants:

1. To grasp more fully the meaning of certain concepts central to sociology: institution, role, role conflict, and value.
2. To see that beliefs and behaviors in one institutional sector have repercussions in other sectors of society.
3. To see how values celebrated in one institutional sphere may be at odds with values in other spheres, thus creating stress in the social order.

4. To see how social action in one institutional setting, designed to produce certain outcomes in other institutional spheres, may have unintended — sometimes undesired — outcomes.

5. *To experience and analyze a teaching strategy based on reflective thinking.*

6. *To see how a single teaching activity can incorporate matters of substance while at the same time it can focus on value analysis and on particular values expressed by students.*

7. *To develop skill in creating teaching activities that use value analysis as the basis for student inquiry.*

8. *To be more effective in assessing the strengths and weaknesses of teaching activities focusing on analysis of values.*[1]

III. CONDUCTING THE ACTIVITY [2]

When taught to high school students, this activity requires approximately three class periods to complete. However, for this purpose, the teaching demonstration has been condensed into approximately forty to fifty minutes.

Prior to starting the demonstration, have the participants fill out the questionnaire *What Do You Think?* [3] It must be completed in advance of the discussion so that responses to the statements will not be influenced by information gained later. Simply tell your class that the data from the questionnaire will serve as the basis for a later discussion. Ideally, the questionnaire should be administered at least one day in advance of conducting the activity so that the data can be tallied outside of class time. If you administer it on the day the activity is begun, you will need to make arrangements to have the data tallied prior to its use during the second part of the demonstration.

Assign "Activity 9/The Decision-Maker" (pages 68–72) for reading in advance of conducting the exercise.

Discussion during the first part of the demonstration should focus on the materials that participants read, and should be open ended with little attempt made for closure.

The following suggested questions can be used to organize the discussion:

1. *What is the immediate problem that Bob Metky faces?*

The problem, simply put, is that Bob must make a decision about locating the new cement plant, either on Site 1, one and one-half miles north of St. Joseph, or on Site 2, eleven miles north of St. Joseph.

[1] Numbers one to four are content objectives; five through eight are pedagogical objectives.

[2] Adapted from the Instructor's Guide for *Inquiries in Sociology* (Boston: Allyn and Bacon, 1972). Copyright © 1972 American Sociological Association. Reprinted with permission.

[3] You will need to make one copy for each participant of the questionnaire *What Do You Think?* (see page 197) in advance of carrying out this exercise.

2. *What are the different points of view that Bob Metky must consider in making his decision?*

In answering this question, participants should be aware of some of the "inputs" that bear on the decision-making process. In doing so, they will start to see the interrelatedness of various aspects of institutional structures. The institutions of the polity, the economy, and the family are represented in the various positions presented in the reading. Following are some viewpoints that will influence the decision on where to locate the new cement factory.

a. *The county view* (polity): Buchanan County is definitely in favor of having the plant located on Site 1. Site 2 is outside Buchanan County. Location there would deprive the county of the tax revenues to be gained from the new twenty-million-dollar plant.

b. *The St. Joseph view* (polity): The residents of St. Joseph are opposed to locating the plant on Site 1. It is so close to the city limits that they fear that air pollution will be a major problem. Moreover, the expansion of the city northward in the direction of the plant is likely to be restricted. The plant is also highly automated, so few jobs will be created in the area. Since the site is located outside the city limits, St. Joseph will not benefit from increased tax revenues. In short, the city has nothing to gain and a great deal to lose. It is interesting to note that two units of the polity, the city and the county, are in conflict on this issue.

c. *The business view* (economy): The business view, of course, favors locating the plant on Site 1. The report from the consultants' firm favors this site over Site 2. Although the report does not rule out Site 2, company profits would be maximized by selecting Site 1. Site 1 has better limestone deposits, good rail and road facilities, and access to the Missouri River. Furthermore, Buchanan County will share in the cost of the Site 1 development and will grant tax concessions.

d. *The state view* (polity): The state stands to benefit economically regardless of which site is chosen. The state, however, is still in a difficult position. Since the Kansas City Air Pollution District does not extend as far north as St. Joseph, the state has no jurisdiction over the plant's operation. However, the city of St. Joseph is bringing pressure to bear on the State Air Conservation Commission to intervene, at least to the extent of putting pressure on Compac Industries to locate the plant on Site 2. Buchanan County wants the state to stay out of the matter, claiming that benefits to the county far outweigh the potential air pollution problem.

e. *The family view* (family): The position of Bob Metky's family does not come through clearly in the materials examined by the participants. Bob's wife is civic-minded and we might thus assume that she would be concerned about the air pollution problem associated with Site 1. However, she is also anxious to see Bob promoted to the presidency of Compac Industries — a promotion that may depend on his putting company interests above all others. Family income also seems to be a factor. With their son away at college and two other children to be cared for at home, Bob could well use the increased salary that goes with the president's chair.

f. *The societal view:* The societal view strongly favors locating the plant on Site 2, thus reducing the air pollution problem. In this way, society can have its cake and eat it too. Society would definitely benefit from the increased productivity of the economy, the increased tax revenues that could be applied to needed social improvements, and, in fact, even by the concrete materials produced by the plant — materials necessary for more building projects, and thus, further growth. If the plant is located on Site 1, benefits to the society would have to be examined against the harmful effects of air pollution.

3. *What, then, is Bob Metky's personal dilemma?*

In answering this question, participants are expected to make use of two concepts — role and role conflict. If Bob Metky had only one role to play, say, that of business executive, his decision would be an easy one. He would select Site 1, maximize company profits, and enhance his chances of being named to the presidency of Compac Industries. But Bob must play many roles, roles that involve conflicting interests concerning the plant's location. In his role as concerned citizen, he might be inclined to select Site 2, thus saving St. Joseph from the pollution problem — a problem that he knows is of increasing national importance. His role as church member might also call for the selection of Site 2. How can he authorize a plant that will pollute the atmosphere and endanger the health of the residents of St. Joseph and still believe that each man is his brother's keeper? His role as family member, however, might dictate the selection of Site 1. His wife wants him to be president of the company (the implication is that he, too, wants the presidency) and money is needed for Jeff's college education. There is, then, no question that Bob Metky faces role conflict.

4. *If you were in Bob Metky's position, where would you locate the new cement plant?*

Now, with the issues clearly stated, participants can state their own opinions about the proper location of the cement plant. The position they take is, of course, unimportant. It is important, however, that in taking a position, participants clearly state how they are resolving the value conflict that Bob Metky is facing.

After the participants have expressed their opinions on where the cement plant should be located, you can focus the discussion on two aspects of the data obtained from the questionnaire (*What Do You Think?*) administered earlier: (1) analysis and interpretation of the results and (2) analysis of the value issues involved. Since some participants may be sensitive to certain value issues, individual rights should be taken into account in the discussion.

Begin this part of the activity by redistributing the questionnaires to the participants. (Since the questionnaires were anonymous, it is unlikely that a participant will receive his own questionnaire.)

The following question might be used as a point of departure for the discussion: *Look over the items on the questionnaire. Is there anything about these items that is striking or interesting?*

Undoubtedly, participants will have numerous observations to make about the items. Some participants may suggest, for example, that each item implies a value. Others may note that the items appear to be concerned with various institutions, such as the family, the polity, etc. These are valid observations but of more importance at this point is that participants discover the fact that, except for three statements (numbers 6, 9, and 14), the items can be arranged in eight pairs as follows: 1-5, 10-13, 7-16, 3-17, 15-19, 2-12, 4-11, and 8-18. Each pair of items involves statements of potentially conflicting values. If participants fail to identify the pairing principle, tell them. Then ask them to try and identify the paired items. There is no need to belabor the point; identifying three or four pairs should make it clear.

Results from the Questionnaire

When the pairing principle has been identified, have the participants look at the Data Sheet (Figure 3-6) — a listing of eight paired statements from the questionnaire. Participants should have little difficulty realizing that each item contains a pair of opposite and possibly conflicting value statements. They should also be able to identify the institution (or institutions) involved in each pair. In Pair C, for example, the idea that the institution of education should be concerned with developing the uniqueness of the individual may conflict with the idea that the needs of society should determine the goals of education.

Now attention can be focused on recording on the Data Sheet the results from the questionnaire and examining the pattern of participants' responses to the paired items. Since there will be more data to discuss than you can reasonably handle in the time devoted to this activity, you may prefer to select ahead of time the items you wish to consider. Your selection should, of course, reflect the interests of the participants. Further, it will probably help to sustain interest if you report the results for each pair when it is to be discussed rather than if you announce the results for all the items at one time. Direct participants to record the results in the appropriate boxes on the right-hand side of the Data Sheet.

Discussing Pair B

Since the suggested approach to discussing the results is roughly the same for each pair of value statements, the following discussion of fictitious data for Pair B will serve to exemplify the procedures that might be used. An outline of the issues and institutions involved in the remaining seven pairs is given later.

The value statements in Pair B are as follows:

10. *Students' rights to equal educational opportunities should be guaranteed throughout the United States.*
13. *Each community should have the right to run its own schools.*

FIGURE 3-6. *Data Sheet*

		Agree	Dis-agree

PAIR A

1. Parents should have the sole right to decide the number of children they will have.
5. Population growth should be regulated.

PAIR B

10. Students' rights to equal educational opportunities should be guaranteed throughout the United States.
13. Each community should have the right to run its own schools.

PAIR C

7. Education should be concerned with developing the uniqueness of individuals.
16. The needs of society should determine the goals of education.

PAIR D

3. Important government decisions should be made only after consideration by many informed groups.
17. Effective government requires that persons in authority should have the power to make immediate decisions.

PAIR E

15. Everyone should respect the sacredness of human life.
19. The United States government should be prepared to use force to defend the national security of the country.

PAIR F

2. To protect consumers from exploitation, prices should be examined and regulated by government.
12. Business firms should have the right to sell their products for whatever the market will bring.

PAIR G

4. Efforts should be made to reduce poverty in the United States.
11. People should work for income they receive.

PAIR H

8. Residents in a neighborhood should have the right to determine who shall live there.
18. Families should have the right to select the neighborhoods in which they will live.

You might begin the discussion by asking: *Can you identify the institution or institutions involved?* The items in Pair *B* are basically concerned with a possible conflict *within* the institution of education. Now, with the institution identified, report the data for Pair *B*. Next ask the participants: *Do the data reveal any inconsistencies or conflicts?* Participants should easily see that in Pair *B*, as with the other paired statements, a value conflict is involved. Basically, it centers in the possibility that if communities have the right to run their own schools, differences between school systems in such things as discriminatory practices in hiring teachers and enrolling students or in economic resources and willingness of community members to spend these resources on education may well result in quantitative and qualitative differences in educational opportunities between school systems. Such differences may well mean that, although equality of educational opportunity exists *within* a given community, inequalities *between* school systems may prevail. In other words, local control of education, a widely held value, comes into conflict with another widely held value: equality of educational opportunity in the society as a whole. With this in mind, some participants may argue that the value issue stated in Pair *B* involves *both* the institutions of the polity and of education. Insofar as agencies of the polity intervene to correct inequalities in local school systems, particularly with regard to racial discrimination, they are correct. Indeed, their observation is important since it further illustrates the complexity of interrelationships between institutions.

Further, in discussing each pair of statements, you should check the meaning or meanings attributed to them by participants. For example, participants' interpretation of the statements in Pair *B* may well diverge from the general discussion provided here. Such variations in meaning may partially account for the manner in which some participants answered items in the questionnaire. Moreover, differences in the interpretation of the implications of each statement may be a basis for conflict between groups of participants within your class.

To facilitate discussion of the possible outcomes of the data for Pair *B*, the general patterns into which the results might fall must be considered. Suppose that the questionnaire had been administered to thirty participants. In general, we would expect their responses to be distributed according to one of the following patterns:

Type I.

	Agree	Disagree
Item 10	26	4
Item 13	21	9

In this instance the data suggest that a majority of participants agree with both statements. Moreover, the results suggest that a majority of participants approve of values that are possibly inconsistent. Given such inconsistency, participants should be pressed to examine the implications of the value conflicts implied in their responses.

Type II.

	Agree	Disagree
Item 10	4	26
Item 13	9	21

These data suggest that most participants disapprove of what are in fact two values that are widely held within the society as a whole. Thus, although these participants resolve the possible value conflict by rejecting both values, their position is nevertheless at odds with the wide acceptance of these values in the society as a whole. Again participants should be pressed to explore the implications of their position.

Type III.

	Agree	Disagree
Item 10	26	4
Item 13	9	21

Type IV.

	Agree	Disagree
Item 10	4	26
Item 13	21	9

The response patterns in Types III and IV are the obverse of each other. In Type III, a majority of participants approve of the value of equal opportunity for all but disapprove of local control of schools. In Type IV, the reverse is true. Clearly, in these instances, the majority of participants have resolved the possible value conflict by expressing disapproval of one or the other of the value statements. Nevertheless, since both values expressed in Pair *B* are widely held in society, the implications of the positions taken by a majority of the participants can be explored.

The importance of examining instances where the participants resolve a possible conflict by rejecting a value that may be presumed to be more or less widely held in society can be illustrated by examining fictitious data for Pair *G*. Suppose the responses were distributed as follows:

	Agree	Disagree
4. *Efforts should be made to reduce poverty in the United States.*	26	4
11. *People should work for income they receive.*	9	21

In this instance, participants have resolved a possible value conflict by rejecting one of the values implied. These data, however, may point to the fact that, currently, many people and particularly the young are challenging the verities of the "American way of life." Because of this, the conflict implied in the data for the example above may not be between the values themselves, but between those who claim that the idea implied in Item 11 is valuable and those who claim that it is not. Reflecting on results like these should prove fruitful not only in terms of the complexity of interrelationships between institutions, but also in terms of the process of change within the value structure of society.

Type V.

	Agree	Disagree
Item 10	16	14
Item 13	17	13

Clearly, interpretations applied in the previous examples may also be applied to the pattern of results shown in Type V. Some participants may, for example, be approving of one value and disapproving of the other. If this is so, it is possible that no value conflict is implied. Or a few participants may agree with both statements. Participants who responded in this way would fit the case described in Type I and thus a value conflict is implied. Only by checking individual responses to the items would it be possible to determine which of these (and other possible) interpretations was valid. However, one other possible interpretation remains. It may be that the data suggest a cleavage within your class regarding the importance of the values in Pair B. In other words, approximately half the class approve of the values and half disapprove of the values. If this were the case, a lively and fruitful discussion of the implications of the results should follow.

By now it should be clear that it is extremely difficult to outline all the contingencies that may arise in analyzing and interpreting the results from the questionnaire. As far as possible, you should try to review the results from the questionnaire before conducting this part of the activity so that you are familiar with the extent to which the results from your group conform to the patterns described above. If this is done, formulating ahead of time a sequence of questions that will press participants to examine thoroughly the implications of the results from the questionnaire should be easier. Further, participants' understanding of the complex interrelationships between institutions should also be enhanced.

Discussing the Other Pairs

The following material outlines the issues and institutions involved in the seven remaining pairs of value issues included in the questionnaire. As you discuss the responses for a particular pair of items, it may be necessary to alter slightly the general format suggested in the preceding analysis of Pair *B*.

PAIR *A*

1. *Parents should have the sole right to decide the number of children they will have.*
5. *Population growth should be regulated.*

Items 1 and 5 point to a possible value inconsistency between the institutions of the polity and the family. If the class or individual participants agree with both statements, they may find their values in conflict. For example, to control the rapid increase in world population, governments may have to pass legislation of various sorts that put limitations on the number of children families may have. With the development of effective birth control devices, this is a real possibility. However, this may run counter to our value concerning the right of individual parents to determine the number of children they want.

PAIR *C*

7. *Education should be concerned with developing the uniqueness of individuals.*
16. *The needs of society should determine the goals of education.*

Items 7 and 16 point to a possible value conflict within the institution of education. Participants may agree with both statements without realizing that the two positions may not be compatible. In a highly complex society, social needs of the society may dictate the pattern of education. If the society needs certain kinds of talents, for example, it may be that the personal preference of the individual may by necessity receive second priority.

PAIR *D*

3. *Important government decisions should be made only after consideration by many informed groups.*
17. *Effective government requires that persons in authority should have the power to make immediate decisions.*

Items 3 and 17 point to a value conflict within the institution of the polity. On the one hand, a stable and responsible governmental system may rest on decisions being made only after careful consideration by many informed groups. Such is the case when legislation is proposed by an executive, put into law by a legislative body, and its constitutional implications considered by a judicial body. This process may, however, stand in the way of effective decision-making in times of crisis. Unless specific institutionalized arrangements are established to handle the crisis situation, the belief in slow and deliberate process may hinder effective action.

PAIR *E*

15. *Everyone should respect the sacredness of human life.*
19. *The United States government should be prepared to use force to defend the national security of the country.*

Items 15 and 19 present a possible value conflict between the institutions of religion and polity. If one believes in the use of force to defend the U.S. national security, he may eventually be placed in the position of having to sanction the taking of human life. Such is the case in time of war when we pray for victory (the destruction of the enemy) while at the same time we try to maintain basic religious beliefs concerning human life.

PAIR *F*

2. *To protect consumers from exploitation, prices should be examined and regulated by government.*
12. *Business firms should have the right to sell their products for whatever the market will bring.*

Items 2 and 12 concern a possible value conflict between the polity and the economy. On the one hand, a basic tenet of capitalism is that prices are determined on the free market, according to the law of supply and demand. On the other hand, we tend to believe that the consumer should not be exploited. Business and industry are entitled to fair profit, but government regulation may be necessary if prices get out of hand.

PAIR *G*

4. *Efforts should be made to reduce poverty in the United States.*
11. *People should work for income they receive.*

Items 4 and 11 cut across the institutions of the economy, the polity, and the family. Although participants may agree that efforts should be made to reduce poverty, they may also agree that people should work for income they receive. Many of the poor, however, are unable to work due to age, illness, lack of job skills, or family responsibilities. In addition, although many people in the poverty category do indeed work, they are still unable to earn a sufficient income. Those participants, then, who agree with both statements 4 and 11 might be asked how they would resolve their value inconsistencies.

PAIR *H*

8. *Residents in a neighborhood should have the right to determine who shall live there.*
18. *Families should have the right to select the neighborhoods in which they will live.*

Statements 8 and 18 cut across the institutions of the family, the polity, and the economy. In this case, the free right of a family to locate where it pleases runs counter to the belief that residents of a neighborhood have the right to band together to keep out unwanted families. Although participants may agree with both statements and thus hold conflict values, it is more likely that in this case the value conflict will be *inter*participant, and not *intra*participant. In exploring the various positions on this issue, you can illustrate the interrelatedness of the family (unit wishing to relocate), the polity (open-housing laws have been passed on this issue), and economy (housing may be priced so high in the neighborhood that unwanted families may be unable to move in, in spite of open-housing legislation).

IV. REFLECTIONS ON THE LEARNING AND TEACHING

A. *Analysis of Learning Outcomes*

To appraise our success in achieving certain learnings in this activity, we can ask: *Do participants have a surer sense of the abstract terms we call concepts: institution, role, role conflict, and value?* Meeting this objective is difficult because such words are well-worn, imprecise symbols in everyday use. For example, we are likely to use the word "institution" to refer to the local home for senior citizens or to the high school or to a nearby prison. But, from the sociological perspective, these are local organizations that exemplify a pattern of relationships *instituted* to achieve certain social ends. What we institute are rules governing men's relationships; they result in social structures that repeat themselves from place to place and time to time. Thus *a* family is not an institution, but *the* family is. The city manager, the mayor, and the council do not constitute an institution. They exemplify it — the common understandings and procedures that define the civic role and the relationships between governors and governed. Institutions are "frozen answers to fundamental questions."

To sustain a society, certain basic problems must be handled. There is the problem of rearing the young and inducting them into the secrets of society. There is the need of every group to institute means of garnering and allocating the produce of soil and sea. There is the question to be faced of how we can reconcile the inevitable disputes among men and prevent the Hobbesian war of each against all. And there is the problem of instituting ways of answering questions about ultimate meaning and ways of enforcing the moral code that guides men's relationships. Thus the concept *institution* carries a freight of connotations that should, in some degree, become a useful tool in people's thinking.

As with all of us, Bob Metky's life is framed by its institutional context: family (husband, father, and the larger kin network); education (public school, the University of Iowa); economy (farm work, the aircraft firm, salesman, vice president with Compac Industries — to say nothing of his role as consumer); religion (mentioned with a perhaps telling brevity); polity (mandatory public schooling, navy service, the legal framework within which his company operates, his public service, civic role, citizens' and the public commission's concern about air pollution). As with all of us, what is required or desired in one institutional setting may not be completely compatible with expectations elsewhere.

As with the word "institution," the concept of *role* is part of our mundane repertoire of symbols loosely used. In this activity, we use the term in its sociological sense. Role here means the culturally stipulated way in which a person in a given social position is expected to act toward a category of others. Thus, of all fathers, there is a set of expectations defining appropriate behavior toward the category we call children. In each institutional setting, Metky has one or more roles. To the extent that expectations defining these roles are incompatible, Metky has problems to resolve. If his roles as citizen and religious communicant stress the equality of men before God and the law, his role as a businessman pushes toward inequality: securing wealth and power that set him apart from others. If within the family, matters of the heart control conduct, the world of business requires a cool, competitive hard-headedness. Interests clash. Roles conflict.

To join the concepts treated in this activity, we can say that in different *institutional* contexts, *roles* may reflect incompatible *values*. By values we simply mean conceptions of the desirable.

A second aim would be achieved if participants gain a keener sense of the interlocking of human institutions. In New York City, the tie between polity, economy, and family is clear when we learn that more than one-fourth of the city's budget goes for welfare. The link between economy and religion was stressed by Karl Marx when he alleged that religion was an opiate, deflecting people's legitimate concerns for this-worldly welfare to an other-worldly interest in salvation. And the German sociologist Max Weber once contended that elements of the Protestant ethic were a necessary (but not sufficient) condition for the emergence of capitalism.

In this activity, participants uncover a connection between the *polity* (laws governing air pollution, the State Air Conservation Commission, the citizens of St. Joseph) and the *economy* (the problem of site selection and maximizing profits). This is the obvious interinstitutional linkage, but the impact of the imminent decision touches other sectors. Company profits and personal promotion (stemming from a decision guided only by economic criteria) would advance family interests. On the other hand, religious principles embodied in the golden rule and, say, in the Sermon on the Mount, may be compromised by a hard-headed, profit-oriented decision.

An appreciation of such antithetical elements is a third learning objective. We have in this activity two sets of data showing institution-anchored values/roles in conflict. One is the case of Bob Metky, in which the analysis turns on an individual's problems of decision-making. The other set takes off from data that aggregate people's responses to statements which, when paired, may reveal antithetical positions. Since these are participants' responses, they may seem more immediate and personal than the conflicts Metky faces. Yet they reveal, when treated in the aggregate, group attributes. And insofar as expressed values are incompatible, they disclose fissures in the institutional structure. Take, for example, a fictitious group of thirty participants who respond in the following way to items 10 and 13:

		Agree	Disagree
10.	Students' rights to equal educational opportunities should be guaranteed throughout the United States.	16	14
13.	Each community should have the right to run its own schools.	17	13

Looking at the group as a whole, we find that over one-half take the "states' rights" position on statement 13, and that just over one-half of the same group favor federal intervention to ensure equality of opportunity (statement 10).[4] Barring thoughtless inconsistencies, such a division points to divisiveness — a potential for conflict. The conflict is both inter- and intrainstitutional. Different levels of government and education are at odds, and federal law (as at Little Rock and elsewhere) intervenes in state and local educational systems.

A fourth desired outcome lies in the answer to this question: *What might be the unintended — perhaps undesired — consequences of action initiated in one institutional sector?* In the Metky case, it was precisely to spot both intended and unanticipated outcomes that management consultants were hired to advise Compac Industries. A central concern of the sociologist is to tease out such undeclared and undetected consequences of social patterns. Thus, we may find that the selection of superior teachers for advanced training (chosen with the aim of improving education) has the effect of shifting them to administrative positions or to other employment, so impoverishing rather

---

[4] One would hope that participants might note that such aggregated data do not necessarily point to the distribution of individual choices. These data do not tell us about the person's two positions on the issues. It is conceivable (if unlikely) that among the seventeen agreeing on local self-determination, sixteen were those who also favored federal intervention. (They might have seen the two positions as reconcilable. They could have been thoughtlessly inconsistent. Or perhaps they misread the statements.) To see the individual distribution of opinions, we would have to tally responses in this fashion:

NUMBER RESPONDING IN VARIOUS WAYS	ITEM 10	ITEM 13
3	agree	agree
14	agree	disagree
10	disagree	agree
3	disagree	disagree

This gives us a better basis for determining the extent of inter- and intrainstitutional tension, and the possible conflict between civic and educational roles. In this instance, we clearly have a divided group. At the other pole would be the case in which all thirty respondents gave the same pattern of responses.

than improving school instruction.   Might the cement-plant decision result in a new set of zoning laws?   Might a decision not to build deprive a financially faltering school system of hoped-for tax support, so inducing moves toward consolidation with other districts, creating busing problems, and altering peoples' decisions about where they would build or rent their homes?   If the government agencies should lead the fight on grounds of air pollution, is it conceivable that those favoring Site 1 might clamor for government to clean its own house, eliminating coal-fired furnaces in office buildings and public utilities?

Such questions as these may be worth participants' attention as alternate courses of action are debated in decision-making processes.

B.   Analysis of Teaching Strategies

The following questions and brief discussions may be useful as participants analyze the teaching strategy used in this activity:

1.   *What data serve as the basis for inquiry?*

In this activity, the data on which the inquiry is structured take two forms.   First are the fictitious data about Robert Metky and the inputs that bear on his decision of where to locate the new cement plant.   Second are the data from the questionnaire which tap some of the values held by the participants and expose some possible value conflicts.   Thus, both fictitious and real data are used to illustrate institutional interrelatedness, possible intra- and interinstitutional conflicts, and personal value conflicts.

2.   *What justification is there for using reflective thinking and value analysis as a teaching/learning strategy for this activity?*

An interesting aspect of this activity is that it incorporates matters of substance while at the same time focuses on values that support the various roles that Bob Metky plays.   It also focuses on particular values expressed by the participants.   Thus, a teaching/learning strategy that generates considerable interest is used to achieve several important, yet abstract, substantive objectives.   Moreover, in addition to the substantive objectives and the high interest level associated with value analysis, there is considerable merit in having people examine through a process of reflective thinking the belief structure that they and others hold.   Of course, nothing is inherently new in using reflective thinking as a teaching strategy.   Many teachers have been using this method for years, perhaps without realizing its distinctiveness.

To ask participants to think reflectively typically involves having them examine the belief structure or values that they hold.[5]   Since values operate at different levels of generality (e.g., national, state, local, group, specific individual) and since they are not arranged in a priority hierarchy, the values held are often inconsistent, perhaps even conflicting.   These value inconsistencies are seldom part of our consciousness, since in a specific situation we usually select from among our many values that which supports our

[5] Lawrence E. Metcalf, "Urban Studies Reflectively Thinking," *Social Education*, 33 (1969), pp. 656–661.

immediate behavior. Thus, in any given situation, alternative modes of behavior may be limited by an unawareness of the various values applicable to that specific situation. The participant who is able to examine rationally a situation in which alternative courses of action are available and then make an informed decision about proper action or inaction has developed a valuable skill. Critical examination of value questions can help promote this skill.

3. *What sequence of events is involved in the activity?*
    Events in this lesson move from consideration of an impersonal (fictitious) situation involving role conflict and associated value conflicts to a more personal analysis of possible value conflicts experienced by the participants themselves. At the same time, of course, substantive objectives are being achieved. Thus, the activity moves from role conflicts and value conflicts experienced by someone else, Bob Metky, to an analysis of the values expressed by members of the group. This attempt to personalize instruction through value analysis does, however, break away somewhat from the traditional role of the teacher — a role that calls primarily for the teaching of substantive content and inculcation of values. Further, the subjects being discussed are very immediate and personal for those involved. Your participants may enjoy speculating about the advantages and disadvantages of this type of activity and about how the problems they identify may be overcome.

4. *Would the outcomes of this activity be significantly different if the sequence of events were reversed (analysis of the data from the questionnaire first, followed by analysis of the hypothetical case) or if one part of the activity were eliminated?*
    Although the rationale for the sequence is explained above, it might be valuable for your participants to consider how the inquiry and ultimate objectives achieved might be different if the sequence were reversed or if one part of the activity were eliminated. Is the connection between the analysis of the case of Bob Metky and the analysis of the questionnaire sufficient to justify considering them in a single teaching activity?

V. APPLICATION

In order to apply the knowledge and skills gained from participating in and analyzing this activity, participants might be asked to engage in some of the following activities:

1. Create a teaching activity that requires students to think reflectively about the values they hold.
2. Locate other evidence that could be used to develop further one or more of the concepts considered in this activity.
3. Develop a teaching activity using value analysis to achieve substantive objectives in the discipline of particular importance to them.
4. Create a teaching activity that achieves one or more of the substantive objectives for this activity but which does so through a process other than value analysis.

QUESTIONNAIRE: WHAT DO YOU THINK? [6]

The nineteen statements below touch on various aspects of social life. Simply check whether you agree or disagree with each statement. This is not a test so there is no reason to record your name. Since the questionnaire will be collected, you will want to keep a record of your response to each item.

		Agree	Disagree
1.	Parents should have the sole right to decide the number of children they will have.	———	———
2.	To protect consumers from exploitation, prices should be examined and regulated by government.	———	———
3.	Important government decisions should be made only after consideration by many informed groups.	———	———
4.	Efforts should be made to reduce poverty in the United States.	———	———
5.	Population growth should be regulated.	———	———
6.	The rate of social change is so great it frightens me.	———	———
7.	Education should be concerned with developing the uniqueness of individuals.	———	———
8.	Residents in a neighborhood should have the right to determine who shall live there.	———	———
9.	The churches in the United States have been too slow to join the struggle against social injustice.	———	———
10.	Students' rights to equal educational opportunities should be guaranteed throughout the United States.	———	———
11.	People should work for income they receive.	———	———
12.	Business firms should have the right to sell their products for whatever the market will bring.	———	———
13.	Each community should have the right to run its own schools.	———	———
14.	Our society is going to be torn apart by rising tension and unrest.	———	———
15.	Everyone should respect the sacredness of human life.	———	———
16.	The needs of society should determine the goals of education.	———	———
17.	Effective government requires that persons in authority should have the power to make immediate decisions.	———	———
18.	Families should have the right to select the neighborhoods in which they will live.	———	———
19.	The United States government should be prepared to use force to defend the national security of the country.	———	———

[6] From Student Handout 2-1, in Instructor's Guide for *Inquiries in Sociology* (Boston: Allyn and Bacon, 1972). Copyright © 1972 American Sociological Association. Reprinted by permission.

ACTIVITY 10

Watchung

I. BACKGROUND

The Watchung activity from "Habitat and Resources," Unit 5 of the High School Geography Project course *Geography in an Urban Age*, is a short activity designed to introduce high school students to some fundamental man-land relationships.

Prior to engaging in the Watchung activity, high school students first studied how habitats can be classified according to the degree of change imposed by man. They then explored how cultural traditions, technology, and population affect the ways man uses similar habitats in different parts of the world. With this background, they are ready for the Watchung exercise — predicting where certain human activities might be found in a habitat at two different points in time.

II. PARTICIPANT OBJECTIVES

Experience with and analysis of this activity should enable participants:

1. To discuss how man organizes his rural and urban settlement activities in relation to local terrain and bedrock conditions.
2. To describe patterns of land use by analyzing data provided in topographic maps and matching aerial photographs.

3. To predict future patterns of urban settlement from data provided in United States Geological Survey Quadrangles and matching aerial photographs.
4. *To use an inquiry process requiring topographic map and aerial photographic data effectively in their own classrooms.*
5. *To develop other inquiry approaches using data similar to those in this activity and using data different from those in this activity.*
6. *To select and arrange materials and activities in sequence to ensure cumulative learning.*
7. *To verify the validity of the inquiry approach by analyzing the hierarchy of inquiry processes.*[1]

III. CONDUCTING THE ACTIVITY

In this activity, participants will predict relationships between habitat and people, using an area in north central New Jersey as the example. They will read about landforms, rocks, and soils of the area, predict certain settlement patterns, verify these with a topographic map and aerial photographs, and predict certain settlement patterns for a later period in history.

Ask participants to read the short description of the physiographic conditions and patterns of the Watchung region (pages 73–75) and to think about the questions posed on page 76. The answers to these questions might seem obvious but for this activity they serve two purposes: (1) to prepare participants for the generalizations to be made, and (2) to encourage them to think about human-use decisions that influence gross patterns of land use.

Make sure that participants understand the cut-away diagram of the Watchung Mountains (Figure 2-28) and the contour map of the Watchung area (Figure 2-29). Your class must be able to read and interpret these figures in order to complete the exercise.

Participants should have no difficulty understanding the cut-away diagram of the Watchung Mountains since it is a simple drawing of an oblique air view of the region. However, they may experience some trouble with Figure 2-29, the contour map. If so, you can point out the following things.

Any given contour or line on a contour or topographic map passes through points of equal height above sea level. Every fifth line contains numbers that indicate the line's elevation (in feet) above sea level. These are called indicator contours. Where contour lines are close together, slopes are steep; where contour lines are farther apart, slopes are gentle. If you travel from south to north on the map in Figure 2-29, you will first encounter a steep slope at about the two-hundred-foot contour; the slope levels somewhat at the four-hundred-foot indicator. As you go on, you find that the northward facing slope is more gradual than the one that you have just crossed from the south. You then reach a

---

[1] Numbers one to three are content objectives; four through seven are pedagogical objectives.

somewhat level valley floor at the two-hundred-foot contour. As you continue north, you will encounter a similar sequence of steep slopes, a somewhat level ridge top, and a gently sloping northward face of the ridge.

Check to see that participants understand the differences between slopes formed on basalt and those formed on shale and that they understand the differences between the soils derived from these rocks.

When you are satisfied that participants are familiar with the background material, ask them to read the section entitled "Predicting 1956 Settlement Patterns and Highways" (page 76) and complete the activity according to the instructions given in the reading. You can have participants work individually or in pairs. Caution them not to look at Figures 3-7 and 3-8 in advance of completing their work maps. You might tell them that when high school students engage in this activity, the teacher distributes the map and photos only after students have made their predictions on the contour maps. Allow about ten minutes for participants to make their predictions and to verify their choices.

When they have completed the 1956 map exercise, discuss the predictions and the reasons which participants give for their choices. The following information should aid you:

Figure 2-30: Agricultural Areas. Choice A. Low-lying, gently sloping land over shale bedrock.

Figure 2-31: Rural Settlement. Choice C. Related to agricultural areas.

Figure 2-32: U.S. Highway 22. Choice B. (Choice A might have been selected with considerable logic.) You may wish to refer participants to Figure 2-27 ("Physiographic Regions of New Jersey") on page 74 and ask them about the connections this highway makes to the major urban settlements east and west of the Watchung area. Probe their reasons for locating the highway with respect to landforms and topography.

Figure 2-33: Urban and Industrial Areas, 1956. Choice D. Related to main transportation routes just south of the arc of the Watchung ridges.

When you have completed discussion of the 1956 predictions, ask your class to read the section entitled "Predicting 1963 Major New Highway and New Urban and Industrial Areas" (page 84) and, as before, follow the instructions given. Participants will use only one source (Figure 3-9) to verify the 1963 prediction as opposed to the topographic map *and* the aerial photograph used to verify the 1956 predictions.

Again, discuss with participants their predictions and reasons, using the following information:

Figure 2-34: Major New Highways. Choice D. Note that this new dual limited access highway serves both the local areas of urban expansion and those areas to the east and west.

Figure 2-35: New Urban and Industrial Areas, 1963. Choice B. Note that Choice B is an extension of Choice D in Figure 2-33. Some participants may have selected either Choice A or Choice D because Choice B extends up the steep slope of one of the Watchung ridges. Discuss briefly the implication of urban expansion onto the ridges. The following questions might further guide the discussion: (a) Why are the eastern slopes of the mountains used in preference to the western slopes? (b) Where is the quarry located and for what might it be used?

Elicit from participants information about how the 1956 man-land relationships were modified to produce the 1963 relationships. This part of the discussion will emphasize the general implications of land use change. For example, what were the overall changes in land use in the Watchung area? What kinds of land provided the area required for the new highway? for urban expansion? for industrial expansion? Which of the apparent land uses diminished in area at the expense of others? Why is it necessary to understand land use competition when studying about land use changes? Which kinds of land compete for similar uses?

IV. REFLECTIONS ON THE LEARNING AND TEACHING

A. *Analysis of Learning Outcomes*

1. *What have participants learned about the relationship of man's activities and the surface of the earth from their examination of the data presented in this activity? How can they phrase these learnings in terms of generalizations?*
    Local terrain and bedrock exert strong influences on man's organization of rural and urban settlement activities, including linkages with rural and urban settlement activities outside a region. It is important to remember, however, that other natural environmental factors (variables) also influence settlement patterns. Such variables have not been studied in this activity; however, question six on page 76 states that parts of the Watchung area are forested. The presence of forests suggests that sufficient rainfall occurs in this area to make some agricultural activity possible. Participants should be aware that although shale can produce structural qualities in soil which make it amenable to cultivation, they were not given any direct information on the productive capabilities of these soils or on agricultural land management practices.
    It is likely that participants possess some general knowledge of the geography of north central New Jersey. Most people know of its proximity to New York City, of its megalopolitan characteristics, and of its overall population density. Or it may be that participants' knowledge of the area is negative, i.e., that the area is not sparsely populated, that it is not losing population, that it is not a desert, that it is not an Arctic area, etc. Negative knowledge is also useful when making predictions.
    General information supports specific information that is provided in an activity and is of assistance when one analyzes simple causal relationships between landform characteristics and settlement characteristics. It is important, however, to caution participants against developing generalizations that are environmentally deterministic about an area.

As a result of examining some fairly fundamental and generalized data (reading material, maps, and aerial photographs), participants should be able to make the generalization that rugged or steep land surfaces inhibit settlement activities while more gentle surfaces encourage them.   If other important variables had been considered, participants might have arrived at different conclusions from those which were obtained for the Watchung area.   For example, in the Colombian Andes, settlements are frequently located on uplands and even on very steep slopes in order to avoid the unhealthy conditions of poorly drained tropical lowlands.   Important rice-producing areas are located on terraced hillsides in the Philippines, and one of the most important tea producing regions of the world is located on the steep slopes of the Assam hills in India. The Watchung area generalization is supported, however, by the fact that the most densely populated urban and agricultural areas of the United States are associated with lowlands or gently sloping areas.

It is important to remember that man-land relationships are significant but that they vary among areas and depend upon local conditions.

2.   *Are U.S.G.S. topographic maps and aerial photographs valuable data sources for predicting expansion or contraction of human settlement activities?*

The U.S.G.S. topographic sheet and the aerial photographs used in this activity will verify the initial predictions and support the initial generalizations with a considerable degree of accuracy.   The visual evidence supplied by these data sources indicates the gently sloping or level agricultural land that will provide areas for urban and industrial expansion and routes for new major transportation arteries.

3.   *What additional data would be helpful in making more accurate predictions for the 1956 settlement patterns?*

Considerable local data would have to be assembled to improve the predictions, data such as detailed local bedrock conditions, the potential of land areas for residential and industrial sites based upon accessibility to traffic arteries, local ground water supplies, sewage facilities, utility hook-ups, detailed slope characteristics, zoning regulations, tax policies, local attitudes toward various types of industry, local weather and climatic conditions, etc.   These data can be obtained only by local field work and archival research.

4.   *How can we verify that the relationships between man's activities and the surface of the land change over a period of time?*

To see if man-land relationships change over a period of time, one must study a habitat at two different points in time.   In this activity, participants learned that settlements increased on the Watchung ridges from 1956 to 1963.   New highway construction improved accessibility to the area.   Those who could afford the amenities of a view from the eastern face of the Watchung ridge and the freedom from urban congestion and pollution settled in the ridge areas.   Newcomers were willing to pay for improved access roads and for digging deep wells into the basalt to obtain water or for piped-in water which is costly.

Early rural and urban settlers take advantage of attractive environmental situations that permit settlement at the lowest cost. Subsequent settlers must spend more money to modify a less attractive environment in order to live there.

Similar analogies can be drawn from the advantages and disadvantages of city and suburban living.

5. *How do the exceptions to the relationships discovered above validate or invalidate the generalization that gently sloping to level land encourages agricultural, urban, industrial, and transportational land uses?*

Although it is sound to infer relationships of topography and human settlement patterns, we have learned that relationships such as those expressed in this activity may lead to erroneous generalizations when applied to other geographic areas. Nonetheless, an examination of a world map will support the initial generalization. What might be implicit in this activity is the need to use logical and sequential methods of geographic inquiry before arriving at generalizations about a particular area. Jan O. M. Broek argues that "many disputes about the validity of observed regularities could be eliminated if opponents took careful note of the scale on which the investigation was conducted. . . . The nature of the problem should determine the scale of the inquiry, and the latter should in turn guide the degree of magnitude of the generalization." [2]

6. *Are there interrelationships among the various land uses within this area? What indications do we have of the linkage of this area to adjacent areas?*

Industrial land uses and residential development are closely associated with each other. Industrial land uses will generally be located along major traffic arteries or on roads accessible to these arteries. Topography and bedrock will influence the location of towns, industrial sites, railroads, and highways.

The road network density and the occurrence of multiple lane highways indicate the relative intensity of settlement in the region and indicate linkages.

B. *Analysis of Teaching Strategies*

1. *Are the information and materials presented in this activity sufficient to ensure valid generalizations that can lead to the formulation of hypotheses?*

To complete the Watchung exercise, participants read some background information on topography and soils and then predicted from contour maps the most likely areas for various settlement activities. From the choices available on the maps, was the participant able to discover basic causal relationships between landforms and settlements? If no choices were outlined on the maps, would the task of verifying choices from data on the topographic map and aerial photographs be as easily accomplished? Suppose the participant was required to make generalizations about causal relationships on a topographic map of the United States. What kind of generalizations would he be able to make in this case?

[2] Jan O. M. Broek, *Geography: Its Scope and Spirit* (Columbus, Ohio: Charles E. Merrill Books, 1965), p. 75.

Structuring observable data so as to limit choices makes possible simple correlations of land use and topographic categories. Structuring reduces the complexity of the problem, focuses attention on variables or exceptions, and, in general, saves time that can be devoted to more detailed tasks. Then comparisons and contrasts between land-use categories (such as agriculture, rural settlement, urban settlement, industrial occupance, and transportation) and topographic categories (ridges and gently sloping surfaces) can be made in order to arrive at generalizations. If the land-use forms were held constant, the generalizations sought in this activity might be invalid.

However, the degree of specificity does not interfere with the logical stages of the inquiry process. If we had a different problem, we would simply seek different generalizations and structure the data accordingly. For example, strip mining for coal is associated with outcrops of carboniferous deposits and we could predict that mining settlements would be located in nearby valleys.

2. *How could participants analyze this activity according to stages in the inquiry process?*

Before asking participants to engage in this analysis, it may be well to remember they may have a minimal knowledge of the inquiry process. Therefore, it is suggested that you discuss a model of inquiry with which you are familiar.

The hierarchy of inquiry processes can be placed on the chalkboard and can serve as a basis for a discussion of inquiry. Initially, the examples cited for each level should come from a problem derived from an activity other than the Watchung activity. Then you can ask participants to apply the Watchung inquiry stages to the model.

Although there are several models of inquiry, you might use Gagné's[3] inquiry levels of "learned intellectual capabilities," which have been synthesized by Hills, as shown in Table 3-9.

You can analyze the Watchung activity in terms of the Gagné model in the following way: After acquiring information on bedrock types and the landforms and soil that result from them, the participant makes a simple *observation* on a contour map, *identifies* the basic landform categories on it (ridges and gentle slopes), *defines* these in terms of rock type and soil, *compares and contrasts* them to the settlement or occupance patterns that might occur, and states a *generalization*, such as "rural or urban settlements are more likely to be found on the gently sloping Piedmont than on the steep Watchung ridges."

As a result, he can *predict* that farms will occupy the most extensive level areas, that roads will follow the lowlands and valleys, and that urban and rural settlements and industrial areas will occur along the highways. In addition, he can predict that industrial areas will be associated with urban settlements.

Data presented in the topographic map and aerial photographs are used by the participant to *verify the predictions.* Once the predictions are verified, he can *develop*

[3] Robert M. Gagné, "Process in a Social Science Curriculum," unpublished paper, April 6, 1968, p. 3. As quoted by James L. Hills, "Building and Using Inquiry Models," in Phillip Bacon, ed., *Focus on Geography*, 40th Yearbook (Washington, D.C.: National Council for the Social Studies, 1970), p. 308. Table reprinted by permission of the National Council for the Social Studies.

TABLE 3-9. *Hierarchy of Inquiry Processes*
(After Gagné)

Making Decisions[a]
Testing Hypotheses
Formulating Hypotheses
Developing Models
Verifying Predictions
Predicting
Generalizing
Comparing and Contrasting
Defining
Identifying Categories
Observing

[a] N.B.: Each level subsumes all levels below it and is subsumed under each level above it in the hierarchy of cognitive processes depicted in the chart.

models of where future expansion or contraction of land uses might occur, e.g., urban, industrial, and transportation uses at the expense of agricultural uses, if he accepts the fact that population is increasing in this area.

Now he can *formulate a tentative hypothesis:* Urban, industrial, and transportation land uses will encroach upon agricultural land uses until resistance to this encroachment occurs. The former uses may therefore be forced to occupy marginal lands in order to expand.

To *test the hypothesis,* he examines the 1963 aerial photograph (Figure 3-9) and finds this has, in fact, occurred; his hypothesis is confirmed.

An understanding of the problem (*making decisions* based on examination of theory and empirical evidence) results in the participant's ability to describe and explain the idea that the relationships between man's activities and the surface of the land change over a period of time and also vary from place to place.

3. *Can participants modify this activity into a traditional reception learning activity?*
   What are the advantages or disadvantages of this method in comparison with an
   inquiry method?
   The activity could be changed into a more traditional learning activity by combining the reading material with a sequence of maps and aerial photographs and eliminating the process of predicting locations. This would be one way of showing the relationship of man's activities to his environment during two time periods. A teacher could ask students to explain why the changes occurred.
   Discuss the differences as well as the advantages or disadvantages of this method.

FIGURE 3-7. *Watchung Mountain Area Topographic Map*

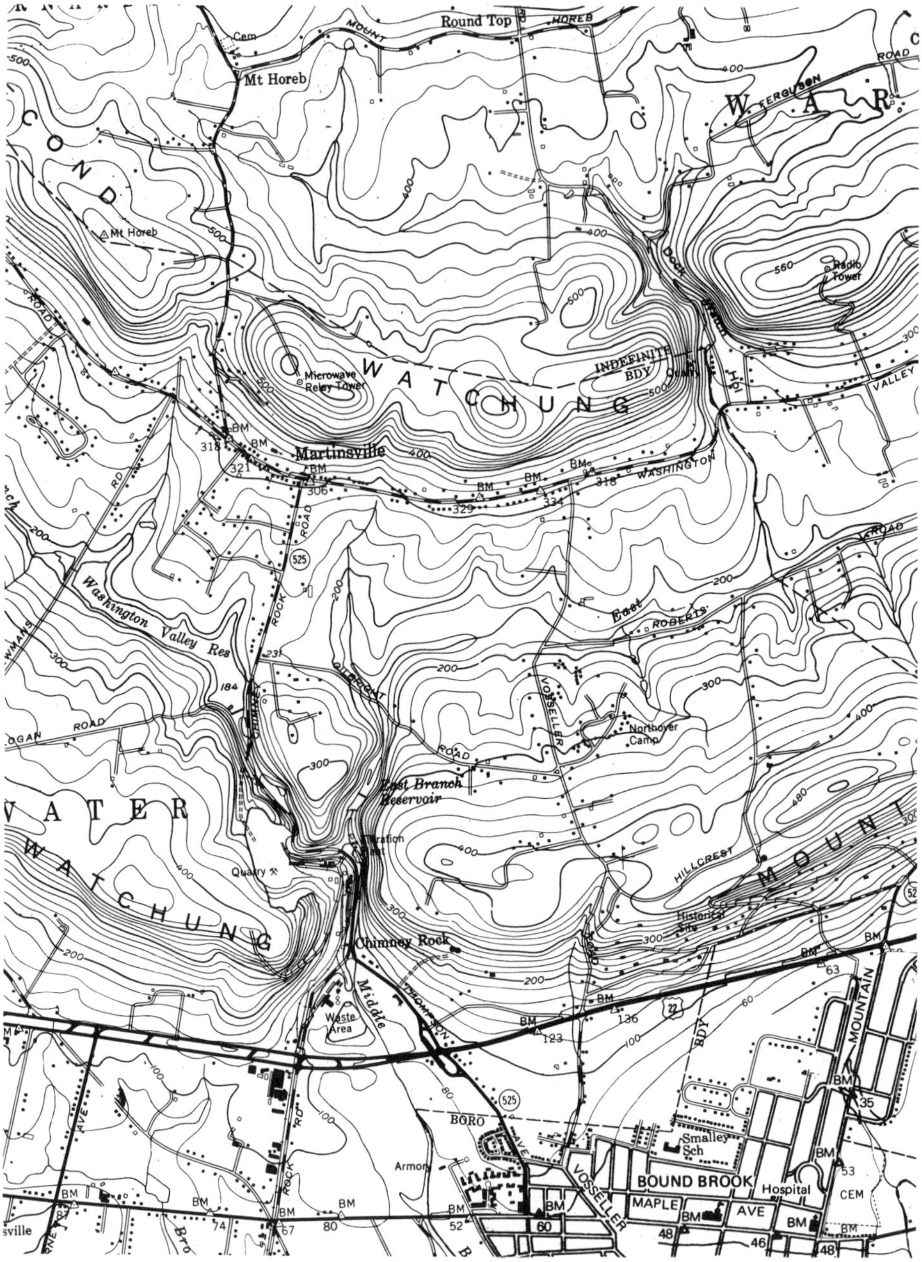

FIGURE 3-8.   *1956 Aerial Photograph of Watchung Mountain Area*

FIGURE 3-9. *1963 Aerial Photograph of Watchung Mountain Area*

V. APPLICATION

The following are suggested applications for further experience and analysis with inquiry models that explicate the hierarchy of inquiry processes.

1. Hills suggests two well-known approaches to the inquiry or discovery method:[4] (a) the Suchman[5] model, where the student asks the questions and the teacher controls the data sources, and (b) the Taba[6] model, where the teacher asks the questions and the students control the data.

   i. Discuss with participants how inquiry is used in other activities in this book.
   ii. Ask participants if they can modify the Watchung activity to produce another model of inquiry.
   iii. Ask participants to prepare a short inquiry activity on their local area.

2. Ask participants to develop a series of questions about a local problem area; for example, rezoning a single family residential area for highrise apartments; allowing boating and swimming in a local water supply reservoir; choosing potential sites for a new shopping center; or siting a sanitary land fill for solid waste disposal. Pay particular attention to the manner in which participants formulate questions. Their success in using an inquiry method should result in better questions which will lead to problem identification and solution by both participants and their students.

3. Ask participants to adapt the Watchung activity for a third-grade class. How will the structure of the sequencing differ from that used in this activity?

4. Ask participants to develop an inquiry activity on predicting future megalopolitan areas of the United States for a twelfth-grade social studies class. Tell them to pay particular attention to differences in scale from the Watchung area and to be aware of how these differences will affect data sources, generalizations, and formulating hypotheses.

5. Ask participants to develop a replication of the Watchung area but to place it in either a subtropical desert or a subarctic area of the United States. What variations in cause-effect relationships would occur? How would the activity be restructured, if at all, in terms of materials, reading assignments, and sequencing?

[4] Hills, "Building and Using Inquiry Models," pp. 306–307.

[5] Richard J. Suchman, *Developing Inquiry* (Chicago: Science Research Associates, 1966).

[6] Hilda Taba, "Implementing Thinking as an Objective in Social Studies," in *Effective Thinking in the Social Studies*, 37th Yearbook (Washington, D.C.: National Council for the Social Studies, 1967), Chapter 2.

ACTIVITY **11**

The Social Context
of Leadership

I. BACKGROUND

This activity can be found in the SRSS episode *Leadership in American Society: A Case Study of Black Leadership.* In the episode, high school students analyze situational factors related to several historical black leaders and to several contemporary black leaders and their organizations. The purpose of this exercise is to help high school students recognize how social situations themselves contribute to the type of leadership behavior necessary to deal with such situations.

II. PARTICIPANT OBJECTIVES

Experience with and analysis of this activity should enable participants:

1. To arrive at a more sophisticated conception of leadership — one that goes beyond common-sense psychological simplicities.
2. To identify social factors that shape performance in the leader's role.
3. To develop skill in analyzing the content of biographies, documents, and other written materials.

4. *To conduct lessons in which high school students can identify and examine the social implications of individual behavior.*
5. *To use teaching techniques that will enable high school students to develop a social perspective on historical and contemporary materials.*
6. *To develop instructional materials that lend themselves to objective, systematic analysis.*[1]

III. CONDUCTING THE ACTIVITY

There is no advance preparation necessary for this activity. Ask participants to read through the introductory material on the method of content analysis (pages 85–87). You can then take a few minutes to discuss with them how the method is to be applied to the readings, so that they can identify the situational components of leadership which affected the roles played by Dr. Martin Luther King, Jr., as head of the Southern Christian Leadership Conference, and Stokely Carmichael of the Student Nonviolent Coordinating Committee.[2]

If any of the participants do not understand the technique of content analysis, work through the example (Figure 3-10) with them. The situation in this example is taken from a questionnaire that high school students complete at the beginning of the episode to help them see the way in which leadership roles can be affected by situations.

[1] Numbers one to three are content objectives; four through six are pedagogical objectives.
[2] The acronym SNCC (which at the time of publication of the episode in 1969 stood for Student Nonviolent Coordinating Committee) later came to stand for Student National Coordinating Committee.

FIGURE 3-10. *[High School] Student Leadership Questionnaire*[a]

Answer each of the following questions by writing in the names of members of your class who you think would do a good job in each situation. In the space numbered (1), write the name of the person you think would be the *very best*. In the space numbered (2), write the name of the person who would be *next best*. In the space numbered (3), write the name of your *third choice*.

Do not read the questions until the teacher tells you. Answer each question in order. Do not jump ahead. You may write in the names of any of your classmates or your own name.

1. Suppose your school has a new principal who is quite strict. During the school year a number of student privileges are taken away and a few students are expelled

[a] From Student Handout 1, in Instructor's Guide for *Leadership in American Society: A Case Study of Black Leadership* (Boston: Allyn and Bacon, 1969). Copyright © 1969 American Sociological Association. Reprinted by permission.

for breaking minor rules. Finally, the principal announces that no modern dancing, mini-skirts, or long-haired males will be tolerated at the annual homecoming dance, and that the dance will end one hour earlier than usual. Your class decides to form a committee to meet with the principal. The students want the principal to be more lenient, less strict. Which student would do the best job in talking with the principal?

(1) _____

(2) _____

(3) _____

FIGURE 3-11. *Completed Situational Components of Leadership Diagram (for Example)* [a]

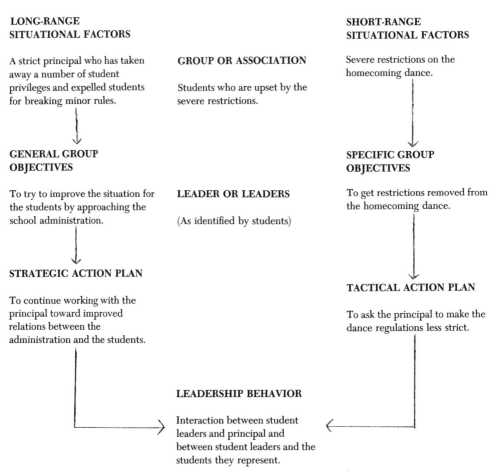

**LONG-RANGE
SITUATIONAL FACTORS**

A strict principal who has taken away a number of student privileges and expelled students for breaking minor rules.

GROUP OR ASSOCIATION

Students who are upset by the severe restrictions.

**SHORT-RANGE
SITUATIONAL FACTORS**

Severe restrictions on the homecoming dance.

**GENERAL GROUP
OBJECTIVES**

To try to improve the situation for the students by approaching the school administration.

LEADER OR LEADERS

(As identified by students)

**SPECIFIC GROUP
OBJECTIVES**

To get restrictions removed from the homecoming dance.

STRATEGIC ACTION PLAN

To continue working with the principal toward improved relations between the administration and the students.

TACTICAL ACTION PLAN

To ask the principal to make the dance regulations less strict.

LEADERSHIP BEHAVIOR

Interaction between student leaders and principal and between student leaders and the students they represent.

Read the situation and then have participants supply the information to complete the "Situational Components of Leadership Diagram" (Figure 2-36, page 86). You can place the diagram on the chalkboard and fill it in as participants make suggestions. Your class should be able to develop a diagram something like the one shown in Figure 3-11.

After you feel that participants understand the method of content analysis, ask them to read the biographical material about Martin Luther King, Jr., and Stokely Carmichael (pages 87–94).

For the demonstration, have the participants meet in groups of three or four to complete Figure 2-36. Assign the readings to different groups and ask that each group reach a consensus on how to complete the diagram. This part of the activity should take no more than ten or fifteen minutes. When the groups have finished, you can either have spokesmen report on their group's findings or discuss the activity with the class as a whole.

The statements about the readings (Figure 3-12) are from the Instructor's Guide to the SRSS episode. They are very terse summaries of the main points introduced in the readings. It is quite likely that at least some of your participants will have additional information about the men and the organizations and will thus view the situational components from a broader framework and in a deeper historical context than high school students are able to do.

As you lead the discussion, see if responses come close to (or are more sophisticated than) the episode's summaries.

A problem may arise in analyzing the readings; that is, the participants may become immersed in the content matter — the lives and times of the civil rights leaders — and lose sight of the concept of leadership. You may have to remind them, if the discussion wanders too far afield, that the same problem can arise in teaching the SRSS episode in their own high school classes. It may become necessary to limit discussion and keep things focused on the sociological perspective of leadership.

IV. REFLECTIONS ON THE LEARNING AND TEACHING

A. *Analysis of Learning Outcomes*

By analyzing the cases of King and Carmichael, participants should gain a fuller understanding of the meaning of leadership and its social definition. Yet it is worthwhile to reflect further on the activity, encouraging participants to exchange ideas on the implications of the experience. You can do this by raising and pursuing various questions. What does it mean to say that a man is a leader? What social influences affect performance in the leadership role? What skills have been learned in analyzing documentary materials?

What do we mean when we say that a person is a leader? Is the leader-follower relationship a one-way street? The common-sense answer is that the leader is a person who tells others what to do. It is a unilateral relationship. The leader controls others' responses. And the higher one goes in the power structure, the freer this exercise of unilateral power.

FIGURE 3-12.

Martin Luther King, Jr.[a]

Group or Association: The Montgomery Improvement Association (MIA); later the SCLC.

Long-range Situational Factors: Deepening mood of despair and disillusionment that gripped American blacks after World War II, and the desire to bring about change through new forms of collective action.

Short-range Situational Factors: An aroused black citizenry who had become impatient over continuing injustices and who were determined to move rapidly to full citizenship.

General Group Objectives: To gain for blacks racial justice and the full benefits of citizenship through the use of nonviolent protest demonstrations.

Specific Group Objectives: To end racial discrimination and segregation (in the South) on buses, in public restaurants and other facilities, etc. To obtain more courteous treatment of and better employment opportunities for blacks. To secure the passage of the Civil Rights Act of 1964. To obtain open housing in northern cities.

Strategic Action Plan: Maintaining an effective bus boycott (Montgomery) until segregation on the buses was ended. Organizing the black community for collective action against discrimination and segregation.

Tactical Action Plan: Nonviolent protest demonstrations — mass meetings, boycotts, marches, sit-ins, etc. Legal-judiciary measures. Speeches and writings.

Leadership Behavior: Coordinated and directed the Montgomery bus boycott (1955–56), which served as a model for mass demonstrations. Organized the SCLC (1957) to coordinate and execute attacks on segregation. Led demonstrations in Birmingham (Ala.), Atlanta (Ga.), St. Augustine (Fla.), led the March on Washington (1963), etc. A gifted writer and a forceful, moving speaker, he stimulated public opinion. By leading the protest demonstrations and responding nonviolently to physical attacks, he showed great courage and dignity and won national respect.

Stokely Carmichael

Group or Association: Young people, black and white, drawn from the ranks of middle-class students and the poor (with emphasis on black leadership); SNCC.

Long-range Situational Factors: Deepening mood of despair and disillusionment that gripped American blacks after World War II, and the desire to bring about change through new forms of collective action.

Short-range Situational Factors: Brutal force used on civil rights workers and the slow pace of the federal government.

General Group Objectives: To build forms of black economic and political power.

Specific Group Objectives: To put black candidates in office; to encourage blacks to control the educational and economic organizations within the ghettoes.

Strategic Action Plan: Militant direct action; voter registration; building local leadership and strongly emphasizing Black Power.

Tactical Action Plan: Individual programs, demonstrations, etc.

Leadership Behavior: Taking part in demonstrations and writing the ideology of Black Power.

[a] From Instructor's Guide for *Leadership in American Society: A Case Study of Black Leadership* (Boston: Allyn and Bacon, 1969). Copyright © 1969 American Sociological Association. Reprinted by permission.

If this is so, however, how did it happen that President Richard Nixon's nominations to the Supreme Court in 1971 — Judges Haynsworth and Carswell — did not carry the day? What did Tolstoy mean when he said in *War and Peace* that a king was history's slave? Or what did Napoleon's statement mean: "I am their leader, therefore I must follow them"?

Reflecting on such questions, participants should be less easily persuaded of the common-sense notion that the higher in the scale of power one is, the greater his independence of action in controlling others.

Some years ago, the German sociologist Georg Simmel suggested that we should consider the influence of slave over master. What did he mean? Is not the master the leader, infinitely empowered to control the slave's destiny? But a condition of effective performance is the master's ability to maintain the slave in a state of vigorous health. This is compelled by the slave-master relationship. Beyond this, brutal and inconsiderate treatment must elicit slowdowns and grudging, even rebellious, behavior that cannot fail to influence — if not to dictate — the master's responses. Beyond this, still, the relationship itself acts to define the master's role. Brutality is brutalizing — for master as well as for slave. The war in Vietnam provided conditions making for a kind of leadership that could exterminate — the word was "waste" — defenseless women, children, and aged at Mylai. In the process, the conquerors were not untouched by the vanquished. To treat other human beings as though they are expendable things is to strip the "leader" of human attributes.

If the leader is influenced (even controlled) by the led, he is also affected by the broad social context in which he exercises his leadership. President Nixon would be a thumping failure in the U.S.S.R., and Mahatma Gandhi would not have lasted long as leader of the Third Reich. Thus, participants in this activity will come to recognize that Donne's often-quoted statement ("No man is an island, entire of itself") applies to the mighty as well as to the meek. Followers are not impotent ciphers manipulated by utterly self-determining leaders. Leadership refers to a role that is socially created and socially limited.

The sociological perspective on leadership developed in the episode can be summarized as follows:

1. Leadership is the ability or power to influence the actions of followers.
2. There are three different kinds of power: (a) authority, (b) persuasion, and (c) coercion.
3. One person can exercise the three kinds of power, e.g., the student-body president.
4. There are both formal and informal leaders.
5. In order to study leadership, it is necessary to have some objective way to identify leaders.
6. The two general techniques of identifying leaders are self-reporting and observation. Each of these techniques has different methods. The interview (oral) or questionnaire (written) can be used in the self-reporting technique, which is the technique used in the *reputational method*. In observing leadership behavior, the investigator either does his own observing

or relies on others. He can either hide his identity or make himself known, depending on how the group might react to his presence.

7. There is a popularly held belief that leaders have special personality traits. However, research using scientific criteria has not been very successful in identifying personality traits associated with leadership in a wide variety of situations.

8. The sociologist focuses on the group and social situations that affect leadership. Those who look at leadership in this way are sometimes said to have a "sociological perspective."

9. Groups consist of people who depend on one another as they work toward some *common* goal.

10. The actions of leaders contribute to the fulfillment of the groups' functions.

11. Leadership may be performed by one or shared by many members of a group.

12. Different kinds of groups have different kinds of leaders.

13. The leadership of a group depends on the social situation in which the group is located.

14. When a social situation changes, leadership often changes.

15. To understand leadership it is necessary to know about the social situation, the group, and the activities of chosen leaders.[3]

A second learning outcome is achieved if participants can answer the question: *What are the social factors that shape performance in the leader's role?* There are many ways of seeking answers to this question. We could use a checklist of socially defined biological traits, asking how sex, age, or race condition leadership. (Being young, black, and male were doubtless preconditions for Stokely Carmichael's performance as leader.) Or we could run through a roster of social institutions, asking in what ways religion, family background, or political and economic influences play a part in shaping leadership. (In selecting political candidates, the right mix of institutional identities becomes important.) In this activity, we have used another framework for analysis: social situational factors (remote and immediate), group objectives (general and specific), and means of achieving them (general strategy and specific tactics).

This framework makes sense if we think of a group (a micro-system) as embedded in a larger organization (macro-system). This larger social system sets certain conditions, certain boundaries for the groups embedded in it. For example, what goes on within a classroom depends in some measure on the situation created by the whole school of which it is a part. And the operations of the school are affected, in turn, by the community situation in which it is set. Thus there are circles within circles. The remoter circles exercise broader, long-range influences. Those closer at hand create the short-range situational factors.

Groups in the civil rights movement are subject to both sets of influences. Within this context, they articulate their general and specific goals.

They also work out means for achieving these goals: on the one hand, general strategies; on the other hand, tactics deemed appropriate for achieving specific ends. It is in this context of remote and immediate influences, general and specific goals, strategic and tactical means, that the leadership role is defined.

[3] From the Instructor's Guide for the SRSS episode *Leadership in American Society: A Case Study of Black Leadership* (Boston: Allyn and Bacon, 1969). Copyright © 1969 American Sociological Association. Reprinted by permission.

Obviously a third desired learning outcome of this activity, *the development of skill in analyzing documentary material,* cannot be picked up by exploring only two sets of data. But one learning essential to that skill should emerge from this experience; that is, the recognition of the need for devising an intelligible framework for analysis that will enable the investigator to cull wheat from chaff as he attacks the data with a set of specific questions in mind. One might hope, also, that participants will think about and be able to test alternative frames for analysis.

B.   *Analysis of Teaching Strategies*

To determine how well participants achieved the pedagogic objectives of this activity, you might pose a few questions.

How can the social implications of individual behavior be explored in the classroom? Content analysis is obviously one technique that participants could use in their classrooms to help high school students improve their ability to view human behavior in a social context. The instructional strategy suggested for the content analysis is one of guided inquiry. The data to be studied are extracted from limited sources and, although there is room for some variation in interpreting relevant data, the investigation should be structured so that focus on the social determination of behavior will be maintained.

What can research tools like content analysis contribute to social studies inquiry? Content analysis, a form of secondary observation, is a research method for describing the content of historical, literary, or scientific materials in an objective, systematic, and accurate way. Like many other methods of research, it is not a perfect tool, but it does help to minimize researcher bias and to standardize procedures of analysis. If this research method is to be applied successfully, the following features must be incorporated:

1. *A theoretical orientation for examining the materials.*
2. *A system of categories for classifying the materials that are examined.*
3. *A systematic way of sampling relevant materials.*[4]

To consider specific teaching techniques, you might ask participants: *How can attention to the social dimensions of behavior be maintained?* The device of the diagram is useful in this regard, but the essential factor in keeping attention focused upon the matter at hand is the skill of the teacher in asking questions. In a discussion such as this, a teacher can use leading questions, probe student responses, and so forth, to clarify factual information. But if the teacher also wants to keep student interest and involvement at high levels, then it is necessary to employ students' ideas in phrasing questions, to maintain an open, receptive posture, and to stimulate participation by passing students' questions

---

[4] From the Instructor's Guide for *Leadership in American Society: A Case Study of Black Leadership* (Boston: Allyn and Bacon, 1969), p. 14.

on to other students for consideration or by asking for reactions to the contributions of other students.

V. APPLICATION

You may find the following suggestions useful in helping participants extend the concepts and teaching strategies featured in this activity to other instructional situations.

How can the technique of content analysis be used in different kinds of social studies investigations? Devices such as the diagram used in this activity can be employed to analyze other kinds of written material. In addition to searching for answers to a set of possible questions, content analysis can be carried out by using frequency counts of those indicator words that reveal an author's views or the intensity of bias.[5]

Participants might also develop a teaching unit or units using content analysis to study social situations described in literature, television programs, or films.

The system of analyzing leadership situations can be applied to new and emerging leaders in the black civil rights movement or in other situations.

[5] For additional information on content analysis, see: Bernard Berelson, *Content Analysis in Communicative Research* (New York: The Free Press of Glencoe, 1952); Dorwin Cartwright, "Analysis of Qualitative Material," in L. Festinger and D. Katz, *Research Methods in the Behavioral Sciences* (New York: Dryden Press, 1953), pp. 421–47; Aaron V. Cicourel, *Method and Measurement in Sociology* (New York: The Free Press of Glencoe, 1964); and Claire Selltiz, et al., *Research Methods in Social Relations* (Henry Holt and Co., 1960).

ACTIVITY 12

The Game of Farming

I. BACKGROUND

"The Game of Farming" is an adapted version of a classroom activity found in "Manufacturing and Agriculture," Unit 2 of the High School Geography Project course *Geography in an Urban Age*. Before beginning this activity, high school students have considered hunger as a world problem and have explored the adequacy of agricultural resources to meet the problem. They have also dealt with situations of individual farmers in different parts of the United States, Poland, and Central America.

II. PARTICIPANT OBJECTIVES

Experience with and analysis of this activity should enable participants:

1. To analyze the difficulties a farmer has in controlling factors which influence the production and market value of farm produce, and to analyze the relative importance of these factors in the 1880's and 1920's.
2. To discuss the possible relationships between the uncertainty of American farming and the need for federal legislation to regulate farm prices.
3. To view farmers as people who make resource allocation decisions.
4. *To use an educational game effectively.*

5. *To discuss the advantages and disadvantages of educational games.*
6. *To evaluate an educational game in terms of certain criteria.*
7. *To develop their own educational games.*[1]

III. CONDUCTING THE ACTIVITY

"The Game of Farming" relies upon decision-making and competition to simulate farming conditions in western Kansas as they existed at two different time periods. Pairs of participants role play farmers. Each pair must decide which allocation of limited financial resources will result in the most effective crop production on their farm. They make decisions for the year 1880, receive outcome information that permits calculation of their financial resources at the end of the year, repeat the process for 1881, and subsequently follow the same procedure for 1920 and 1921.

Begin the activity by telling participants that they will play a game in which they will role play farmers and make decisions about what crops to produce on their farms. Pair the participants and ask them to read pages 95–96 and to follow the instructions for the game for 1880. You may wish to review these pages and answer any questions that arise.

When the participants have made their allocations for 1880, each pair is ready to find out how successful its operation has been. Read the following outcome for 1880:

Most of the area receives ample rainfall in 1880. Crop diseases and insects inflict serious damage only on corn and oats. Both crop and livestock prices are good. The following multipliers reflect these conditions:

	Multiplier
Wheat	5
Oats	1
Barley	2
Rye	2
Corn	1
Dairy cattle	2
Beef cattle	1.5
Sheep	1.5
Hogs	2

Feel free to modify the multipliers somewhat; for example, you could assign four to wheat and three to sheep. It is important only to keep alterations consistent with the preliminary statement describing the overall situation. You can modify the multipliers for each year the game is played if you wish.

After the participants have totaled their outcomes for the year 1880, you may wish

[1] Numbers one to three are content objectives; four through seven are pedagogical objectives.

to carry on a brief discussion of the results each pair obtained. However, players should move on quickly to their allocation decisions for 1881. After they have made their decisions, read the outcomes for 1881 that follow. (Again, changes in multipliers may be made as long as they are consistent with the statement that precedes them.)

In 1881, most areas in the county experience the lowest rainfall ever recorded. Corn is a near total loss. Winter-sown crops are not severely damaged by the drought. Pastures are damaged in late summer but sustain cattle through the period of low market prices. Thus, we have the following multipliers:

	Multiplier
Wheat	2
Oats	0
Barley	2
Rye	0.5
Corn	0
Dairy cattle	1.5
Beef cattle	1
Sheep	1
Hogs	1

After a brief discussion of the results obtained for 1881, tell participants to read page 102 which describes changes that took place between the 1880's and the 1920's and which provides instructions for playing the game for 1920. They should then fill out the 1920 allocation sheet (Figure 2-40). When this has been done, read the following outcome information for 1920:

The price of wheat remained at the 1919 level, while the prices for other crops went down in 1920. Only sugar beets experienced a substantial price increase. Prices for hogs, beef cattle, and sheep showed a sizable decline but dairy prices increased significantly. Growing conditions were good and yields were generally high. An epidemic of hog cholera was ruinous to some farmers, and hail caused extensive damage to certain fields of small grain crops.

	Multiplier
Unirrigated crops	
Wheat	3
Barley	1
Sorghum	2
Irrigated crops	
Corn	2
Sugar beets	4
Alfalfa	2
Livestock	
Dairy cattle	4
Beef cattle	2
Sheep	2
Hogs	1

After an exchange of results for 1920, the participants should proceed to the 1921 allocation decisions. The 1921 outcome information follows:

Rainfall was average for Settler County in 1921 and most crop yields were above average. Although wheat was badly hurt by winter freezing, the decline of farm prices was of greater importance to Settler County farmers. For example, wheat prices fell to less than $1.00 per bushel, and prices for other crops were less than half the 1920 prices. Only prices for dairy products held at relatively high levels. Sheep prices were the lowest since 1908, and beef cattle prices were down 50 percent.

Multiplier

Unirrigated crops
   Wheat 0
   Barley 1
   Sorghum 1
Irrigated crops
   Corn 0.5
   Sugar beets 1.5
   Alfalfa 0
Livestock
   Dairy cattle 2
   Beef cattle 1
   Sheep 1
   Hogs 1

The effectiveness of most educational games in attaining conceptual objectives depends upon a post-game analysis or processing session. Information is available in the following section for assisting participants in analyzing the learning outcomes of "The Game of Farming."

IV.   REFLECTIONS ON THE LEARNING AND TEACHING

Achievement of many of the participant objectives listed earlier depends upon both an experience with the game and an analysis following the game. The following analysis is divided into two parts: one considers the learning outcomes and the other explores the teaching strategies implicit in the activity.

A.   Analysis of Learning Outcomes

Although it is impossible to discuss all that may have been learned from the experience, participants may suggest such things as an increased understanding of the risks involved in farming and the factors influencing farm production, a new feeling about farmers, and an awareness of some problems inherent in decision-making. Little attention needs to be given to factual information participants may have learned, such as the price of wheat in 1915 or the fact that western Kansas tends to have marginal precipitation for grain farming.

More pointed questions may be needed to bring out the most significant learning outcomes. The four questions that follow should help elicit these learnings:

1. *What was the major problem farmers in western Kansas faced in the early 1880's?*

Nature was neither very predictable nor very kind to farmers in this part of the United States at that time. Plant diseases, insect pests, and lack of rainfall served to destroy crops and reduce farm production. Such occurrences might lead one to conclude, erroneously, that a form of environmental determinism was in operation.

You can discuss with participants how the problem of natural disasters diminished in importance over time. The use of irrigation facilities during the 1920's put a different perspective on the man-land relationship. Kansas farmers now had the technological capability to control the most devastating of natural disasters, i.e., drought. Farmers of the 1920's also had new farm machinery available to them. If mention is made of insecticides, hybrid seed strains, and new fertilizers, it becomes clear that the influence of natural elements varies in terms of the science and technology available to control them.

2. *What was the major problem confronted by western Kansas farmers in the early 1920's?*

Although the price factor was given some attention in the 1880's section of the game, it becomes the center of attention during the 1920's. Demand for American produce during World War I and immediately thereafter was quite high. However, with European farms at a high production level after the war, a surplus of farm produce decreased prices. The inability of the individual farmer to control surplus production in order to ensure fair prices for agricultural produce should be brought out. This idea provides a basis for discussing price as a function of supply and demand in a free market and the inclination of producers to do whatever possible to exert some control over market mechanisms. The desire for control may help explain the trend toward large business enterprises and farm organizations in the American economy. Farmers have been influenced to form such organizations and to enter the political arena in order to protect their interests.

3. *How would participants describe the decision-making process they experienced in playing the role of farmer?*

Participants might first mention that decision-making was difficult for 1880 because of the lack of information on which to base their allocations. The outcome information provided at the conclusion of that year made the decisions somewhat easier for 1881 since they now possessed more knowledge of conditions in western Kansas. The more detailed information of the situation for the 1920's and the price performance graphs for livestock made it possible to approach the decisions of the 1920's with a greater likelihood of predicting outcomes. Bring out the fact that decisions are made in terms of anticipated outcomes but that these outcomes are not predictable with a great degree of certainty. Participants may mention that one influence on the decision-making process was the game restriction that two people had to agree on a decision. One or both individuals may have found it necessary to modify their original suggestions in order to reach agreement.

4. *Are changes of attitude with respect to farmers likely to result from playing "The Game of Farming"?*

Participants may become more aware of the element of risk in the lives of farmers and that farmers make complicated decisions. Since the game focuses on risks and decision-making as components of farm life, it may serve to modify the stereotype that farming is primarily a life of physical labor and is a generally dreary existence.

B. Analysis of Teaching Strategies

1. *What important factors are involved in using an educational game effectively?*

Three factors are of importance in educational games: relevance, management, and processing.

Relevance refers to the increased effectiveness obtained when an educational game is used in the context of a course of study. The success of a game in achieving conceptual objectives depends on its relevance to the topic of study or to the unit in which it is used. It is possible, of course, to use educational games in the same way that some teachers use films. That is, they are used when available, without reference to the current subject of study. However, to be truly effective, an educational game should be used in context so that important concepts can be illustrated. Without proper attention to the factor of relevance, games will not only lose their potential value as an instructional technique for helping students to develop concepts, but they may be viewed by students and others interested in education as simply a diversionary strategy that wastes time. Such views will result in decreased rather than increased student interest in games.

Proper *management* is also needed if an educational game is to be used effectively. Management requires careful advanced planning. A teacher must understand the sequence of steps necessary to carry out the game and must have the proper game elements on hand at the time they are needed. For example, the rules may require rearrangement of room furniture so that the game can proceed smoothly. Another aspect of management is making sure that players clearly understand the rules of the game before beginning to play. There are always some players who are ready to begin before others are ready, but the overall effectiveness of the game requires a teacher to be very sensitive to those who may not have grasped some element of the rules or some understanding of the context of the game.

After the game has been played, it is important to set aside enough time to analyze what has been learned. This *processing* session is sometimes called "debriefing." Without attention to ideas, students may fail to realize that they have learned principles of social science that can be generalized. In addition, debriefing reinforces concepts and should facilitate retention. Equally important in the processing session is the opportunity to bring out other types of learning, such as attitudes that may have changed or skills that may have been developed from participating in the game. Emphasis on decision-making and group process skills at the conclusion of the game should help students improve in subsequent decision-making and group work.

2. *What are the major advantages and disadvantages of educational games?*

The major advantage of educational games is their ability to involve students directly in the learning process. Although a need for variety provides partial justification for educational games, use in school classrooms simply for variety's sake minimizes their value in serving both cognitive and affective objectives. In the long run, educational games find justification in their contribution to a more meaningful and lasting learning of social science principles. Active involvement in manipulating data is more likely to help students view the principles of social science from a functional standpoint than is learning by traditional rote procedures. Active student involvement often has a third outcome that should not be ignored, i.e., students will develop more positive attitudes toward school. Such positive attitudes may influence students to continue study in the social sciences.

The most obvious disadvantage of educational games is the extensive expenditure of class time they require. Teachers who are conscientious about communicating a great many ideas and a wide variety of information often are reluctant to devote extended periods of class time to educational games. More information and ideas can be presented in the same amount of time through conventional teaching procedures than through the use of educational games. By trying one or two games and assessing the results, teachers can find out for themselves whether the advantages outweigh the disadvantages.

3. *What things should one look for when determining the value of an educational game?*

Many educational games are now available commercially and more will be appearing in the future. To assess the effectiveness for the classroom of a particular game, the following questions should be considered:

a. Does the game deal with ideas that are relevant to your educational objectives?
b. Are the conditions that must be established before beginning play too complicated? Some games require players to master a considerable degree of background information, usually by reading. The addition of elaborate rules to such information provides an ineffective basis for beginning an educational game.
c. Are the chance factors so paramount that players fail to become involved in making the decision themselves or in working cooperatively with other students? In some games, the decisions that are made and the outcomes of the decisions are indicated by means of very arbitrary actions, such as the roll of dice. Other games are set up in ways that permit some degree of player decision-making. If improved decision-making is an educational objective, then clearly this is an important criterion in evaluating the potential effectiveness of a game. When all facets of a game are completely determined by chance, one resultant learning may be that knowledge is virtually useless in making decisions. This clearly would be an undesirable attitude for schools to generate.

d. Is the game likely to foster an undesirable degree of competitiveness? Since virtually all games derive their motivation from competition, it is important to look at the degree of competitition involved and to examine the possibility of obtaining undesirable results. For teachers who wish to foster cooperative attitudes, the excessive competitiveness of some games may preclude their use. Closely related to competitiveness is the possibility that animosity will develop among students. In other words, the motivational feature of an educational game can be so overpowering that for some students healthy competition may be replaced by open hostility.

4. *How can one develop an educational game like this one?*
   The first thing to be considered in developing an educational game is stating clearly the problem or types of problems players will face. In the case of "The Game of Farming," the problem is always the same. Each player must allocate his limited resources among several possible crops and livestock. He is given information about his resources at the beginning of the game, i.e., he has $1,500 to start his farm. To the extent that one round of decisions adds to or subtracts from these resources, he has greater or fewer resources to begin the second round of play.

   The player's perspective is provided by indicating the time and place at which the play commences. Any other constraints on his play are indicated via this perspective also. For "The Game of Farming," western Kansas is identified as the location, and the 1880's and the 1920's as the time periods.

   Another major aspect of developing a game is the creation of rules for expending resources. In "The Game of Farming," an attempt was made to make these rules correspond fairly closely to reality. Thus the cost of producing forty acres of corn was placed at $200 and the cost of producing forty acres of other produce or livestock at $100. At the same time, it was indicated that hogs require no acreage of their own. Likewise, provision was made for renting additional land.

   One difficulty with the creation of rules that are close to reality is that the game rules will become too detailed and too complex. Note that in the interests of simplifying this game, the following "unreal" rules were used: $100 units are used exclusively; cattle are assumed not to require additional investment; and there is no provision for saving part of one's resources.

   Another critical element of a game is the outcome information — the determination of gain or loss for the players. In "The Game of Farming," a technique called a "multiplier" was used to balance the results. Thus a multiplier of three changes a $300 investment into a $900 outcome. Likewise, a multiplier of zero changes a $200 investment into an outcome of nothing. It should be noted that this or any other way of determining outcomes must yield information that is kept from the player until after the critical time of decision.

   Thus five elements are built into a game like "The Game of Farming." They are the player's problem, the player's resources, the player's perspective, rules for expending resources, and an outcome determinant. Once these have been prepared, each round of the game can be repeated as often as desired and the game experience can be concluded with a processing session.

The player's problem, perspective, and resources are fairly simple for "The Game of Farming," primarily because all players are the same. If a game is constructed for more than one type of player, it is necessary to develop the appropriate problem perspective and resources for each. The fact that two participants work together as one player simply adds a social element to the game. It is possible to have as many as three or four people who must reach consensus on the decisions that must be made by the player.

V. APPLICATION

1. There are three conceptual themes highlighted in "The Game of Farming": man-land relationships, supply and demand, and interaction of economic interests with political action. You might ask participants to select a social studies topic other than farming and use it to exemplify one of these concepts. For example, a participant might choose a familiar historical period and indicate the information he would need to develop one or more of these concepts. Or he might decide on a culture region for a regional geography class or an environmental pollution issue for a problems of democracy class to study the concepts.

2. Ask participants to evaluate one of the following educational games, using the criteria of relevance, elaborateness of rules, treatment of chance factors, and treatment of competitiveness:

> Ghetto
> Dangerous Parallel
> Black and White
> Monopoly

3. Have participants develop an educational game that is based on familiar subject matter and concepts. They will need to formulate player problems, player resources, player perspectives, rules of the game, and provision for determining outcomes. They should also include questions to be used in processing the game.

4. Participants might compare the primary characteristics of games with the main features of simulations by using "The Game of Farming" and one of the simulations developed in this book.

PART IV

Evaluation

Evaluating Student Achievement and Course Effectiveness

EVALUATION AND OBJECTIVES

The instructor of this course faces the same two evaluation problems that the high school social studies teacher faces: grading his students and judging the effectiveness of his teaching methods and his course materials. To deal with the first problem, a teacher needs information about individuals. To work with the second, he needs information about groups. Both problems will be considered in this chapter.

The point of departure for this discussion of evaluation will be the objectives listed for the activities in Part Three of this book. Questions about the way objectives are formulated are related to the issue of behavioral objectives. We will also investigate the need to evaluate affective as well as cognitive objectives. It should become clear that objectives such as the ones included in this book are similar to objectives pursued in high school social studies classes.

A major emphasis of this chapter is on ways of obtaining information in order to make evaluation judgments about students and courses. Three techniques of primary importance in obtaining data are explored: standard multiple-choice and essay questions to measure cognitive abilities; questionnaires and scaling instruments to study opinions, beliefs, and attitudes; and checklists to obtain information about performance objectives. One needs to use a variety of data sources in order to make effective evaluation decisions.

INDIVIDUAL EVALUATION:
THE PROBLEM OF GRADING

Evaluation is often equated with the testing that is done for the purpose of grading. Grading is a process that makes distinctions among students with regard to attainment of course objectives and other matters. It is a difficult task and one that often is not done well. To be able to grade effectively, a teacher should be fully cognizant of the issues underlying the process of making distinctions among students.

In their many years of schooling, participants have had numerous experiences with the erratic process of being graded. They probably feel that each of their teachers followed a unique procedure in determining grades. They may feel uncertain about the criteria used in making the judgments. Some of their teachers may have emphasized test scores while others felt that "effort" and "class involvement" were most important. Even when just test scores were used, a given score meant a "B" to one teacher and a "C" to another, an indication that teachers use different standards in assessing the quality of student performance. A third difference among teachers that participants may have experienced concerns decisions about who will participate in the grading process. Some teachers do all the grading themselves, whereas others involve their students.

If the participants of this course were to be asked what criteria they think should be used to determine *their* grades, their responses would likely include "attainment of the course objectives." Most of the objectives listed for the HSGP and SRSS activities in this book are related to one of three more general objectives:

1. The ability to understand and use certain concepts, such as social stratification and region.
2. The ability to conduct or develop certain types of teaching activities, such as simulations.
3. The desire to use certain types of instructional materials and procedures in a teaching situation.

Attainment of one or more of these objectives would be a legitimate basis for assigning grades in this course. The first objective focuses on understanding and applying ideas. High school social studies courses usually have a number of similar cognitive objectives. The second objective parallels the skill objectives in secondary school social studies classes, while the third objective is an affective or attitudinal objective that also has counterparts in high school geography or sociology courses. The reduction of specific objectives to these three general types and the following discussion of the types should help participants become alert to the kinds of objectives that serve as criteria for grading.

Of the three general objectives listed above, it is easiest to measure attainment of the first. It often happens that a particular objective becomes *the* criterion for grading simply because of its ease of measurement. Thus, participants are probably most familiar with the testing procedures that tap evidence of factual knowledge. Many of them may have had unhappy experiences with true-false, matching, and "fill in the blank" questions that require primarily the recall of miscellaneous information. The measurement of understanding is more difficult. However, most participants are familiar with multiple-choice questions and essay questions that measure understanding of a process or principle.

It is considerably more difficult to measure attainment of the skills suggested by the second objective cited above. Most teachers are not able to find the time and circumstances for students to demonstrate these abilities. It is even more difficult to evaluate the demonstration since a complex set of behaviors is called for.

When the third general objective is used as a basis for grading, a different kind of problem occurs. Although attitudinal objectives are surely both significant and legitimate, grading on the basis of how well such objectives are achieved encourages deception. Students are likely to fake the responses they think are expected. It is extremely difficult to measure attitudes reliably when students realize they will be punished or rewarded on the basis of their responses.

As a result of the difficulties indicated, the more easily measured objectives, those dealing with knowledge and understanding, are most likely to be used when deciding grades for students. As a result, some of our most important educational objectives, those of a performance or attitudinal nature, are not used as criteria for determining grades. When we cannot tell whether students have attained an objective, it is fairly certain that we will not use this objective as a basis for grading judgments. It is this sort of situation that turns teachers toward simpler and more conventionally measurable objectives.

In addition to using course objectives as criteria for grading, a teacher may unconsciously use attitudinal criteria. One attitude that may influence grading is the willingness of the student to do whatever the teacher asks of him. Most grading systems based on contracts between teacher and students, however desirable in other terms, rely on student willingness to do designated tasks, such as coming to class, paying attention, and completing homework. In such cases, teachers reward the effort shown by students by appropriate grading without being aware that they are using attitudinal criteria.

A more hidden affective consideration is the evaluator's attitude toward his student. When a teacher knows who the writer of an essay question is, he sometimes adjusts the grade upward or downward in terms of his expectations for that particular student. Teacher bias may become even more evident when he evaluates students in such performances as oral reports or the carrying out of simulation activities. Like other people, teachers tend to have positive feelings toward some personalities and negative feelings toward others. Unless carefully watched, such tendencies can have a significant bearing on the grading process.

There is no question that the priority given to grading in American education has some negative consequences for student learning. The desire to differentiate students from one another for grading purposes leads many teachers to emphasize esoteric details rather than to concentrate on the major ideas and skills they wish to communicate in their course. Unusual amounts of time are spent in devising tests that will spread students out on a continuum so they can be more easily placed in A, B, C, and D categories.

The "pass-fail" system is sometimes offered as a solution to the problems of grading. To begin with, it should be recognized that pass-fail is but a two-category form of grading.   Students are put into a pass category or a fail category.   One of the advantages of the pass-fail system is that it clearly emphasizes objectives.   For example, driver's license tests are passed by a large majority of young people.   The emphasis on either passing or failing focuses attention on the information and skills needed for safe driving.   Students know in advance that they must master certain skills and this undoubtedly helps them pass the test.

In the academic setting, pass-fail efforts often revert to a more extended grading system.   When a pass-fail system has been in effect for a time, standards for passing tend to become minimal.   Consequently, both students and teachers feel a need to acknowledge superior performance, and so a grade of superior is introduced.   Thus, pass-fail does not really avoid the grading problem.   However, to the extent that pass-fail grading forces teachers and students to clarify their thinking about what is to be accomplished, there will be more emphasis on learning.

The question of who should make grading decisions is worth discussing with participants.   When students become involved in such decisions, the evaluative criteria on which grades are based must become more explicit and more public.   Most discussions about using students in the grading process assume that a particular student will help make the decisions about the grade he should receive.   Teachers who have encouraged student participation have found that their students are fairly realistic in estimating their own grades.   Active involvement tends to make students more responsible for their performance.

As important as involving the individual in his own evaluation is the desirability of including other students in the evaluation process.   As we move from exclusive reliance on written examinations to oral and performance measures, there simply is not enough time for a teacher to help each student evaluate his learning.   Teachers who have tried to lead a class discussion, while at the same time keep track of the quantity and quality of individual student participation, will recognize the virtual impossibility of the task.   They need the help of their students.   Consequently, in the discussion of objectives and ways to measure their attainment, we have assumed that high school students and college students should and will be involved in the evaluation process.

Many educators wish that the nagging problem of grades would go away.   Even if grades were to be abolished by decree, however, a need to accumulate evaluation data on the performance of individual students would still exist.   Whether teachers and administrators need such data is a moot question, but it is undeniable that students need the information.   For a learner to improve in his ability to understand an idea or to do something new, he must receive continuous feedback on the correctness or appropriateness of his responses.   This need for learner feedback is the primary reason for obtaining evaluation data on individual performances.   If individuals are to assume increasing responsibility for their own learning, it is necessary for teachers to aid in developing diagnostic instruments and other measures so that students can assess their progress.

The following applications of the points presented in this discussion of grading could be suggested to participants:

1. Indicate the factors you would consider in determining the grades to be assigned participants in this course.
2. Indicate the factors you think should determine a semester grade in a senior high school problems of democracy course.
3. What bases would you suggest for student evaluation of oral reports in a geography or sociology class?

GROUP EVALUATION:
THE PROBLEM OF IMPROVING INSTRUCTION

Parallel to the use of individual evaluation data for improving student performance is the use of group evaluation data for determining the effectiveness of teaching procedures and materials. Such data can provide reliable guidelines for improving instruction.

Preoccupation with the administrative function of evaluation has diminished the use of evaluation for providing feedback on the effectiveness of the materials and strategies used in teaching. If a teacher will determine both before and after teaching how his group performs on specific objectives, he can obtain useful information that will help him make his objectives more realistic. Such knowledge will also give him clues for modifying the materials and strategies he has employed. The result in both cases should be an improvement in his teaching and, very likely, an improvement in learning by his students.

To evaluate the effectiveness of course procedures and materials, group data rather than data on individual students are needed. Averaged student opinions are valuable when we raise questions such as the following: "Is this a good book?"; "Should it be used again?"; "Is this course effective? If not, how should it be changed?"; "Was I effective? If not, how should I change?" Group scores are also useful in helping teachers diagnose the strengths and weaknesses of each class.

Successful teachers have always had ways of finding out whether an idea they are trying to communicate is actually understood by most of their students. Such informal diagnostic data gathering can be supplemented by more formal and systematic procedures for finding out what the class has learned or failed to learn so that reteaching can take place.

For example, data about what the class knows and does not know can be obtained before teaching. With this information a teacher can avoid repeating what students already know.

More specifically, questions derived from course objectives can be administered at the beginning of the course and at its conclusion. With average group scores on questions before and after instruction, one can make judgments about the adequacy of the achievement indicated. A decrease or no change in the percentage of students answering a question correctly may indicate a failure to achieve a particular course objective.

In this course, questions dealing with one concept could show a much greater gain than questions dealing with another concept.   For example, the following questions might be asked:

1.   Which of the following would be considered an objective indicator of social class in the United States?
    A.   Political beliefs
    B.   Self-image of status
    C.   Occupational prestige
    D.   Years of school completed

2.   Which of the following is the greatest obstacle to social change?
    A.   Attitudes
    B.   Education
    C.   Technology
    D.   Economic measures

The percentage of participants getting question one right might increase from thirty-five percent before teaching to sixty percent after teaching, while the percentage for question two remains at about fifty percent for both the pretesting and the post-testing. Such results would suggest the relative inadequacy of the materials and procedures used to teach about "obstacles to social change" in comparison with "objective indicators of social class."

Several questions derived from the same objective can yield even more conclusive evidence that changes in instructional procedures and materials need to be made.   This use of test data is quite similar to the diagnostic use of tests for identifying areas that require remedial work for individuals.

Group data derived from questionnaires and attitude scales have even greater potential value for course improvement.   Unlike the problem that can occur when we use attitudinal criteria as the basis for grading individuals, the use of group data ensures anonymity of individuals and thereby overcomes the drawback of obtaining honest expressions of attitudes.   When students can respond anonymously, they seem to be more willing to indicate what they are likely to do in a given circumstance.

One objective of this course is to encourage prospective teachers to use a variety of innovative teaching materials, such as simulations and inquiry activities.   The inclination of participants to attempt such activities as teachers can be assessed by using attitude scales.   Clearly, if participants can express their views anonymously, more of them are likely to give true expressions of their interest in extending learnings from this course to the high school classroom situation.

Measures of group attitudes can be used to indicate achievement of some of our most important objectives.   Thus group data are really the only practical kind of data for measuring the full range of objectives of any instructional unit or course.

The following applications of the points made in this section of the chapter should serve to clarify and reinforce the ideas for participants:

1. Prepare a few questions related to the objectives of two SRSS or HSGP activities. Administer the questions before and after teaching. What conclusions can you draw about the relative effectiveness of the activities?
2. What criteria would you suggest for evaluating a new black studies course at your high school?
3. What differences, if any, exist between the evaluative criteria for a professional course such as this course and a general education course in sociology at the high school level?

THE PROBLEM OF OBJECTIVES

Despite considerable emphasis by departments of education and school administrators, teachers seem to teach without paying much attention to objectives. Most teachers have some idea of what they want students to learn, yet they seldom formulate expected outcomes in an explicit way. This teacher tendency to ignore formal objectives has at least two serious consequences for instruction.

First, unclear objectives encourage teachers to use inappropriate teaching procedures and materials. It is difficult to devise effective methods for helping students to learn when the ideas or skills to be learned are fuzzy. This does not mean that objectives once formulated should be fixed in an unalterable form. Teachers who are conscious of, and can articulate, what they hope students will learn are in a position both to plan effectively and to modify objectives to meet actual classroom conditions.

A second consequence of unclear objectives is the difficulty encountered in evaluating their attainment. Most test questions that teachers devise require students to recall information rather than demonstrate new understandings or skills. Far too many teachers are willing to accept informational competence as evidence of understanding. Consequently, evaluation measures reinforce what, at best, are insignificant objectives. Clearly formulated objectives would reveal the inadequacy and irrelevance of certain test items as evaluation tools.

The unwillingness of many teachers to formulate objectives might be a backlash against the excessive demands of the advocates of behavioral objectives: these behavioralists require carefully prescribed objectives for all circumstances. If all objectives were stated in approved behavioral terms, there might be little time left for teaching!

Detailed behavioral objectives represent an extreme shift from the virtually meaningless generalizations that were once commonly accepted ways of stating objectives. Old geography objectives might have included statements such as "to develop an appreciation for the peoples of Asia" or "to understand the influence of the physical environment on human activities." In previous times, sociology objectives might have been formulated in terms such as "to know the major characteristics of the American family as an institution" or "to appreciate the influence of racist attitudes on social mobility."

Because of the difficulty of pinpointing the meaning of such words as "appreciating," "understanding," and "knowing," educational leaders began to insist that objectives be formulated in terms of specific actions to be taken by the learner so that it could be demonstrated that he "knows" or "appreciates." Unfortunately, the urge to make objectives more meaningful and therefore more useful in guiding instruction did not always succeed. Even though more time was devoted to stating objectives, the activity often became an exercise in using acceptable verbs in the place of unacceptable ones. Instead of "understand," "appreciate," or "know," such verbs as "identify," "clarify," "calculate," and "describe" were substituted.

It is important to note, however, that the shift in verb usage has been significant because it has placed emphasis on what the learner is expected to do. Action verbs imply that the learner will be able to provide a meaningful demonstration of his learning. For objectives to be effective guides for learning and evaluating, they should be thought of in terms of things students might learn to do. To think of objectives this way avoids the confusion that sometimes exists between what we hope students will learn, on the one hand, and what the purpose of an educational activity is, on the other.

The confusion between purpose and desired learner behavior often arises when teachers are asked to prepare lesson plans. The mechanics of the lesson are sometimes mistaken for the educational objectives. Thus, "to show a film on discrimination" becomes a substitute for what students are expected to learn about discrimination. Some of the original statements of objectives for the activities of this book were formulated as purposes rather than as desired learner behaviors. For example, one "Game of Farming" activity objective was stated as "to illustrate the use of gaming as a teaching technique." The intended objective is "to use an educational game effectively." The latter formulation has the learner in mind whereas the former has the teacher in mind.

Perhaps the most unfortunate negative consequence of behavioral objectives is the implication that all educational objectives, no matter what their purpose or level of generality, should or can be stated in specific behavioral terms. This belief is unfortunate because objectives for a total school program clearly need to be of a different order of generality than objectives for a lesson plan. The three course objectives listed on page 232 are at a high level of generality. They are clearly useful in this form and do not need specification beyond appropriate examples for them to be meaningful.

The first two general objectives on page 232 are formulated at lower levels of generality than most of the activities in this volume. The objective of understanding and using certain concepts appears at more specific levels in the following forms:

To classify [social stratification] criteria as objective or subjective (page 123).

To identify social factors that shape performance in the leader's role (page 210).

To examine the importance of least cost and maximum profit considerations as influences on manufacturing location decisions (page 113).

In the same way, the general objective related to the ability to conduct certain types of teaching activities appears more specifically in several activities as follows:

To use an educational game effectively (page 219).

To develop skill in using audio recordings as instructional media (page 157).

To develop techniques for engaging high school students in problem-solving by using their ideas and judgments as data sources (page 123).

An objective reaches its most specific point when it describes a type of behavior that permits the gathering of evaluation data about the learner's attainment of the objective. At this level of evaluation, we should be able to specify (1) what we expect a student to be able to do, (2) what questions or stimuli we expect to use in getting the student to demonstrate his attainment, and (3) what level of sophistication or excellence we expect him to demonstrate. Even the most general objectives should be reducible to the point where these three criteria apply. When this is the case, objectives are truly behavioral.

It is always advisable to check an educational activity or unit to see that it does, in fact, promise attainment of its stated objectives. It is also advisable to examine intended educational experiences to identify unstated objectives implicit in the experience. The divorce of objectives from planned educational activities should lead us all to have a healthy suspicion of the value of the stated objectives.

The discussion in this section has shown us that we frequently separate objectives from the learning experiences designed to accomplish them. As a result, statements of objectives rarely represent the learning outcomes likely to ensue from a given instructional activity. We develop many of our educational activities without the guidance of clearly formulated objectives. It is also common for us to prepare objectives as an afterthought to meet an externally imposed requirement. Consequently, it is not surprising that the relationship between stated objectives and planned educational experiences is sometimes unclear.

The following activities represent applications of the ideas about objectives indicated in this section:

1. Examine the objectives indicated for an activity in this book and
    A. Identify those objectives that employ vague terms that would be difficult to reduce to participant behaviors.
    B. Reduce one objective to behavioral terms by using the three criteria indicated above.

2. Select an activity you experienced in this class and examine its objectives to determine which may be unlikely outcomes. Also indicate likely outcomes not mentioned in the objectives.

3. Critically evaluate a list of course objectives in terms of emphasis on the learner and behavioral vagueness.

OBTAINING EVALUATION DATA

We have spoken of three types of objectives: the ability to understand and use certain concepts, the ability to conduct or develop certain types of teaching activities, and the desire to use certain types of instructional materials and procedures. This section will discuss ways of measuring understanding, performance, and attitude. Most measurement efforts in the past have emphasized informational recall in the name of understanding. The most critical measurement problem today is the development of learner tasks that measure attainment of significant understanding, performance, and attitudinal objectives.

Measuring Understanding

Both objective questions and essay questions are used to measure student understanding. Objective questions provide limited choices for the student. He must select a "correct" response from several provided (multiple-choice or matching questions) or determine the "truth" of a statement (true-false questions). Certain questions require the student to fill in a blank with a word or phrase; they come closer to the more open response sought in an essay question. The "objectivity" of objective questions derives from the manner in which they are scored. The answer the student selects is compared with the response that has been predetermined as the correct one. Variation in responses to most essay questions precludes formulation of a single predetermined correct answer. Consequently, scorers may disagree with respect to the worth of a student answer to an essay question.

ESSAY QUESTIONS

Low scorer reliability is the major disadvantage of essay questions. Grades for the same essay are likely to differ from teacher to teacher. It is also possible that a teacher will assign two different scores if he grades the same essay at two different times. With essay tests, too, the writing ability of the student is often evaluated rather than his substantive knowledge.

The main advantage of essay tests is that they provide the student with the opportunity to formulate conclusions and to support them. Well-prepared questions can stimulate thoughtful responses that provide evidence of thought processes as well as of conclusions. Even the best objective questions do not measure process well.

Since time prohibits the asking of more than a few items in an essay test, questions that deal with the most important and central topics should be devised. It is important to provide explicit directions for the test so that all examinees will address themselves to the intended question. To disguise their lack of understanding of a topic, some "testwise" students will write as if they have misunderstood the directions. Words like "compare" and "contrast" are preferable in the instructions to such terms as "discuss" or "write an essay on."

Procedures for scoring essay responses are critical. It is essential to work out a model answer, outlining the main points to be covered in the question. Credit to be given for each question and for each main point should be determined in advance. It is also important to read the responses anonymously. If a teacher knows who wrote the answer, a "halo" effect may bias the rating. That a student is well-behaved or disruptive in the classroom should not be read into test scores, either consciously or unconsciously.

In addition, it is better to grade answers to the first question on all papers before going on to the second question. This procedure avoids the possibility that the answer to one question will color evaluation on subsequent items. A student's effort on each question should be evaluated independently of his performance on other questions.

MULTIPLE-CHOICE QUESTIONS

Multiple-choice items are preferred to other kinds of objective test questions because they provide a better opportunity for measuring abilities of interpretation and application. When properly constructed, they are also the least ambiguous way of measuring understanding. On the other hand, true-false questions, fill-in-the-blank questions, and matching questions offer little possibility of going beyond informational questioning. They are also subject to considerable ambiguity.

The major difficulty in preparing multiple-choice questions is the casting of significant learning objectives in a format that allows only one correct answer. One method of doing this is by formulating questions in terms of the most likely or least likely cause or consequence. The following questions are examples of this method:

1. Which of the following is most likely to encourage social change?
   A. Matriarchal family structure
   B. Traditional customs and beliefs
   C. Dissatisfaction with current conditions
   D. Strongly entrenched power groups
2. Which of the following would a society be most likely to accept?
   A. A new funeral practice
   B. A new type of radio
   C. A new alphabet
   D. A new way of farming
3. Which of the following usually occurs when a large manufacturer leaves a community?
   A. Retail sales decrease
   B. Neighborhood land values increase
   C. Unemployment decreases
   D. School attendance increases
4. Which of the following would be least likely to be associated with areas of the world where undernourishment is a serious problem?

    A.   High instance of disease
    B.   A highrise apartment house
    C.   A religious building
    D.   A railroad station

Another method of measuring understanding of a concept is to ask students to identify the best of several possible answers. For example, the following question could be asked:

5. In order to find out how students in a school feel about American foreign policy, which of the following would be the most reliable sample on which to base a survey?
    A.   Members of the school's athletic teams
    B.   Students whose first name begins with "R"
    C.   Students who usually make the honor roll
    D.   Students who read at least one library book a week

6. Three settlements of equal size are located on the west coast of Africa. If you want to predict which city will be largest in 1980, which do you think is the most important question to ask?
    A.   Does the settlement have a good port?
    B.   Are there raw materials of value nearby?
    C.   Is the climate desirable for people?
    D.   Is the settlement in a country with a democratic government?

Sometimes a series of questions can be used to measure several aspects of understanding a concept. The following sequence of questions, asked after presenting the initial statement, could elicit student understanding of social change.

Farmers in parts of southern Nigeria use hoes instead of plows. The farmers produce crops mainly for food for their own families and not for cash income. Their families include distant relatives; the structure of the family is based on marriage customs different from ours. The soils are generally not very fertile. As a result, fields must be left idle for some time after a crop is harvested. Thus the farmers cultivate first one field and then another. There are no work animals because the tsetse fly brings a disease that kills work animals.

7. Which of the following parts of the way of life of these people is most likely to resist change?
    A.   The practice of leaving some fields idle
    B.   Their use of hoes rather than plows
    C.   The practice of producing for family use rather than for sale to others
    D.   Their marriage customs

8. On which of the following grounds could a proposal to invest all foreign-aid money in tractors and plows be most soundly criticized?
    A.   It would do nothing about the more basic tsetse fly problem.
    B.   The people apparently have little interest in raising their living standard.

    C.   The people are probably unable to use and maintain the tractors properly.

    D.   The practice of leaving fields idle shows that these people are unable to farm efficiently.

9.   What is the probable attitude of these people toward the customs described in the paragraph?

    A.   "If we put up with the inconvenience, things will get better."

    B.   "This is the natural and proper way to do things."

    C.   "If we had more education, things would improve."

    D.   "With a lot of hard work, maybe we can be more like Americans."

There are several pitfalls to be avoided in constructing multiple-choice questions. Many teachers include irrelevant clues in their answer options to questions. In addition, so that they will not leave themselves open to criticism, teachers are likely to make the correct answer more elaborate than the incorrect options. Alert students are thereby clued in to the correct response when they may, in fact, have had no idea of which answer was correct. Another tendency some teachers have is to include absurd responses, thereby effectively reducing a four-option question to a one- or two-option question. When the difficulty of writing good multiple-choice questions becomes apparent to them, many teachers tend to settle for simpler questions of the "who," "where," and "when" variety. To avoid such traps, teachers should maintain a file of those questions that have been successful in measuring student understanding so that the effort of writing multiple-choice questions is not dissipated in one use.

Measuring Attitudes

QUESTIONNAIRES

In addition to measuring cognitive objectives, we need to obtain measures of student attitudes if we are to make effective evaluations. We have already noted the problems associated with using attitudinal questions in tests given for grading purposes. However, some of our educational objectives *are* attitudinal and teachers *do* have a legitimate interest in finding out whether individual student attitudes have been changed by a course. For example, one intention of a geography course may be to encourage students to become more sympathetic toward or appreciative of practices followed in other cultures. In such a course, the following question might provide a measure of this attitude:

10.   Some of the peoples of East Africa insert a hollow tube into the veins of their cattle and draw out blood. The blood is then used as a part of their diet. What is your opinion about such a practice? (There is no correct answer to this question.)

    A.   "It does not appeal to me, but it probably makes sense to the people involved."

    B.   "Using cattle for milk and beef is a more natural thing to do."

    C.   "These people probably do not know that cattle provide milk and beef."

    D.   "These people are probably not aware that this will hurt the cattle."

Materials produced by both SRSS and HSGP strive to make students more aware of multiple solutions to problems, especially the more complex causational and practical decision-making problems. The following example represents one way of measuring an attitude of openness:

The following questions ask for your opinion. *Your* views are what count. Choose the option that best represents your opinion.

If all sources of information were available, which of the options below (A, B, C, or D) would you choose for questions 11–17?

   A.   I am confident there is one right answer or reason.
   B.   There is probably one right answer or reason.
   C.   There are probably two or three acceptable answers or reasons.
   D.   There are probably several generally acceptable answers or reasons.
_____ 11.   Which nation in North America has the most people?
_____ 12.   What has made Chicago a large city?
_____ 13.   What should Farmer Jones in Benson County (Iowa) grow this year?
_____ 14.   Why did the United States enter World War II?
_____ 15.   Where would be the best place in the United States to locate a plywood factory?
_____ 16.   Where should the new boundary of Eastern Nigeria be drawn?
_____ 17.   In a state where there are two congressmen, where should the boundary be drawn so that each district has about the same population?

Items 18 and 19 ask for your opinion about two statements. Choose the option (A, B, C, or D) that best represents your opinion.

   A.   I strongly agree with the statement.
   B.   I agree.
   C.   I disagree.
   D.   I strongly disagree.
_____ 18.   For most things that happen in the world, there is more likely to be one cause than several causes.
_____ 19.   Encyclopedias and textbooks are likely to give the same answers about when something happened.

It is important to note that not all attitude measures are directly related to the attainment of course objectives. We may wish to find out from students whether an assigned reading was too difficult, whether a film seemed worthwhile, or whether the organization of a lesson seemed clear. Group data that are anonymous help us to make decisions about the effectiveness of materials and procedures; they are not related to the attainment of objectives. A student evaluation questionnaire for this book might take the following form:

Your help is needed in improving the materials and procedures used in this course. Please fill out this questionnaire so the necessary modifications can be made. Do not put your name on this form.

The table of contents lists the major activities in this book. Use the activity numbers to indicate your answers to the following questions:

1. _____ Which activity did you find *most* interesting?
2. _____ Which activity did you find *least* interesting?
3. _____ From which activity do you think you learned the *most?*
4. _____ Which activity was the *least* worthwhile?
5. _____ Which activity was the *most* difficult for you?
6.   State the major reason why you found this activity the *most* difficult.
7.   Write suggestions you have for improving the book.

SCALING INSTRUMENTS

Some attitudinal measures which at first seem to be unrelated to our educational objectives are on closer examination clearly relevant. Asking students about their interest in an educational medium or educational experience has a direct bearing on one of our most basic objectives — the development of student interest in their educational experiences. Although it is often not stated explicitly, one educational objective of a geography course or a sociology course is the development of student interest in these subjects. Without interest, there is little likelihood that students will seek additional experiences in these subject areas.

One way to gauge student interest is to use a scale consisting of four options, labeled A, B, C, and D. The options represent points on an interest continuum, from (A) *dull* to (B) *generally uninteresting* to (C) *generally interesting* to (D) *very interesting.* (Some teachers prefer scales with a neutral middle option; however, there seems to be no valid reason for preferring a five-point scale to a four-point scale.) The instrument should list topics or ideas that students will study. For example, participants in this course or workshop might be asked to rate the following topics, using the options A to D, in terms of how interesting the topic might be to study:

_____ 1. Social class
_____ 2. Leadership
_____ 3. Farming
_____ 4. Manufacturing
_____ 5. School boundaries
_____ 6. Chinese Communism

In order to determine changes in student interest, the scale, like other measures, should be administered before and after a unit or course is taught. In each administration, students register the degree of interest they have for the topics listed. To obtain the score for each topic, the number of A's, B's, C's, and D's are first tabulated. A weighted value is then assigned to each of the four options. If the "very interesting" response receives a "4" value, the "dull" response would receive a "1" value. This value is then used to multiply the number tabulated for each option. The class mean for each topic can be determined by totaling the weighted values and dividing the result by the number of students responding.

TABLE 4-1.

Topic	Pretest Class Mean	Post-test Class Mean
1. Politics	2.62	2.65
2. Farming	2.02	3.05
3. Japan	2.70	2.69
4. Manufacturing	2.33	2.57

The data shown in Table 4-1 were collected from an interest scale administered before and after a teacher taught a geography unit on manufacturing and agriculture.

Topics 1 and 3 in Table 4-1 were not a part of the unit of study and showed little, if any, gain in student interest. Topics 2 and 4 were emphasized in the unit and did show substantial gains. Moreover, additional valuable information about Topics 2 and 4 was revealed in the results. Both topics received equal class time, yet Topic 2 generated considerably more interest. A teacher who values high student interest in his subject can profit from such evaluation data by adapting the procedures or materials used in Topic 2 to future topics of study.

Another attitude that can yield valuable evaluation data and can be measured with an interest scale is the worth of a particular unit or course to students. We can ask students if they think they learned something worthwhile from their study. A scale for this purpose might include points from (A) *no worth* to (D) *great worth*. Student opinions about what they have learned are helpful in measuring attainment of objectives that would be difficult to measure otherwise.

Another attitude measurement scale that can be used for evaluation is the semantic differential scale. Charles E. Osgood, a psychologist, developed this technique for use in his research on meaning.[1] The instrument is used to explore the images or meanings that people attach to ideas or things, from brands of cigarettes to socialism. For whatever is being rated, a teacher selects several bipolar adjectives or adjective phrases that will define the dimensions of meaning. Each pair of adjectives is separated by a seven-point scale on which the student registers his attitude. (In his book, Osgood discusses pairs of adjectives on which data have been obtained; however, teachers can devise their own adjective opposites.) For example, to assess the image that students have of sociology, a form like that shown in Table 4-2 could be used.

Scoring and interpreting data from the semantic differential scale is easier if the pairs of adjectives are arranged so that any change that occurs between the first administration and the second administration moves from right to left on each continuum. For instance, if you are interested in finding out how "smart," how "important," and how "educated" students think farmers are and if you want to develop more favorable attitudes on all three continua, you would place "smart," "important," and "educated" in the left-hand column. "Stupid," "unimportant," and "uneducated" would be placed in the right-hand column.

[1] Charles E. Osgood, et al., *The Measurement of Meaning* (Urbana, Ill.: University of Illinois Press, 1957).

TABLE 4-2.

Sociology

Good								Bad
Serious	___	___	___	___	___	___	___	Funny
Easy	___	___	___	___	___	___	___	Difficult
Smart	___	___	___	___	___	___	___	Stupid
Important	___	___	___	___	___	___	___	Unimportant
Noisy	___	___	___	___	___	___	___	Quiet
Useful	___	___	___	___	___	___	___	Useless

After students have registered their attitude toward farmers or sociology or communists, a class average for each continuum is determined. A teacher scoring results for the "important-unimportant" continuum would begin by assigning a value from 1 to 7 to each of the seven spaces between the adjectives. The student markings in the space to the far right would carry the value of "1" and markings to the far left a value of "7." Each intermediate space would carry an appropriate value between these extremes. The teacher would then total the number of students who marked space 1 and multiply that number by one, total the number of 2's and multiply this total by two, and so on through the seven spaces. Dividing the sum of all the weighted values by the total number of students will give the average for the class for that continuum.

After determining the mean (average) value for each continuum, a class profile for the concept can be drawn by connecting the mean points. If the same instrument is administered before and after an instructional unit, the two profiles can be compared.

Figure 4-1 illustrates changes in the attitudes of a class that studied a unit on economic geography. The results of this semantic differential test indicate that students held a consistently more positive attitude toward farmers after instruction than before.

The questionnaire "What Do You Think?" (page 197) used in Activity 9/The Decision-Maker illustrates yet another type of attitude measuring device — the Likert scale.[2] This instrument is probably the most easily constructed and widely used scale presently available for measuring attitudes. To construct this scale, a teacher formulates statements that will reveal attitudes relevant to the topic being studied and provides students with a range of choices for registering their opinions. Unlike the simple "agree-disagree" choice provided in the decision-maker questionnaire, most Likert-type scales have five or more response choices. On a five-point continuum, respondents can react to each statement by marking "strongly agree," "agree," "uncertain," "disagree," or "strongly disagree."

For attitude statements to be effective, they must be meaningful and interesting to students. (If the Likert technique is unsuccessful, it is usually because the statements have failed to arouse much interest in the respondents.) The statements must be worded appropriately so that respondents will not quibble about the meaning or want to change

[2] For a discussion of this kind of scale, see A. N. Oppenheim, *Questionnaire Design and Attitude Measurement* (New York: Basic Books, 1966).

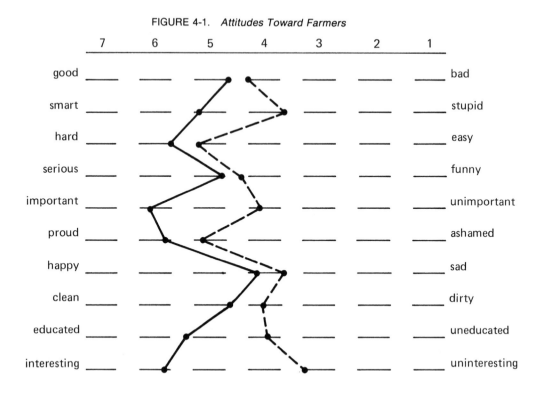

FIGURE 4-1. *Attitudes Toward Farmers*

Legend:	Pretest class profile	– – – – –
	Post-test class profile	————

them. If large numbers of students select the "uncertain" response or simply skip statements, the given statements are probably not functioning well.

After students have registered their reactions to the statements on the scale, a class mean is determined for each statement in the same way that means were figured for the semantic differential scale and the other attitudinal scales already discussed. Each of the five response positions is assigned a weight from "1" to "5." If a high score on the item or statement indicates a favorable attitude, then statements expressing that attitude should be scored "5" for "strongly agree" down to "1" for "strongly disagree." Unfavorable statements must be scored "1" for "strongly agree" up to "5" for "strongly disagree."

There is no easy way to graph the results of the Likert scale. However, changes that take place in the attitudes of a group from preunit to postunit evaluation can be seen by comparing the class means obtained in the two administrations.

Measuring Performance

Performance objectives are the most difficult objectives from which to obtain sound evaluation data. Most of the activities in this book list both product performance and process performance objectives. Product objectives relate to improving student ability to produce or to develop a new activity, for example, a simulation. Process objectives refer to student ability to use instructional procedures and materials, for example, to lead a small group discussion or to use slides to foster inquiry. Standards for evaluating a product are relatively easy to prepare, whereas standards for evaluating a process are much more difficult to delineate. Checklists are used to measure both kinds of performance objectives, but the dynamic character of process evaluation makes it far more difficult to measure.

PRODUCT EVALUATION

The evaluation of planned educational experiences, such as simulations, requires identification of the significant characteristics that define the product. Numerous criteria for "effective" educational simulations exist; for example, inclusion of significant concepts, existence of roles that incorporate the conceptual variables, careful formulation of the problem to be resolved, grounds for disagreement or conflict among the role players, and provision for analyzing the results of the simulation. These criteria are evident in Activity 2/Metfab and in Activity 9/The Decision-Maker, although in the latter simulation, conflict is built into the role of a single person. Checklists are then constructed on the basis of the criteria.

      Ideally, examples of different levels of product quality should be included with the list of product characteristics. Thus, it would be useful in judging level of attainment for a teacher to have examples of an excellent simulation, an average simulation, and a poor simulation to use in much the same way that he compares student responses on an essay question to the model answer. In practice, however, it is usually the students themselves who provide the examples of varying quality. A teacher might use student examples from one class as models to judge another class.

      The similarity between procedures for evaluating simulations and procedures for grading essay questions should not escape notice. The major points to be dealt with in an essay response (product) must first be identified. Then examples A, B, C, D, and E help the evaluator grade each succeeding product he examines. Without identification of criteria or major characteristics, the evaluator may discover that his criteria change as he proceeds. Without qualitative examples for guidance, he will find it difficult to distinguish high quality products from mediocre products.

PROCESS EVALUATION

A second type of performance objective describes a process or ability to be developed. One process objective implicit in most role playing simulations is development of effective group decision-making. Evaluating group decision-making abilities requires analysis of the process and identification of the abilities that seem to be involved. These more specific abilities become the basis for preparing behavioral checklists. For example, a checklist for group decision-making might take the following form:

1. Contributes to group deliberations:
   _____ very seldom
   _____ adequately
   _____ too often
2. Facilitates clarification of the problem and movement toward its resolution:
   _____ fosters confusion and group disorientation
   _____ seems unaware of this goal
   _____ occasionally fosters clarification and movement
   _____ regularly fosters clarification and movement
3. Helps other group members state their views:
   _____ never
   _____ occasionally
   _____ regularly
   _____ regularly and skillfully
4. Represents a role he has been assigned:
   _____ not at all
   _____ somewhat
   _____ very effectively

Because of the dynamic character of process evaluation, a teacher may discover that he needs to refine his checklist as he goes along. He should not hesitate, however, to begin the evaluation with a crude checklist, for the very act of use leads to further identification of specific abilities and to further refinement of the testing instrument.

It is important to involve students in the acts of evaluating performance objectives and refining checklists. As a student demonstrates attainment of performance objectives, student observers can record evaluation data on the checklist. Performance judgments can then be shared to aid the student (and other class members) in improving subsequent efforts.

Using students to evaluate attainment of performance objectives has several desirable educational outcomes. Students will gain a clearer understanding of what an objective means if they help in devising a behavioral checklist, then actually gather data and refine the list, and finally provide feedback to fellow students. In turn, students who are being evaluated learn more about themselves and are encouraged to improve subsequent performance behavior.

   The following activities represent applications of the suggestions made in this section:

1. Turn to the Appendix (pages 252–58) and analyze the set of test questions given there with the following question in mind: How appropriate is this test as a measure of achievement in this course or workshop?
2. Select an objective listed for a sociology or geography activity in this book and identify the test questions that seem relevant to the objective. Which questions are trivial? Which appear to be relevant to the objective but, in fact, are not?
3. Identify several questions that fail to meet the criteria for item construction discussed in this section.
4. Prepare a Likert scale instrument appropriate for this course or workshop. Use at least ten attitude statements.
5. Rate the activities in this book on a four-point scale, from dull to very interesting; also, rate them from worthless to very worthwhile. What appears to be the relationship between interest and worth?

Appendix

Analyze the following set of test questions with this thought in mind: How appropriate is this test as a measure of achievement in this course or workshop? These questions are not intended to serve as a test for the contents of this book.

1. A leader is a person who has the ability to
   A. solve individual problems.
   B. control the actions of others.
   C. express one's opinion clearly.
   D. predict the behavior of others.
2. Which of the following is most likely to encourage social change?
   A. Matriarchal family structure.
   B. Traditional customs and beliefs.
   C. Dissatisfaction with current conditions.
   D. Strongly entrenched power groups.
3. What is the basis for the authority a person has over others?
   A. Physical force.
   B. His personality.

    C. His formal position.

    D. His informal position.

4. The spread of European culture has taken place
   A. over land routes more than over sea routes.
   B. primarily in a southerly direction.
   C. fastest in areas closest to Europe.
   D. almost simultaneously in several distant parts of the world.

5. Farm machinery is *not* usually found in areas of
   A. high per capita income.
   B. low population density.
   C. commercial agriculture.
   D. noncommercial agriculture.

6. What was the purpose of the Communists in encouraging Chinese peasants to express grievances against their landlords by holding "struggle meetings"?
   A. To use the peasants to accomplish the Communists' goals.
   B. To increase the sense of power and importance of the peasants.
   C. To promote a deeper understanding between the peasants and landlords.
   D. To emphasize the differences in power between the peasants and landlords.

7. Which of the following is most descriptive of social change?
   A. No culture ever really changes.
   B. Beliefs and values change more rapidly than technology.
   C. All aspects of society and culture tend to change at about the same rate.
   D. Changes in technology are accepted more rapidly than changes in values and beliefs.

8. Which of the following is a problem in the use of occupational prestige scales?
   A. Different occupations receive different scores.
   B. The scales cannot include all occupations in the labor force.
   C. Occupations with different prestige often receive the same scores.
   D. The scales do not provide information about social status of the occupations.

9. Prior to the year A.D. 1000, cities that resembled each other were usually located
   A. close together.
   B. in the Southern Hemisphere.
   C. in different countries.
   D. in rugged mountains.

10. Which of the following would a society be most likely to accept?
   A. A new funeral practice.
   B. A new type of radio.
   C. A new alphabet.
   D. A new way of farming.

11. Which of the following types of purchased material inputs would have the least effect on the location of a manufacturing plant?
   A. Materials that have a uniform delivery price.
   B. Materials for which the delivery price varies with the distance from the supplier.

C.   Material inputs that account for a small share of the final value of the product.

D.   Material inputs that account for a large share of the final value of the product.

12.   Which of the following is the greatest obstacle to social change?

A.   Attitudes.

B.   Education.

C.   Technology.

D.   Economic measures.

13.   Which of the following would be considered an objective indicator of social class in the United States?

A.   Political beliefs.

B.   Self-image of status.

C.   Occupational prestige.

D.   Years of school completed.

14.   As the group and the task to be performed become more stable, the leadership of the group tends to

A.   become more centralized.

B.   become less centralized.

C.   maintain the same degree of centralization.

D.   be performed by more group members.

15.   Some of the peoples of East Africa insert a hollow tube into the veins of their cattle and draw out blood. The blood is then used as a part of their diet. What is your opinion about such a practice? (There is no correct answer to this question.)

A.   "It does not appeal to me, but it probably makes sense to the people involved."

B.   "Using cattle for milk and beef is a more natural thing to do."

C.   "These people probably do not know that cattle provide milk and beef."

D.   "These people are probably not aware that this will hurt the cattle."

16.   Which of the following usually occurs when a large manufacturer leaves a community?

A.   Retail sales decrease.

B.   Neighborhood land values increase.

C.   Unemployment decreases.

D.   School attendance increases.

17.   What black leader was awarded the Nobel Peace Prize?

A.   Roy Wilkins.

B.   Elijah Muhammad.

C.   Adam Clayton Powell.

D.   Martin Luther King, Jr.

18.   Which of the following is *not* necessary for content analysis to be successful?

A.   A systematic way of sampling relevant materials.

B.   A theoretical orientation for examining the materials.

C.   A systematic way of making the materials agree with the conclusions.

D.   A system of categories for classifying the materials that are examined.

19. Transportation costs are an important consideration in the location of a factory because
    A. parking lots must be provided for employees.
    B. materials must be moved to the factory and finished products moved to the market.
    C. large per-mile cost differences exist among truck, railroad, and airline carriers.
    D. finished products cost more to transport than materials.

20. When deciding where to locate a manufacturing plant, it is desirable for one to assess for each location the
    A. total production costs.
    B. market potential.
    C. total profits.
    D. impact of governmental regulations.

21. In order to find out how students in a school feel about American foreign policy, which of the following would be the most reliable sample on which to base a survey?
    A. Members of the school's athletic teams.
    B. Students whose first name begins with "R."
    C. Students who usually make the honor roll.
    D. Students who read at least one library book each week.

22. Which of the following is indicated by research on occupational prestige?
    A. There is a clear-cut and fixed prestige ranking of occupations.
    B. Occupational prestige varies within each community.
    C. There is no agreement at all with regard to prestige ranking of occupations.
    D. There is general agreement on prestige ranking of occupations, but the rankings change gradually.

23. What is the most important single indicator of social class membership?
    A. Wealth.
    B. Occupation.
    C. Social acceptance.
    D. Place of residence.

24. A manufacturer who locates a factory solely on the basis of obtaining maximum sales assumes that
    A. transportation and production costs are approximately equal everywhere.
    B. demand for the product is approximately equal everywhere.
    C. demand for the product is independent of the factory's location.
    D. sales of the product are independent of pricing schedules.

25. For every dollar of income white families received in 1967, how much income did black families receive?
    A. $.20
    B. $.40
    C. $.60
    D. $.80

26. Under what condition is widespread resistance to social change most likely to increase?
    A. When it encounters the problem of illiteracy.
    B. When it threatens to fragment family ties.
    C. When it brings about a feeling of national pride.
    D. When it substitutes efficiency for craftsmanship.

27. As it spreads from one culture to another, an idea is likely to
    A. change its form somewhat.
    B. be unrecognizable as the same idea.
    C. become more useful in the new culture than it was in the old.
    D. remain in its original form.

28. Cities that resemble each other today were probably built
    A. before 1500.
    B. between 1500 and 1700.
    C. between 1700 and 1900.
    D. after 1900.

29. Rice is a more appropriate crop than wheat or corn for the densely populated areas of the world because of its
    A. greater labor requirements.
    B. more demanding climatic requirements.
    C. higher caloric yield per acre.
    D. use in cattle and swine feeds.

30. Which of the following is least important for a planned social change to be effective?
    A. Strong leadership with power.
    B. Popular support for the leadership's program or plan.
    C. A social problem serious enough to arouse general discontent.
    D. Determination to enforce a great deal of change in a short period of time.

31. Before 1949, the Nationalist government of mainland China chiefly represented the interests of the
    A. peasants.
    B. Communist rebels.
    C. land reform teams.
    D. wealthy strata of society.

32. For social change to be successful, it must
    A. aim at realistic goals.
    B. proceed at a rapid pace.
    C. be directed by a central authority.
    D. change the total pattern of relationships.

33. Which of the following would be least likely to be associated with areas of the world where undernourishment is a serious problem?
    A. High instance of disease.
    B. Low per-capita income.

C. High rate of literacy.

D. Low population density.

34. Which of the following buildings would most probably be built in the traditional architectural style of a country?

A. An office building.

B. A highrise apartment house.

C. A religious building.

D. A railroad station.

35. Which of the following is least important to a manufacturer in assessing labor as a locational factor?

A. Wage rates.

B. Labor productivity.

C. Labor supply.

D. Union dues.

Questions 36 and 37 are based on the following table:

	Father's Occupation	
Son's Occupation	Blue collar	White collar
Blue Collar	40	10
White Collar	60	90

36. What type of relationship is shown between father's occupation and son's occupation?

A. High positive.

B. Low positive.

C. High negative.

D. Low negative.

37. Compared with white-collar fathers, blue-collar fathers are

A. less likely to have sons.

B. less likely to have white-collar sons.

C. more likely to have white-collar sons.

D. about as likely to have white-collar sons.

38. The system of social stratification in the United States depends upon

A. wealth only.

B. political power only.

C. family background only.

D. a combination of criteria.

39. How important is education as a means of achieving upward mobility in American society?

A. Very important.

B. Slightly important.

C. Irrelevant.

D. A handicap.

40. Social scientists generally identify the basic differences in life style among social classes in terms of
  A. occupational prestige.
  B. income and education levels.
  C. the clothing that the head of the family wears to work.
  D. patterns of housing and home decorating, the schools children attend, etc.

41. Which parts of two large cities in different culture regions of the world will probably look most alike?
  A. The central business district.
  B. Residential areas at the edges of the cities.
  C. Residential areas near the central business district.
  D. Areas of religious worship.

42. What are the two general techniques of identifying leadership?
  A. Reputation and observation.
  B. Interview and questionnaire.
  C. Self-reporting and reputation.
  D. Self-reporting and observation.

43. Which of the following is *not* part of the social situation of a group?
  A. The goals of the group.
  B. The composition of the group.
  C. The extent to which the group is being maintained.
  D. The extent to which the group is achieving its goals.

44. Which of the following is a reason for using a national sample in studying occupational prestige?
  A. To obtain prestige scores for more occupations.
  B. To have a larger number of people rating the occupations.
  C. To minimize bias due to differences in age and experience.
  D. To give more people a chance to participate in the study.

45. The introduction into Culture X of a new way of doing things is most likely to succeed when
  A. people are told how well it worked in the original culture.
  B. corresponding changes are introduced in related parts of Culture X.
  C. it involves the most basic behaviors in Culture X.
  D. a law is passed putting it into effect.

Index

Teacher:
  as selector rather than creator of material, 13–14
  behavior of, 148
  effectiveness, 148
  expectation of, 148
Teacher's Guide, Introduction to, 1–14
Teacher training through national projects, 13
Teaching strategies, 7–8
  Culture Change: A Trend toward Uniformity, 176–179
  Decision-Maker, 195–196
  Dilemma of the Tribes, 147–148
  Eye of Childhood, 111–112
  Game of Farming, 224–227
  Hunger, 135–137
  Metfab, 117–122
  Occupational Prestige Rating Questionnaire, 128–129
  School Districts for Millersburg, 152–155
  Settling Accounts, 160–161
  Social Context of Leadership, 217–218
  Watchung, 203–205
Testing programs for social studies materials, 12
Topographic map, 203–204

U
Understanding, measurement of, 240–243
Uniformity as trend in cultural change, 54–67

See also Culture Change: A Trend toward Uniformity.
Urban settlement, predicting, 199

V
Value analysis, 195–196
Value conflict, 184, 187, 190, 191, 193–194
Value system revealed by choice of criteria of social importance, 128, 129
Values, defined, 193
Variables:
  environmental, 201
  in determining social stratification, 126
  in factory-placing simulation, 119–121
  selecting, 119–120
Verification of predictions, 204

W
War:
  as topic, 179–180
Watchung, 73–84, 198–209
  background, 198
  conducting activity, 199–201
  follow-up, 209
  learning outcomes analyzed, 201–203
  participant materials, 73–84
  participant objectives, 198–199
  teaching strategies analyzed, 203–205
Work and buying power, 38
World population, 30